BURGERS
SAUSAGES & MORE
OVER 160 BARBECUE FAVOURITES

BY JAMIE PURVIANCE

PHOTOGRAPHY BY TIM TURNER
ILLUSTRATIONS BY LINDA KELEN

ACKNOWLEDGEMENTS

Writing this book felt like throwing a big ole barbecue that lasted about a year. I had the good fortune of planning, cooking and collaborating with many of my favourite people. Some were with me from start to finish. Some stopped by for just a short visit. But each and every person contributed something wonderful to this burger extravaganza.

The first people on the scene were Mike Kempster and Brooke Jones from Weber. They dreamed a big dream for this book and then gave me everything I needed to make it real. Thank you, Mike and Brooke. It is an honour and pleasure to work with you. Susan Maruyama was right there with us every step of the way, sharing superb ideas and her good graces with everyone involved. Several other people at Weber stepped up with grilling inspiration, grilling equipment and all-round support. I want to express my appreciation to Kim Lefko, Kevin Kolman, Jeanine Thompson and Kim Durk. Amy Dorsch and Deanna Budnick also deserve special mentions for their awesome work on the finished look of these pages.

The hardest-working person of all was Marsha Capen. I am awed and inspired by her extraordinary dedication to getting every element just right. As the managing editor, Marsha worked closely with a top-notch design team led by creative director Shum Prats and designer Carrie Tilmann. Marsha also collaborated with the wonderful editor and writer Abby Wilson and the pure genius of their boss, Christina Schroeder. Just one of Christina's brilliant moves was bringing Kerry Trotter on to the writing team. Thank you, Kerry, for your hilarious wit and your unfailing kindness.

I have been working on Weber cookbooks with photographer Tim Turner for more than 15 years. I used to think he was great at his job. Now I think that great doesn't begin to describe his actual level of technical skills, his impressive range of creative solutions, and his impressive artistry with light and lens. I want to send special thanks to Tim's photo assistant, Christy Clow, and the other members of his team, including Joe Bankmann, Matt Gagné, Josh Marrah, David Raine, Meghan Ross and Donte Tatum. For the gorgeousness of the food and the colourful variety of presentations, we can all thank the delightful food stylist Lynn Gagné and her very talented assistant, Nina Albazi.

Wanting to write a cookbook is one thing, but actually doing it in ways that are ultimately successful requires a publishing house with a deep understanding of the business and an unwavering professionalism about how to get it done right and on time. I am grateful that Jim Childs at Oxmoor House supported this book from start to finish. Thank you, Leah McLaughlin, Felicity Keane and Pam Hoenig, for caring so deeply about all aspects and for giving your expertise so generously. I also want to acknowledge others at Oxmoor House whose hard work and collaborative attitudes I really appreciate, specifically Tom Mifsud, Steve Sandonato, Susan Hettleman and Vanessa Tiongson.

When we talk about the food at this year-long barbecue, I have enormous gratitude and admiration for my culinary team (the 'Purviance Alliance'). These people finessed each and every recipe again and again so they taste as great as they possibly can. Many thanks, especially to the following grillers: Lynda Balslev, Brigit Binns, Lena Birnbaum, David Bonom, Angela Brassinga, Linda Carucci, Tara Duggan, Sarah Epstein, Elizabeth Hughes, Allison Kociuruba, Alex Novielli, Rick Rodgers, Cheryl Sternman Rule, Andrew Schloss and Terri Wuerthner. You guys are the best. I hope you will all come back and enjoy our next barbecue together.

FOREWORD

I can't imagine a world without hamburgers. Some of my fondest memories are accompanying my dad to our favourite burger drive-ins for meaty treats, along with sides of fries and shakes. Dad and I also liked to explore. When a new burger place opened, we had to give it a try. I guess you could say that I became an accomplished burger critic before even reaching my teenage years.

At home, though, hamburgers just didn't seem to be nearly as tasty and adventuresome – that is, until my dad started barbecuing them in the backyard. Burgers cooked in a frying pan on the stove were OK, but they were a meal, not a celebration. Burgers cooked on the grill were smoky and fun, and flames sizzled the patties, imparting a special flavour.

Then, when I started barbecuing, I was like most backyard chefs: I started with hamburgers. Burgers were an easy entry point to the world of barbecuing for friends and family, but what I didn't understand was that everyone is a hamburger expert. Grilling hamburgers is like walking out on stage: expectations are high, and preparation, technique and creativity are closely scrutinised

by a semicircle of hungry grill watchers. When I pleased the onlookers with technique – the dimpled patty, the perfectly timed flip and the addition of cheese at the right moment – I felt like a true backyard hero.

Weber's Big Book of Burgers, Sausages & More™ stretches the definition of the hamburger as it takes you on a journey of imaginative burger recipes – but we didn't stop there. You'll also find recipes for hot dogs, sausages, brats, sides, toppings and drinks. Plus, there are plenty of helpful tips to improve your barbecuing technique, so you're sure to have crowd-pleasing results every time.

This book is all about fun and flavour. Use your imagination as you enter a whole new world that is filled with big, beautiful burgers – that's my kind of world!

Mike Kempster

INTRODUCTION

Imagine you are seven years old. It's the first day of second grade, and you're the new kid in class. All morning long you have a sinking feeling that you really don't belong. At lunch, you sit in the cafeteria and watch with scepticism as a few classmates pile potato crisps on their cheeseburgers.

To your surprise, they motion for you to do the same, and they wait as you balance your last delicate crisp in place and hold the top bun over your little tower. In unison, you and your new classmates crush each tower of crisps to smithereens, laugh instinctively, and then bite into the warm cheesy patties that are dripping with meaty juices and flecked with salty crisps. The ladies in the kitchen wearing paper hats shake their heads but break into laughter right along with you. I was that seven-year-old kid, and that was when I started to love burgers and the way they made me feel.

Since then, like a lot of us, I've eaten a ridiculous number of burgers. Most estimates are that Americans eat about 50 billion burgers per year. That's three burgers per week for each and every American. For most of my childhood, a burger meant a predictably basic version involving a thin minced beef patty tucked inside a soft enriched bun. Sometimes they had cheese, sometimes they had lettuce and tomato, but back then we didn't have a lot of burger options. On big birthdays, my parents treated me to dinner at a fancy restaurant where I inevitably ordered some kind of super-deluxe burger, like a double-decker bacon cheeseburger with the house sauce. That was as crazy as burgers got.

In the 1980s and '90s, a funny thing happened … 'alternative burgers' started showing up all over America. The first time I saw chicken burgers at a barbecue, I thought to myself, *this is not quite right. Where's the respect for our beloved hamburger? What's next, a pizza with fish on top?* Well, like pizzas, burgers proved to be very adaptable. It wasn't long before lots of people were raving about burgers made from chicken, turkey and other surprising ingredients. When I moved to California for college and came across fish burgers, I smirked at the idea at first, especially at the weird toppings like alfalfa sprouts and guacamole. But now that pigs were flying every which way, I let go of preconceived notions and just took a bite. My mind changed quickly when I tasted the lightly smoked and charred edges of a moist fish patty held inside a warm bun glistening with butter. Whoa, it was good. Really good.

All the while, beef burgers were getting bigger and better in America. Celeb chefs rescued us from the redundancy of fast-food burgers and made headlines with outrageously expensive versions starring ingredients like Kobe beef, black truffle shavings and béarnaise sauce. As restaurants loaded the humble burger with the trappings of exalted steaks, folks like you and me who throw backyard barbecues showed a new

open-mindedness about burgers of all types and styles. We cleared room on the grill for whatever our guests preferred, even … gasp … vegetarian burgers. We let people put whatever wacky toppings they wanted on their burgers, and if someone wanted a burger without a bun, we toasted to their individual style.

Which begs the question: what is a burger anyway? At Weber, we are not purists when it comes to a definition. In fact I'm not convinced there really is a strict definition. Even the purists disagree about which types of meat and buns qualify. Early versions of the 'Hamburg sandwich' actually used thinly sliced bread, so a burger has been a flexible idea since its beginnings and has always been evolving.

This book covers a full range of interpretations over time – not only for burgers, but also for the great food and drinks that we associate with burgers. You'll find many recipes for hot dogs, sausages and brats, along with a selection of side dishes, toppings and drinks. As with burgers, many of these items now reflect our most modern tastes, and yet the early versions from decades ago remain as popular as ever. In other words, our options haven't really changed as much as they have just grown in numbers and creativity. With each new take on a burger, a hot dog, or even a potato salad, we can ask whether or not it's authentic, but for me the more important question is: how does it make you *feel*? I figure that if it makes me smile like I did when I ate 'crunch burgers' (for the recipe, see page 25) back in the second grade, that is all I really need to know.

5

TABLE OF **CONTENTS**

GRILLING
BASICS

STARTING A
CHARCOAL GRILL

Got a match? You and your charcoal grill, right? All jokes aside, plan on carving out 15–20 minutes to get your fire going.

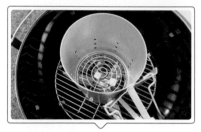

1. LIFE'S EASIER WITH A CHIMNEY STARTER. This metal cylinder with a wire rack and handles provides a snug spot for getting a fire going quickly. Simply fill the space under the wire rack with some wadded-up newspaper or paraffin cubes, then fill the cylinder with charcoal briquettes.

2. LIGHT, CHIMNEY, ACTION. Once you light the newspaper or paraffin cubes, the briquettes will fire up with little risk of a flame-out. You'll see the chimney smoking at first, but don't make a move until the top coals are covered in white ash.

3. GLOVES ON. Wearing insulated barbecue mitts or oven gloves, grab both of the chimney handles and carefully pour the hot coals on to the charcoal grate. That swinging handle is designed to make it safer and easier to aim the coals.

4. COAL PLAY. We like the flexibility of a two-zone fire, where all the coals are pushed to one side of the charcoal grate, providing you with both direct and indirect cooking options. An area of indirect heat will also give you a 'safety zone' – a place to temporarily move food if it begins to flare up over direct heat.

5. JUST ABOUT GO TIME. Put the cooking grate back in place, and cover the grill with the lid. In 10–15 minutes, the temperature of the grill should be close to 260°C/500°F. This is when you want to brush the grate clean.

6. MAKE SURE THE TOP AND BOTTOM VENTS ARE OPEN. While grilling, the vent on the bottom half of the grill should be wide open and clear of ashes, to provide enough air for the fire. Keep the vent on the top open as well, unless you want to lower the temperature a bit by closing the top vent about halfway.

STARTING A
GAS GRILL

Skills required: lid lifting and knob turning. The huge advantage of gas barbecuing is its ease, but there are a few important tips to follow:

1. FIRST THINGS FIRST.
Check the gas cylinder; replace it if it's empty or near empty.

2. LIFT THE GRILL LID AND LIGHT THE GRILL.
Follow your Owner's Guide for lighting instructions.

3. GRILL ON, LID GOES DOWN.
Close the lid and wait 10–15 minutes for the grill to preheat. This creates the oven-like environment needed for efficient cooking and gets the cooking grates good and hot for the perfect sear. It also makes the grates much easier to clean.

DIRECT AND INDIRECT
COOKING

It's time for us to be direct – and indirect – regarding heat.

There are two basic ways of grilling your food: directly over hot coals or fired-up burners, or indirectly, off to the side of the heat source. Direct cooking doles out a hefty blast of heat, which gives food that satisfying, crunchy sear, while indirect heat is gentler, transforming the grill into an oven that cooks your meal more gradually.

Direct heat is best used when cooking thinner, tender items that don't need a lot of time to cook all the way through – your basic hot dogs and beef burger patties would fall into this category.

Indirect heat is the way to go when you want to cook foods more gently from all directions. It's great for roasting fresh sausages and toasting buns, for example.

In many cases, we like to dabble in both types of heat to achieve a good external crust with the preferred internal doneness level to match. This approach leads to more dependable outcomes and not as many awkward 'surprise – it's raw!' moments at the dinner table. To ensure tasty success, start your item over direct heat to sear on both sides, and then move it to the indirect zone to finish up without getting torched. You'll need to build a simple two-zone fire for this, where the hot coals are pushed to one side in a charcoal grill, or where some of the burners are turned off on a gas grill.

In order for all this direct–indirect stuff to work, however, you need to know that the lid is your friend. Keeping it closed as much as possible is what retains the swirling radiant heat you need for indirect cooking, as well as staving off flare-ups in direct use. You'll still need to turn your food, but when the heat can cook the food from the top and bottom simultaneously, grilling tends to go much faster, which, of course, means the eating part arrives more quickly, and that's the whole point of this delicious exercise, isn't it?

CHARCOAL: DIRECT COOKING
With direct heat, the fire is right below the food. The heat radiates off the charcoal and conducts through the metal cooking grate to create those dark, handsome grill marks.

CHARCOAL: INDIRECT COOKING
With indirect heat, the charcoal is arranged to one side of the food, or it is on both sides of the food.

GAS: DIRECT AND INDIRECT COOKING
Using direct heat on a gas grill is simply a matter of grilling the food right over lit burners. To use indirect head, light the burners on the far left and far right of the grill, and grill the food over the unlit burner(s) between them. If your grill has just two burners, light one of them and grill over the unlit one for indirect cooking.

GRILL
MAINTENANCE

Outdoorsy types tend to be pretty low maintenance – grills included. That said, embracing a couple of simple up-keep rituals can keep your grill going, and going strong, for a very long time.

To achieve the coveted grill marks, keep food from sticking, and eliminate the chances of old burnt barnacles on your burger, the cooking grates need to be cleaned before every use. Close the lid and preheat your grill to about 260°C/500°F for 10 minutes. Slip your hand into an insulated barbecue mitt or oven glove and use a long-handled grill brush to do a quick once-over of the grates, dislodging any charred bits left behind from past meals. That quick treatment does the trick.

Keep your grill in tip-top, efficient shape by giving it a more thorough cleaning every month or so. Check the instructions in your Owner's Guide, but start by wiping down the outside of your grill with warm, soapy water. Scrape any accumulated debris from the inside of the lid. Gas barbecuers should remove the cooking grates, brush the burners and clean out the bottom of the cook box and drip pan. Charcoal barbecuers should regularly remove all ash sitting at the bottom of the kettle.

Check your Owner's Guide to get the full report on the ultimate deep clean, up-keep and maintenance for your grill.

A sturdy grill brush with stainless-steel bristles is essential for cleaning your cooking grate. A notched scraper on the brush head is especially good at loosening hardened bits.

TOOLS OF
THE TRADE

These are our must-have tools for creating perfectly cooked, easily flipped, deftly served masterpieces.

PERFORATED GRILL PAN

Use this when cooking foods that are either too small or too delicate for the grates, and say goodbye to saying goodbye to food dropped in the fire.

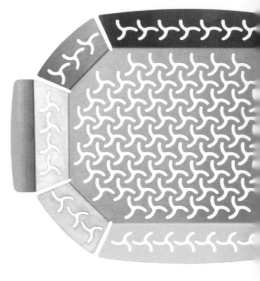

CHIMNEY STARTER

This is the secret to charcoal-grilling success. Pile in briquettes; fill the space underneath with paraffin cubes or wadded-up newspaper; strike a match; and a safe, quickly lit fire is at the ready – lighter fluid need not apply. See 'Starting a Charcoal Grill' (page 10) for more details.

BARBECUE GLOVES

Choose gloves that are insulated and that cover both hand and wrist.

INSTANT-READ THERMOMETER

Get a quick and accurate read on internal temperatures. Easy to find and relatively inexpensive, this all but guarantees grilling success.

5 BURGER PRESS

Become a patty-forming machine with this. Your burgers will be the same size and thickness, which means they will cook at the same rate.

6 GRILL BRUSH

Keep your cooking grates clean with one of these. Your burgers and sausages won't stick or be speckled with old, burnt bits.

7 SPATULA

Long-handled spatulas with offset (bent) necks are what we flip for. These are the easiest for lifting burgers off the grates.

8 GRILL-PROOF GRIDDLE

A griddle brings another kitchen convenience to your grill top for cooking fish and vegetable burgers that are too delicate to put right on an open grate.

9 TONGS

Turn hot dogs, brats and sausages in seconds without piercing them and losing those precious juices. Look for a pair with low tension, a good grip and a lock for storage.

TEN TIPS
FOR GRILLING GREATNESS

1 THOSE WHO PREHEAT WELL, EAT WELL.

Cold grills are no place for burgers and sausages. Without that ample surge of heat to kick off the cooking, food will stick to the grates and you'll miss out on those coveted grill marks. Even if a recipe calls for medium or low heat, the grill should be preheated. Lift the lid, fire up the coals or burners, close the lid, and let the grill do its intensely hot thing for 10–15 minutes – the internal temperature should reach about 260°C/500°F.

2 CLEANLINESS IS GRILL-LINESS.

Unless you prefer your burgers speckled with burnt, crusty old bits of food, a swift sweep of a grill brush over the grates is your second order of business. There's usually 'stuff' left behind after grilling, and, if not removed, it will bind itself to your food, and your food to the grates. So, after a good preheat, grab a sturdy, long-handled, stainless-steel bristled grill brush and give your grates a good cleaning.

3 GET IT TOGETHER, MAN!

Once your grill is preheated and the cooking grates are brushed clean, gather everything you will need and bring it to your grill. That includes tools, oiled and seasoned food, and any additional sauces or sides you're using. Don't forget a clean platter or plates to use as a landing pad for your grilled burgers, sausages and sides. Running back and forth to the kitchen could lead to something great getting overcooked or burnt.

4 PLAY (HEAT) ZONE DEFENCE.

Thinner beef burgers tend to cook pretty quickly over direct heat, as do hot dogs, but sometimes you'll use ingredients that benefit from indirect cooking – think big, raw sausages, or super thick burger patties. In those instances, and many others, a two-zone fire is the way to go. Also, you can brown your items directly above the heat source to get good grill marks, and then slide them on to the indirect, cooler side to finish in gentler, roasting confines.

TEN TIPS

5 THEY JUST NEED SOME SPACE.

Burgers and sausages were designed to feed a crowd, but they don't necessarily want to be part of one. All food cooks a little better on a grill with a little space around it. This allows heat to move freely up and around, as well as giving you some elbow room to wedge tongs or a spatula in between items. Also, leave about a quarter of the grate space clear in case you have to move something quickly to a warmer or cooler spot.

6 GIVE A LID-DLE.

Yes, it's more than just a heavy-duty rain shield. The grill's lid is actually an integral part of the cooking. Leaving the lid on while grilling keeps the interior at a consistent temperature, which makes for better and more predictable results. Also, dripping fat plus too much air whooshing in can trigger flare-ups. Not good. Charcoal barbecuers, remember to keep the lid vents at least halfway open. All fires need at least some air to keep on burning.

7 HANDS OFF THE MERCHANDISE.

When you put a cold, raw patty on a hot cooking grate, it sticks. As the meat begins to cook, it attaches itself to the cooking grate for the first couple of minutes. If you try to turn a patty during this time, you are bound to tear it and leave some meat sticking to the grate. However, if you can manage to wait four minutes or so, that's enough time for the meat to develop a caramelised crust that releases naturally from the grate.

8 KEEP THE GRILL FIRES BURNING.

Charcoal fires, if left to their own devices, reach their hottest temperatures first and then start to lose heat – that rate is determined by the type and amount of fuel used, and your interference. Refuel your fire every 45 minutes or so to keep the temperature up, and move coals around to get your heat zones in order. Always keep the bottom vent free of ash, and the top vent adjusted to your preferred airflow.

9 KNOW WHEN TO PULL THE RIP CORD.

This means getting your burgers and sausages off the grill at just the right moment. The surest approach involves a thermometer slipped into the centre of the meat, but forget about that old, dial thermometer bouncing around your kitchen drawer. For much more reliable readings, trust a digital instant-read thermometer.

10 NOW, WAIT JUST A MINUTE.

As burgers cook, the heat pushes meat juices out to the surface. If you let hot burgers 'rest' for just a minute or two off the grill before diving in, the juices have a chance to be reabsorbed into the meat, and that makes a better burger. On decadent days, drop a thin slice of butter on top of each burger while resting and let the lusciousness seep inside.

BURGERS

5 STEPS TO BURGER BRILLIANCE

1 MEAT MATTERS

Prepackaged 'hamburger' often means you get minced scraps of questionable quality. Once that meat has been compressed in a tray, it will never have the loose, tender texture of a great burger. You are much better off with 'mince', or, if perfection is your goal, buy freshly minced beef from a butcher you trust.

2 THOROUGH SEASONING

Burgers taste significantly better with seasonings dispersed throughout the meat, not just on the surface. Use salt and pepper at a minimum. Wet ingredients like chopped onion, tomato ketchup, mustard and Worcestershire sauce improve not only the taste but also the juiciness. Mix in the seasonings as gently as possible with your fingertips so you don't compress the texture too much.

Consider this one of life's great turning points. Before: burgers were at times dry, tough, tasteless, or the unfortunate all-of-the-above abomination. After: burgers are juicy, flavourful and consistently brilliant. Here's why.

3 PORTION CONTROL

Divide the meat into equal portions. Form each portion into a loose, round ball, then gently flatten it until it's 1.5–2.5 cm/ ¾–2.5 cm/1 inch thick. This is your ideal thickness for giving the surface a nicely charred crust just as the centre is reaching a juicy medium doneness.

4 DIMPLING

Most burgers tend to puff up in the middle as they cook, making the tops rounded and awkward for piling on toppings. To avoid this, use your thumb or the back of a spoon to press a shallow indentation in the centre of each raw patty (or use a burger press). As each patty cooks, it will fill in and flatten out, giving you a level surface instead of a big meatball.

5 HANDLING THE HEAT

The grill has to be hot (200–260°C/400–500°F) and clean. You have to be cool and patient. Close the lid as soon as the patties hit the grate. Give them 8–10 minutes total to reach medium, turning them only once – any more and you run the risk of ripping the surface before it has turned into a tasty crust. Don't ever smash burgers with a spatula! The juices will cause a flare-up.

TEXAS BURGERS WITH CHEDDAR CHEESE AND BARBECUE SAUCE

SERVES: **4** | PREP TIME: **15 MINUTES, PLUS ABOUT 30 MINUTES FOR THE SAUCE** | GRILLING TIME: **8–10 MINUTES**

BEEF

SAUCE
1 tablespoon vegetable oil
½ onion, finely chopped
250 ml/8 fl oz tomato ketchup
4 tablespoons water
2 tablespoons Worcestershire sauce
1 tablespoon dark brown sugar
1 tablespoon chilli powder
1 tablespoon cider vinegar
½ teaspoon garlic powder

PATTIES
700 g/1½ lb steak mince (80% lean)
1 tablespoon chilli powder
½ teaspoon garlic powder
½ teaspoon sea salt

4 slices Cheddar cheese, each about 30 g/1 oz
4 burger buns, split
4 leaves romaine lettuce, shredded
16 sweet pickle slices (optional)

1. In a heavy, medium saucepan over a medium heat, warm the oil. Add the onion and cook for 12–15 minutes until super soft and as dark as possible, stirring occasionally. Add the remaining sauce ingredients and bring to the boil over a medium-high heat. Regulate the heat so that the sauce simmers gently. Cook for 15–20 minutes, until thickened, stirring frequently. Let cool to room temperature.

2. Mix the patty ingredients, and then gently form four patties of equal size, each about 1.5 cm/¾ inch thick. With your thumb or the back of a spoon, make a shallow indentation about 2.5 cm/1 inch wide in the centre of the patties to prevent them from forming a dome as they cook. Refrigerate the patties until ready to grill.

3. Prepare the grill for direct cooking over medium-high heat (200–260°C/400–500°F).

4. Grill the patties over *direct medium-high heat* for 8–10 minutes, with the lid closed, until cooked to medium (70°C/160°F), turning once. During the last 30–60 seconds of grilling time, place a slice of cheese on each patty to melt, and toast the buns, cut side down, over direct heat.

5. Build each burger on a bun with lettuce, a patty, barbecue sauce and pickles, if liked. Serve warm. The extra sauce can be stored in the refrigerator in a covered container for up to 1 week.

For this barbecue sauce, cook the onions until super soft and as dark as possible to extract as much flavour as you can before adding the tomato ketchup and other wet ingredients.

CRUNCH BURGERS

SERVES: **4 (MAKES 8 SLIDERS)** | PREP TIME: **10 MINUTES** | GRILLING TIME: **ABOUT 6 MINUTES**

BEEF

PATTIES

700 g/1½ lb steak mince (80% lean)
1 tablespoon tomato ketchup
½ teaspoon Worcestershire sauce
½ teaspoon onion powder
½ teaspoon sea salt
¼ teaspoon freshly ground black pepper
2 slices Cheddar cheese, each about 30 g/1 oz,
   cut into quarters

8 slider buns, split
tomato ketchup (optional)
16 dill pickle slices
8 handfuls thin crisps, such as Walkers®

1. Mix the patty ingredients, and then gently form eight patties of equal size, each about 1 cm/½ inch thick. Refrigerate the patties until ready to grill.

2. Prepare the grill for direct cooking over medium-high heat (200–260°C/400–500°F).

3. Grill the patties over *direct medium-high heat* for about 6 minutes, with the lid closed, until cooked to medium (70°C/160°F), turning once. During the last 30–60 seconds of grilling time, place a quarter-slice of cheese on each patty to melt, and toast the buns, cut side down, over direct heat.

4. Place a patty on each bottom bun half and top with tomato ketchup (if using), a patty, pickles and a stack of crisps. Put the bun tops on and then press down. Serve immediately.

Go ahead and have some fun with your cheeseburgers. Making a tower of crisps and crushing them into smithereens is bound to bring back the little kid in you.

BURGERS

VERMONT BURGERS WITH MAPLE-MUSTARD GLAZE

SERVES: **4** | PREP TIME: **20 MINUTES** | GRILLING TIME: **9–11 MINUTES**

BEEF

PATTIES

700 g/1½ lb steak mince
  (80% lean)
½ finely chopped onion
2 teaspoons
  Worcestershire sauce
1 teaspoon mustard powder
1 teaspoon sea salt
½ teaspoon freshly ground
  black pepper

GLAZE

3 tablespoons pure maple syrup
2 tablespoons coarse-grain
  mustard
1 tablespoon balsamic vinegar
¼ teaspoon freshly ground
  black pepper

180 g/6 oz Cheddar cheese,
  cut into 4 slices, at room
  temperature
4 pretzel rolls, split
large handful rocket leaves
½ small red onion,
  cut into thin slices
8 rashers cooked thick-cut bacon

1. Mix the patty ingredients, and then gently form four patties of equal size, each about 2.5 cm/ 1 inch thick. With your thumb or the back of a spoon, make a shallow indentation about 2.5 cm/1 inch wide in the centre of the patties to prevent them from forming a dome as they cook. Refrigerate the patties until ready to grill.

2. Prepare the grill for direct cooking over medium-high heat (200–260°C/400–500°F).

3. Combine the glaze ingredients.

4. Grill the patties over *direct medium-high heat* for 9–11 minutes, with the lid closed, until cooked to medium (70°C/160°F), turning once. Once the burgers have been turned, baste with the glaze frequently. During the last 30–60 seconds of grilling time, place a slice of cheese on each patty to melt, and toast the rolls, cut side down, over direct heat.

5. Build each burger on a roll with rocket, a patty, onion and two rashers of bacon. Serve warm.

BACON AND EGG BEEF BURGERS WITH CHEDDAR

SERVES: **4** | PREP TIME: **25 MINUTES** | GRILLING TIME: **9–11 MINUTES**

PATTIES

700 g/1½ lb steak mince
  (80% lean)
¼ finely chopped onion
2 tablespoons tomato ketchup
2 teaspoons Worcestershire
  sauce
1 teaspoon sea salt
¼ teaspoon freshly ground
  black pepper

8 rashers bacon
4 slices Cheddar cheese,
  each about 30 g/1 oz
4 crusty rolls, split
4 large eggs
Sea salt
Freshly ground black pepper
8 slices ripe tomato

1. Mix the patty ingredients, then gently form four patties of equal size, each about 2.5 cm/1 inch thick. With your thumb or the back of a spoon, make a shallow indentation about 2.5 cm/1 inch wide in the centre of the patties to prevent them from forming a dome as they cook. Refrigerate the patties until ready to grill.

2. In a frying pan over a medium heat, fry the bacon for 10–12 minutes until crisp, turning occasionally. Transfer the bacon to kitchen paper to drain. Pour off and discard all but 2 tablespoons of the bacon fat from the pan.

3. Prepare the grill for direct cooking over medium-high heat (200–260°C/400–500°F).

4. Grill the patties over *direct medium-high heat* for 9–11 minutes, with the lid closed, until cooked to medium (70°C/160°F), turning once. During the last 30–60 seconds of grilling time, place a slice of cheese on each patty to melt, and toast the rolls, cut side down, over direct heat.

5. Return the frying pan to a medium heat and warm the bacon fat. Crack the eggs into the pan and cook until the yolks are still slightly runny, about 3 minutes, turning once. Season with salt and pepper.

6. Build each burger on a roll with two tomato slices, a patty, two rashers of bacon and an egg. Serve warm.

This one is for all the breakfast lovers. Who says you can't have bacon and eggs for dinner? After you fry the bacon, leave a little fat in the pan and heat it just until it barely sizzles before you add the eggs. If your eggs are really fresh, the yolks will sit up proudly in the centre and the whites will not spread far and wide in the pan. For really tender eggs, cover the pan while frying. The moisture trapped by the lid will gently steam the tops of the eggs.

BEEF

TEX-MEX BEEF BURGERS

SERVES: **4** | PREP TIME: **25 MINUTES** | GRILLING TIME: **9–11 MINUTES**

PATTIES

700 g/1½ lb steak mince (80% lean)
1 teaspoon onion flakes
½ teaspoon ground cumin
½ teaspoon garlic granules
½ teaspoon chilli powder

Sea salt
Freshly ground black pepper

SALSA

3 ripe plum tomatoes, cored, seeded and
  cut into 5-mm/¼-inch dice
4 tablespoons roughly chopped fresh coriander
  leaves
3 tablespoons finely diced red onion
2 tablespoons seeded and finely diced jalapeño
  chillies
1½ tablespoons fresh lime juice

8 slices sourdough bread, each about 1 cm/½ inch
  thick
Extra-virgin olive oil
4 whole green chillies (from a can), chopped
4 slices Cheddar cheese, each about 30 g/1 oz
120 ml/4 fl oz sour cream

1. Mix the patty ingredients, including ½ teaspoon salt and ¼ teaspoon pepper, and then gently form four patties of equal size, each about 2.5 cm/1 inch thick. With your thumb or the back of a spoon, make a shallow indentation about 2.5 cm/1 inch wide in the centre of the patties to prevent them from forming a dome as they cook. Refrigerate the patties until ready to grill.

2. Prepare the grill for direct cooking over medium-high heat (200–260°C/400–500°F).

3. Meanwhile, combine the salsa ingredients, including ½ teaspoon salt and ¼ teaspoon pepper.

4. Lightly season the patties on both sides with salt and pepper, and brush one side of each bread slice with oil. Grill the patties over *direct medium-high heat*, with the lid closed, for 5 minutes. Turn the patties over and top with an equal amount of chopped chillies and a slice of cheese. Continue grilling until the patties are cooked to medium (70°C/160°F), 4–6 minutes more. During the last 30–60 seconds of grilling time, toast the bread, oiled side down, over direct heat (do not turn).

5. Stir the salsa. Build each burger on a bread slice with a patty, 1 tablespoon salsa, 1 tablespoon sour cream and the remaining bread slice. Serve warm with the remaining salsa and sour cream on the side.

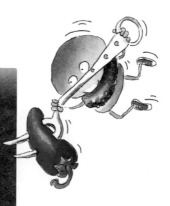

FUN FACT

The word 'Tex-Mex' first entered the English language around 1875, in reference to the Texas-Mexican Railway. Since then, the term has turned much tastier, generally referring to the now mainstream Mexican-influenced cuisine, such as fajitas, chilli, nachos, tacos and burritos.

FOUR-ALARM JALAPEÑO CHEESEBURGERS

SERVES: **4** | PREP TIME: **15 MINUTES** | GRILLING TIME: **8-10 MINUTES**

BEEF

SAUCE
180 ml/6 fl oz mayonnaise
2 canned chipotle chillies
  in adobo sauce, finely diced
2 teaspoons fresh lime juice

PATTIES
700 g/1½ lb steak mince (80% lean)
3 tablespoons tomato ketchup
2 teaspoons Worcestershire sauce
1 teaspoon garlic powder
¾ teaspoon chilli powder
¾ teaspoon sea salt

4 slices pepper jack or Cheddar cheese,
  each about 30 g/1 oz
4 burger buns, split
1 large ripe beefsteak tomato, cut crossways
  into 4 slices
4 pickled jalapeño chillies (from a jar),
  each cut lengthways into quarters

1. Whisk the sauce ingredients.

2. Mix the patty ingredients, and then gently form four patties of equal size, each about 1.5 cm/¾ inch thick. With your thumb or the back of a spoon, make a shallow indentation about 2.5 cm/1 inch wide in the centre of the patties to prevent them from forming a dome as they cook. Refrigerate the patties until ready to grill.

3. Prepare the grill for direct cooking over medium-high heat (200–260°C/400–500°F).

4. Grill the patties over *direct medium-high heat* for 8–10 minutes, with the lid closed, until cooked to medium (70°C/160°F), turning once. During the last 30–60 seconds of grilling time, place a slice of cheese on each patty to melt, and toast the buns, cut side down, over direct heat.

5. Build each burger on a bun with sauce, a patty, a tomato slice and four jalapeño quarters. Serve warm.

WHERE DID THE WORD 'HAMBURGER' COME FROM?

Etymologists will contend that the Hamburg steak, the hamburger's plated knife-and-fork predecessor, is also the hamburger's etymological derivation. Named after the port city of Hamburg, Germany, the Hamburg steak (simply a seasoned chopped steak patty) made its way to America alongside its emigrant creators in the seventeenth century. America's industrialisation and the advent of lunch wagons then provoked the Hamburg steak's historic leap from plate to sandwich, making standing lunches – sans plates or utensils – both possible and plausible. Filling, cheap and convenient, the 'hamburger steak sandwich' was born, and the rest, as they say, is history.

BEEF

ROUTE 66 BURGERS

SERVES: **4** | PREP TIME: **15 MINUTES** | GRILLING TIME: **8–10 MINUTES**

SAUCE
5 tablespoons mayonnaise
2 tablespoons tomato ketchup
1 tablespoon sweet pickle relish
1 tablespoon finely chopped shallot

PATTIES
700 g/1½ lb steak mince (80% lean)
¾ teaspoon garlic powder
¾ teaspoon sea salt
¼ teaspoon freshly ground black pepper

4 processed cheese slices
4 burger buns, split
4 leaves romaine lettuce
1 large ripe beefsteak tomato,
   cut crossways into 4 slices

1. Combine the sauce ingredients.

2. Mix the patty ingredients, and then gently form four patties of equal size, each about 1.5 cm/¾ inch thick. With your thumb or the back of a spoon, make a shallow indentation about 2.5 cm/1 inch wide in the centre of the patties to prevent them from forming a dome as they cook. Refrigerate the patties until ready to grill.

3. Prepare the grill for direct cooking over medium-high heat (200–260°C/400–500°F).

4. Grill the patties over *direct medium-high heat* for 8–10 minutes, with the lid closed, until cooked to medium (70°C/160°F), turning once. During the last 30–60 seconds of grilling time, place a slice of cheese on each patty to melt, and toast the buns, cut side down, over direct heat.

5. Build each burger on a bun with sauce, a lettuce leaf, a tomato slice and a patty. Serve warm.

Like the great ole highway that stretched from Chicago to Los Angeles, these burgers represent a classic Americana style. If you ever drove Route 66 and ate in the mom-and-pop restaurants along the way, you might have had burgers just like these.

BEEF FAJITA BURGERS WITH GUACAMOLE

SERVES: **4** | PREP TIME: **25 MINUTES** | GRILLING TIME: **8–10 MINUTES**

1 tablespoon extra-virgin olive oil
½ red pepper, cut into thin strips
½ yellow pepper, cut into thin strips

GUACAMOLE

1 ripe avocado
1 tablespoon fresh lime juice
1 plum tomato, seeded and finely chopped
1 tablespoon finely chopped fresh coriander
1 tablespoon finely chopped shallot
½ teaspoon sea salt, or to taste

PATTIES

700 g/1½ lb steak mince (80% lean)
1 tablespoon chilli powder
1 teaspoon ground cumin
½ teaspoon sea salt

4 slices pepper jack or Cheddar cheese, each about
    30 g/1 oz
4 sesame seed buns, split

1. In a large frying pan over a medium heat, warm the oil. Add the peppers and cook for about 10 minutes, until softened, stirring frequently. Remove from the heat.

2. Mash the guacamole ingredients. Cover with clingfilm, pressing the film directly on to the surface of the guacamole to prevent it from browning. Refrigerate until ready to serve.

3. Mix the patty ingredients, and then gently form four patties of equal size, each about 1.5 cm/¾ inch thick. With your thumb or the back of a spoon, make a shallow indentation about 2.5 cm/1 inch wide in the centre of the patties to prevent them from forming a dome as they cook. Refrigerate the patties until ready to grill.

4. Prepare the grill for direct cooking over medium-high heat (200–260°C/400–500°F).

5. Grill the patties over *direct medium-high heat* for 8–10 minutes, with the lid closed, until cooked to medium (70°C/160°F), turning once. During the last 30–60 seconds of grilling time, place a slice of cheese on each patty to melt, and toast the buns, cut side down, over direct heat.

6. Build each burger on a bun with a patty, peppers and guacamole. Serve warm.

CHEDDAR-STUFFED BURGERS WITH CHOPPED ONION

SERVES: **4** | PREP TIME: **20 MINUTES** | GRILLING TIME: **9–11 MINUTES**

PATTIES

700 g/1½ lb steak mince
  (80% lean)
½ onion, finely chopped
1 teaspoon sea salt
¾ teaspoon garlic granules
½ teaspoon freshly ground
  black pepper

4 slices Cheddar cheese,
  stacked and quartered to make
  4 blocks, each about
  3 cm/1¼ inches square and
  1 cm/½ inch thick
4 burger buns, split
Tomato ketchup or Sweet and
Spicy Tomato Chutney
(for recipe, see page 235)

1. Mix the patty ingredients, and then gently form eight patties of equal size, each about 8 mm/⅓ inch thick. Place four patties on a work surface and centre a cheese block on top of each. Centre the remaining four patties over the top and press down until each double patty is about 2.5 cm/1 inch thick. Pinch the edges together tightly to seal the cheese inside. Refrigerate the patties until ready to grill.

2. Prepare the grill for direct cooking over medium-high heat (200–260°C/400–500°F).

3. Grill the patties over *direct medium-high heat* for 9–11 minutes, with the lid closed, until cooked to medium (70°C/160°F), turning once (don't worry if a little cheese leaks out). During the last 30–60 seconds of grilling time, toast the buns, cut side down, over direct heat.

4. Build each burger on a bun with a patty and tomato ketchup or chutney. Serve warm.

Use whatever type of Cheddar you like with your burgers. The 'maturity' of the cheese is an indication of its pungency. Mature Cheddar is usually aged for 6–9 months, so it has a stronger taste than mild Cheddar. Extra-mature Cheddar is often aged for 1½–2 years. Regardless of its maturity, a good Cheddar should have a nutty taste and a firm but creamy texture. Its colour is naturally off-white, but a lot of American producers colour it orange with annatto seeds or other ingredients.

CHEESEBURGERS WITH GRILLED APPLE

SERVES: **4** | PREP TIME: **15 MINUTES** | GRILLING TIME: **9–11 MINUTES**

PATTIES
700 g/1½ lb steak mince (80% lean)
1 teaspoon sea salt
¼ teaspoon ground nutmeg
¼ teaspoon freshly ground black pepper

1 large, ripe apple, cored and cut crossways into four 1-cm/½-inch slices
1½ teaspoons extra-virgin olive oil
120 g/4 oz Edam cheese, cut into 8 pieces
4 round pretzel rolls or burger buns, split
Spicy brown mustard
4 lettuce leaves

1. Mix the patty ingredients, then gently form four patties of equal size, each about 2.5 cm/1 inch thick. With your thumb or the back of a spoon, make a shallow indentation about 2.5 cm/1 inch wide in the centre of the patties to prevent them from forming a dome as they cook. Refrigerate the patties until ready to grill.

2. Prepare the grill for direct cooking over medium-high heat (200–260°C/400–500°F).

3. Brush the apple slices on both sides with the oil.

4. Grill the patties over *direct medium-high heat* for 9–11 minutes, with the lid closed, until cooked to medium (70°C/160°F), turning once. At the same time, grill the apple slices over *direct medium-high heat* for 3–4 minutes until tender and nicely marked, turning once. During the last 30–60 seconds of grilling time, place two pieces of cheese on each patty to melt, and toast the rolls, cut side down, over direct heat.

5. Build each burger on a roll with mustard, a lettuce leaf, a patty and a grilled apple slice. Serve warm.

BEEF

WEBER'S EXTREME BURGERS

SERVES: **4** | PREP TIME: **25 MINUTES** | GRILLING TIME: **6–8 MINUTES**

4 rashers thick-cut bacon

MAYO
5 tablespoons mayonnaise
1 teaspoon crushed garlic
Sea salt
Freshly ground black pepper

GUACAMOLE
2 ripe avocados
1 tablespoon fresh lime juice
2 teaspoons crushed garlic

1 kg/2 lb steak mince (80% lean)
1 tablespoon Worcestershire sauce
½ teaspoon smoked paprika
½ teaspoon onion powder
8 thin slices Cheddar cheese
4 burger buns, split
4 leaves round lettuce
1 ripe beefsteak tomato, cut crossways
    into 4 slices about 8 mm/⅓ inch thick

1. In a frying pan over a medium heat, fry the bacon for 10–12 minutes until crisp, 10 to 12 minutes, turning occasionally. Drain on kitchen paper.

2. Whisk the mayo ingredients, including ¼ teaspoon salt and ⅛ teaspoon pepper.

3. Mash the guacamole ingredients, including ½ teaspoon salt and ¼ teaspoon pepper.

4. Mix the steak mince with the Worcestershire sauce, 1 teaspoon salt, ½ teaspoon pepper, the smoked paprika and onion powder and then gently form eight patties of equal size, each about 1 cm/½ inch thick and a little wider than the buns. Refrigerate the patties until ready to grill.

5. Prepare the grill for direct cooking over medium-high heat (200–260°C/400–500°F).

6. Grill the patties over *direct medium-high heat* for 6–8 minutes, with the lid closed, until cooked to medium (70°C/160°F), turning once. During the last 30–60 seconds of grilling time, place a slice of cheese on each patty to melt and toast the buns, cut side down, over direct heat.

7. Build each burger on a bun with garlic mayo, a lettuce leaf, a tomato slice, two patties, as much guacamole as you like, a slice of bacon (torn in half) and more garlic mayo. Serve immediately.

Behold an extreme example of what's good, renowned and entirely decadent about burgers. This cheesy double-decker of grilled beef gets a dollop of garlic mayonnaise smeared on the bun, all of which would make a spectacular sandwich if we stopped right there, but we don't take the word 'extreme' lightly. So bring on the layers of lettuce and tomato. Bring on the glorious guacamole. And as long as we're going over the top, bring on the bacon, too.

BUILDING A
BETTER BURGER

The burger is about as foolproof a meal as we know: open bun, insert patty, close bun, eat. Not much to it, right? Nor should there be, but some small adjustments can yield delicious results.

1 CHOOSE FIRM BUNS

Supermarket brands can be too soft and may fall apart as the juices run. A good bun should be slightly dense but still pillowy. Sound contradictory? The crusty roll pulls off this duality well.

2 MAKE IT TOASTY

Tossing your split buns on the grill for 30-60 seconds creates a dry surface that will absorb juices without total bun disintegration. That slight crunch does a lot for texture, too.

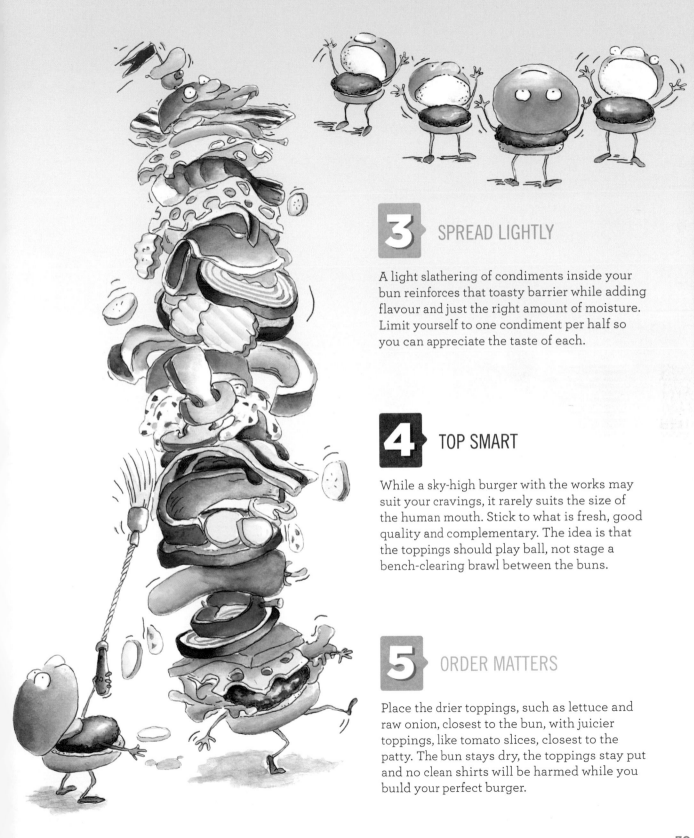

3 ▸ SPREAD LIGHTLY

A light slathering of condiments inside your bun reinforces that toasty barrier while adding flavour and just the right amount of moisture. Limit yourself to one condiment per half so you can appreciate the taste of each.

4 ▸ TOP SMART

While a sky-high burger with the works may suit your cravings, it rarely suits the size of the human mouth. Stick to what is fresh, good quality and complementary. The idea is that the toppings should play ball, not stage a bench-clearing brawl between the buns.

5 ▸ ORDER MATTERS

Place the drier toppings, such as lettuce and raw onion, closest to the bun, with juicier toppings, like tomato slices, closest to the patty. The bun stays dry, the toppings stay put and no clean shirts will be harmed while you build your perfect burger.

BRONCO BURGERS WITH SMOKED MOZZARELLA AND BARBECUE SAUCE

SERVES: **4** | PREP TIME: **15 MINUTES** | GRILLING TIME: **8-10 MINUTES**

PATTIES

700 g/1½ lb steak mince (80% lean)
1 teaspoon ground cumin
1 teaspoon chilli powder
1 teaspoon onion powder
1 teaspoon sea salt
½ teaspoon freshly ground black pepper

4 slices smoked mozzarella cheese
4 burger buns, split
180 ml/6 fl oz Cherry Cola Barbecue Sauce (for
   recipe, see page 237) or shop-bought barbecue
   sauce
4 thin slices onion
16 dill pickle slices

1. Mix the patty ingredients, and then gently form four patties of equal size, each about 1.5 cm/¾ inch thick. With your thumb or the back of a spoon, make a shallow indentation about 2.5 cm/1 inch wide in the centre of the patties to prevent them from forming a dome as they cook. Refrigerate the patties until ready to grill.

2. Prepare the grill for direct cooking over medium-high heat (200-260°C/400-500°F).

3. Grill the patties over *direct medium-high heat* for 8-10 minutes, with the lid closed, until cooked to medium (70°C/160°F), turning once. During the last 30-60 seconds of grilling time, place a slice of cheese on each patty to melt, and toast the buns, cut side down, over direct heat.

4. Build each burger on a bun with barbecue sauce, an onion slice, a patty and pickles. Serve warm.

Serving suggestion: Smoky Barbecued Baked Beans (for recipe, see page 226).

FUN FACT

Pickle perfection is all about the snap. The best dill pickles, according to professional pickle purveyors, pack an audible crunch from 10 paces away, whereas pickles that can be heard from only one pace are known as 'denture dills'.

SUN-DRIED TOMATO BEEF BURGERS WITH SMOKED MOZZARELLA

SERVES: **4** | PREP TIME: **20 MINUTES** | GRILLING TIME: **6–8 MINUTES**

PATTIES

450 g/1 lb steak mince
    (80% lean)
1 shallot, finely chopped
2 tablespoons freshly grated
    Parmesan cheese
2 tablespoons finely chopped oil-
    packed sun-dried tomatoes
1 tablespoon panko breadcrumbs
1 tablespoon chopped fresh
    parsley leaves
1 teaspoon dried oregano

Sea salt
Freshly ground black pepper
4 slices olive bread, each
    about 1 cm/½ inch thick
Extra-virgin olive oil
90 g/3 oz smoked mozzarella
    cheese, thinly sliced
large handful rocket leaves

1. Mix the patty ingredients, including ¾ teaspoon salt and ¼ teaspoon pepper, and then gently form four patties of equal size, each about 1 cm/½ inch thick. Refrigerate the patties until ready to grill.

2. Prepare the grill for direct cooking over medium heat (180–230°C/350–450°F).

3. Brush the bread slices on both sides with oil and lightly season the bread and the patties with salt and pepper. Grill the patties over *direct medium heat*, with the lid closed, for 3–4 minutes. Turn the patties over and distribute the cheese evenly on top of the patties. Continue grilling for 3–4 minutes more, until cooked to medium (70°C/160°F). During the last minute of grilling time, toast the bread over direct heat until slightly golden, turning once.

4. Top each bread slice with a patty and some rocket. Serve warm.

DOUBLE-TRUFFLED CHEESEBURGERS

SERVES: **4** | PREP TIME: **15 MINUTES** | GRILLING TIME: **9-11 MINUTES**

PATTIES
700 g/1½ lb steak mince
   (80% lean)
1½ tablespoons finely chopped
   shallots
4 teaspoons white or
   black truffle oil
1 tablespoon Dijon mustard
1 tablespoon chopped fresh
   parsley leaves
½ teaspoon Worcestershire sauce

Sea salt
Freshly ground black pepper
75 g/2½ oz truffle cheese, cut into
   8 slices, at room temperature
2 focaccia squares, each about
   11 cm/4½ inches, split
4-8 gherkins, thinly sliced

1. Mix the patty ingredients, including ½ teaspoon salt and ¼ teaspoon pepper, and then gently form four patties of equal size, each about 2.5 cm/1 inch thick. With your thumb or the back of a spoon, make a shallow indentation about 2.5 cm/1 inch wide in the centre of the patties to prevent them from forming a dome as they cook. Refrigerate the patties until ready to grill.

2. Prepare the grill for direct cooking over medium-high heat (200-260°C/400-500°F).

3. Lightly season the patties on both sides with salt and pepper, and then grill over *direct medium-high heat* for 9-11 minutes, with the lid closed, until cooked to medium (70°C/160°F), turning once. During the last 30-60 seconds of grilling time, place two slices of cheese on each patty to melt, and toast the focaccia, cut side down, over direct heat.

4. Top each focaccia square with a patty and gherkins. Serve warm.

The first dose of truffle comes from a soft, melting cheese that is speckled with tiny bits of the mushroomy tuber. The second dose comes from oil that is infused with truffle aroma and worked into the meat.

REUBEN BURGERS

SERVES: **4** | PREP TIME: **20 MINUTES** | GRILLING TIME: **13–15 MINUTES**

BEEF

PATTIES
450 g/1 lb steak mince (80% lean)
120 g/4 oz pancetta or lean bacon,
   finely chopped
2 teaspoons wholegrain mustard
1 teaspoon onion flakes
½ teaspoon garlic granules

Sea salt
Freshly ground black pepper

DRESSING
8 tablespoons mayonnaise
2 tablespoons sour cream
1½ tablespoons tomato ketchup
2 teaspoons horseradish
1 teaspoon Worcestershire sauce
1 teaspoon chopped fresh dill
1 garlic clove, crushed
¼ teaspoon white wine vinegar

8 slices rye bread
30 g/1 oz unsalted butter, melted
8 slices Emmenthal cheese, each about 30 g/1 oz
225 g/8 oz sauerkraut, drained

1. Mix the patty ingredients, including ½ teaspoon salt and ¼ teaspoon pepper, and then gently form four patties of equal size, each about 2.5 cm/1 inch thick. With your thumb or the back of a spoon, make a shallow indentation about 2.5 cm/1 inch wide in the centre of the patties to prevent them from forming a dome as they cook. Refrigerate the patties until ready to grill.

2. Prepare the grill for direct cooking over medium-high heat (200–260°C/400–500°F).

3. Combine the dressing ingredients, including ⅛ teaspoon salt.

4. Lightly season the patties on both sides with salt and pepper, and then grill over *direct medium-high heat* for 9–11 minutes, with the lid closed, until cooked to medium (70°C/160°F), turning once.

5. Brush one side of each bread slice with the melted butter, and place them on a work surface, buttered side down. Spread the unbuttered side of the bread with the dressing. Build each burger with a bread slice (dressing side up), one slice of cheese, a patty, another slice of cheese, sauerkraut and a second bread slice (dressing side down). Place the burgers over *direct medium-high heat*, close the lid, and cook for about 4 minutes until the cheese is melted and the bread is toasted, carefully turning once. Serve warm.

Pancetta is easier to chop if it is very cold, so chill it in the freezer for 15 minutes just before chopping.

BAGUETTE BEEF BURGERS WITH BRIE

SERVES: **4** | PREP TIME: **15 MINUTES** | GRILLING TIME: **8–10 MINUTES**

PATTIES

700 g/1½ lb steak mince
    (80% lean)
1½ tablespoons finely chopped
    fresh parsley leaves
2 garlic cloves, crushed
1 teaspoon dried thyme

Sea salt
Freshly ground black pepper
120 g/4 oz Brie cheese,
    rind removed, chilled,
    and cut into 4 chunks
4 slices French baguette,
    each about 1 cm/½ inch thick,
    cut on a sharp diagonal
2 teaspoons unsalted
    butter, softened
4 teaspoons wholegrain mustard
1 small head frisée lettuce,
    pale inner heart only

1. Mix the patty ingredients, including ½ teaspoon salt and ¼ teaspoon pepper, and then divide into four equal-sized balls (don't compact the meat too much). With your forefinger, make a dimple in the centre of each ball of meat and insert a piece of cheese. Close the meat over the cheese. Gently press the meat into oblong patties of equal size (to match the size of the bread slices), each about 1.5 cm/¾ inch thick. Refrigerate the patties until ready to grill.

2. Prepare the grill for direct cooking over medium-high heat (200–260°C/400–500°F).

3. Lightly season the patties on both sides with salt and pepper, and then grill over *direct medium-high heat* for 8–10 minutes, with the lid closed, until cooked to medium (70°C/160°F), turning once. During the last minute of grilling time, toast the baguette slices over direct heat, turning once.

4. Spread the butter on the baguette slices and top each with mustard, a patty and frisée. Serve warm.

FONTINA-STUFFED BURGERS WITH PARMA HAM

SERVES: **4** | PREP TIME: **15 MINUTES** | GRILLING TIME: **10–12 MINUTES**

PATTIES
700 g/1½ lb steak mince
(80% lean)
1 tablespoon finely chopped fresh
sage leaves
½ teaspoon sea salt
¼ teaspoon freshly ground black
pepper
1 teaspoon dried thyme

60 g/2 oz fontina cheese,
cut into 4 pieces
5 tablespoons mayonnaise
½ teaspoon finely grated lemon
zest
4 burger buns, split
120 g/4 oz thinly sliced Parma
ham
large handful rocket leaves

The keys to keeping the
cheese inside a burger are:
(1) using just a little of it and
(2) creating a tight seal all
the way around each patty.

1. Mix the patty ingredients, and then gently form eight patties of equal size, each about 1 cm/½ inch thick. Centre one piece of cheese on top of four patties. Centre the remaining four patties over the top and press down until each double patty is about 2.5 cm/1 inch thick. Pinch the edges together tightly to seal the cheese inside. Refrigerate the patties until ready to grill.

2. Mix the mayonnaise and lemon rind. Cover and refrigerate until ready to use.

3. Prepare the grill for direct cooking over medium heat (180–230°C/350–450°F).

4. Grill the patties over *direct medium heat* for 10–12 minutes, with the lid closed, until cooked to medium (70°C/160°F), turning them once.

5. Build each burger on a bun with lemon mayonnaise, a patty, Parma ham, rocket and more lemon mayonnaise. Serve immediately.

BEEF

BEEF BURGERS WITH CAMEMBERT AND RED ONION JAM

SERVES: **4** | PREP TIME: **15 MINUTES, PLUS ABOUT 30 MINUTES FOR THE JAM** | GRILLING TIME: **9–11 MINUTES**

JAM

2 tablespoons extra-virgin olive oil
2 large red onions, 700 g/1½ lb, sliced
3 tablespoons granulated sugar
200 ml/7 fl oz cabernet sauvignon
2 tablespoons balsamic vinegar

Sea salt
35 g/1¼ oz unsalted butter, softened
8 slices rye bread
700 g/1½ lb steak mince (80% lean)
Freshly ground black pepper
120 g/4 oz Camembert cheese, cut into 8 slices

1. In a large, heavy sauté pan over a medium heat, warm the oil. Add the onions and sugar and sauté for about 15 minutes, until the onions are very soft, stirring occasionally. Pour in the wine and vinegar and cook for 13–14 minutes until almost evaporated, stirring occasionally. Season with ½ teaspoon salt. Keep warm until ready to serve.

2. Butter both sides of each bread slice.

3. Mix the mince, 1 teaspoon salt and ½ teaspoon pepper, and then gently form four patties of equal size, each about 2.5 cm/1 inch thick. With your thumb or the back of a spoon, make a shallow indentation about 2.5 cm/1 inch wide in the centre of the patties to prevent them from forming a dome as they cook. Refrigerate the patties until ready to grill.

4. Prepare the grill for direct cooking over medium-high heat (200–260°C/400–500°F).

5. Grill the patties over *direct medium-high heat* for 9–11 minutes, with the lid closed, until cooked to medium (70°C/160°F), turning once. During the last minute of grilling time, place two slices of cheese on each patty to melt, and toast the bread over direct heat, turning once.

6. Build each burger on a bread slice with a patty, red onion jam, a generous grinding of pepper and the remaining bread slice. Serve warm.

This great sweet-and-sour jam requires cooking the red onions with a bit of sugar until very, very tender and then infusing them with red wine and vinegar. Use any leftover jam for a topping on steaks, leg of lamb or pork chops.

BEEF

PARMESAN BURGERS WITH BALSAMIC TOMATO KETCHUP

SERVES: **4** | PREP TIME: **20 MINUTES** | GRILLING TIME: **11–14 MINUTES**

PATTIES
700 g/1½ lb steak mince
(80% lean)
2 tablespoons balsamic vinegar
2 teaspoons finely chopped fresh
rosemary leaves
3 small garlic cloves, crushed

Sea salt
Freshly ground black pepper

KETCHUP
4 tablespoons tomato ketchup
2 tablespoons balsamic vinegar
1 tablespoon Dijon mustard
1½ teaspoons mayonnaise

30 g/1 oz Parmesan cheese, at
room temperature, shaved into
pieces with a vegetable peeler,
divided
4 slices rustic Italian bread, each
about 1 cm/½ inch thick

1. Mix the patty ingredients, including ½ teaspoon salt and ¼ teaspoon pepper, and then gently form four patties of equal size, each about 2.5 cm/1 inch thick. With your thumb or the back of a spoon, make a shallow indentation about 2.5 cm/1 inch wide in the centre of the patties to prevent them from forming a dome as they cook. Refrigerate the patties until ready to grill.

2. Prepare the grill for direct and indirect cooking over medium-high heat (200–260°C/400–500°F).

3. Whisk the ketchup ingredients.

4. Lightly season the patties on both sides with salt and pepper, and then grill over *direct medium-high heat* for 9–11 minutes, with the lid closed, until cooked to medium (70°C/160°F), turning once. Remove from the grill, immediately top the patties with half of the cheese, and allow to rest for 2–3 minutes.

5. Brush the bread on both sides with oil, and then grill over *indirect medium-high heat* for 30 seconds. Turn the bread over and top with the remaining cheese. Cook for 1–2 minutes until the cheese softens. Serve each cheese-topped patty on a cheese-topped piece of bread with the balsamic tomato ketchup on the side.

CROQUE-MONSIEUR BEEF BURGERS

SERVES: **4** | PREP TIME: **15 MINUTES** | GRILLING TIME: **8–10 MINUTES** | SPECIAL EQUIPMENT: **GRILL-PROOF GRIDDLE**

PATTIES

700 g/1½ lb steak mince
   (80% lean)
2 tablespoons Dijon mustard
1 tablespoon
   Worcestershire sauce
¾ teaspoon sea salt

40 g/1½ oz unsalted
   butter, softened
8 slices sourdough or
   French bread
180 g/6 oz Gruyère cheese,
   grated
¼ teaspoon ground nutmeg
8 thin slices deli ham
Dijon mustard
Gherkins (optional)

1. Mix the patty ingredients, and then gently form four patties of equal size, each about 1.5 cm/ ¾ inch thick. With your thumb or the back of a spoon, make a shallow indentation about 2.5 cm/ 1 inch wide in the centre of the patties to prevent them from forming a dome as they cook. Refrigerate the patties until ready to grill.

2. Prepare the grill for direct cooking over medium-high heat (200–260°C/400–500°F) and preheat a grill-proof griddle.

3. Butter both sides of each bread slice. Mix the cheese with the nutmeg.

4. Grill the patties on the cooking grates over *direct medium-high heat* for 8–10 minutes, with the lid closed, until cooked to medium (70°C/160°F), turning once. After you turn the patties, place two ham slices on each patty to warm. At the same time, cook the bread on the griddle for 2 minutes, turn, top equally with the cheese, and cook for 2 minutes more.

5. Place one slice of bread on each serving plate, cheese side up, and then add a patty. Top with another slice of bread, cheese side down. Serve immediately with mustard and gherkins, if liked.

FUN FACT

The *croque-monsieur* is a classic French ham-and-Gruyère-cheese sandwich that's traditionally spread with béchamel sauce and then grilled to a crisp (in fact, it literally translates to 'crunch, mister'). Seeking even more French decadence? Slap a sunny-side-up fried egg on top, and you've made it a *croque-madame*.

BEEF

BEEF

WILD MUSHROOM CHEESEBURGERS

SERVES: **4** | PREP TIME: **25 MINUTES** | GRILLING TIME: **9–11 MINUTES**

2 tablespoons extra-virgin olive oil
225 g/8 oz assorted mushrooms, such as shiitake,
   oyster and chanterelle, cleaned and cut into slices
2 shallots, thinly sliced
3 garlic cloves, thinly sliced
1 teaspoon chopped fresh thyme leaves
   or ½ teaspoon dried thyme
120 ml/4 fl oz Madeira wine
Sea salt
Freshly ground black pepper
700 g/1½ lb steak mince (80% lean)
2 tablespoons soy sauce
4 thick slices Gruyère cheese
4 French rolls, split
4 tablespoons mayonnaise

1. In a large sauté pan over medium-high heat, warm the oil. Add the mushrooms, shallots, garlic and thyme, and sauté for 10–11 minutes until lightly browned, stirring occasionally. Pour in the wine and cook until it has evaporated, about 2 minutes, stirring often. Remove the mushroom mixture from the heat and season with ¼ teaspoon salt and ¼ teaspoon pepper.

2. Mix the steak mince, soy sauce, ½ teaspoon salt and ¼ teaspoon pepper, and then gently form four patties of equal size, each about 2.5 cm/1 inch thick. With your thumb or the back of a spoon, make a shallow indentation about 2.5 cm/1 inch wide in the centre of the patties to prevent them from forming a dome as they cook. Refrigerate the patties until ready to grill.

3. Prepare the grill for direct cooking over medium-high heat (200–260°C/400–500°F).

4. Grill the patties over *direct medium-high heat* for 9–11 minutes, with the lid closed, until cooked to medium (70°C/160°F), turning once. During the last 30–60 seconds of grilling time, place a slice of cheese on each patty to melt, and toast the rolls, cut side down, over direct heat.

5. Build each burger on a roll with mayonnaise, a patty and the mushroom mixture. Serve warm.

The stalks of wild chanterelles (far left) are a little tougher than the caps but still edible; however, the stalks of cultivated shiitakes (left) are almost always too tough, so cut them off before sautéing the caps in a hot pan.

WEBER'S IDEAL CHEESEBURGERS

SERVES: **4** | PREP TIME: **15 MINUTES** | GRILLING TIME: **9–11 MINUTES**

PATTIES

700 g/1½ lb steak mince (80% lean), preferably
   minced to order by your butcher
2 tablespoons finely diced onion
1½ teaspoons Dijon mustard
½ teaspoon Worcestershire sauce
½ teaspoon dried oregano

Tomato ketchup
Sea salt
Freshly ground black pepper
30 g/1 oz unsalted butter, softened
4 burger buns, split
4 slices mature Cheddar cheese, each about
   60 g/2 oz
4 leaves round lettuce
16 dill pickle slices

1. Mix the patty ingredients, including 1 tablespoon tomato ketchup, ½ teaspoon salt and ¼ teaspoon pepper, and then gently form four patties of equal size, each about 2.5 cm/1 inch thick. With your thumb or the back of a spoon, make a shallow indentation about 2.5 cm/1 inch wide in the centre of the patties to prevent them from forming a dome as they cook. Refrigerate the patties until ready to grill.

2. Prepare the grill for direct cooking over medium-high heat (200–260°C/400–500°F).

3. Lightly season the patties on both sides with salt and pepper. Butter the cut side of the buns. Grill the patties over *direct medium-high heat* for 9–11 minutes, with the lid closed, until cooked to medium (70°C/160°F), turning once. During the last 30–60 seconds of grilling time, place a slice of cheese on each patty to melt, and toast the buns, cut side down, over direct heat.

4. Build each burger on a bun with a lettuce leaf, a patty, pickles and more tomato ketchup, if liked. Serve immediately.

Serving suggestion: Classic Buttermilk Onion Rings (for recipe, see page 228).

THE GLORY OF MUSTARD

In life, we consider it prudent to live by the golden rule. That is, put mustard on everything.

From smooth and vibrant to spicy and granular, mustard and mankind have moved together through history. Ancient Romans used ground mustard seeds in sauces; Greeks treated scorpion bites (yikes) with the stuff; and healers of all eras relied on mustard ointments for medicinal cure-alls.

The *mères* and *pères* of the modern marvel we love come from thirteenth-century Dijon, France, where ingenious folk whipped up a spread of the ground seeds, wine, vinegar and spices – the predecessor of the spicy, nuanced Dijon-style we know today.

The word 'mustard' has a number of possible origins, but one comes from its rightful home of old Dijon. The town's coat of arms bore the phrase *Moult Me Tard* ('I ardently desire'), which became associated with its delicious export and was eventually whittled down to moutarde, or, anglicized, 'mustard'.

WHO INVENTED THE HAMBURGER?

Was it 'Hamburger Charlie' Nagreen with the bread-enveloped meatballs in Seymour, Wisconsin? Or could it have been the Menches brothers with the burger sandwiches in Hamburg, New York? Like a century-long game of hamburger Clue, the hunt for the true inventor of 'America's National Sandwich' has turned up no shortage of likely suspects.

The late nineteenth and early twentieth centuries, however, did provoke a plethora of alleged originators – all with fiercely contested credentials. Let us present you with just a few claims to hamburger fame.

Fletcher 'Old Dave' Davis said that he did it first in the 1880s at a lunch counter in Athens, Texas, where he served fried minced beef patties between two slices of homemade bread. From there, his hamburger invention got its first widespread national exposure at the 1904 World's Fair in St Louis, Missouri. Oh, and for what it's worth, in 2006 the Texas State Legislature went ahead and designated Athens as the 'Original Home of the Hamburger'.

Around the same time that Old Dave allegedly invented the hamburger, 15-year-old Charlie Nagreen started selling a similar product at the 1885 Outagamie County Fair in Seymour,

Wisconsin: meatballs that were smashed between bread slices. The town of Seymour still stands staunchly by the claim, even erecting a 3.5-m (12-foot) statue of 'Hamburger Charlie' proudly presenting his famous burger for all to affirm.

And then there were the Menches brothers of Akron, Ohio. While little Charlie the entrepreneur was busy slinging meatballs in the Midwest, Frank and Charles Menches were pioneering minced beef patties in the East. Legend has it that during a stop at the Erie County Fair in Hamburg, New York, the two travelling concessionaires ran out of their standard sausage sandwich, so they started serving beef patties between two pieces of bread. They declared it 'the hamburger', supposedly naming it after the town in which they sold their first.

Other folklore attributes the hamburger's invention –

specifically, the first-known hamburger on a bun – to Oscar Weber Bilby of Tulsa, in 1891. While there is little documentation to prove this, the mystery further multiplied when Oklahoma's governor proclaimed 12 April 1995 as 'The *Real* Birthplace of the Hamburger in Tulsa Day'.

Lastly (but that doesn't mean *anything*), came Louis' Lunch in New Haven, Connecticut. Founder Louis Lassen purportedly sold the United States' first hamburger in 1900 from his small lunch wagon: a vertically grilled minced beef patty on white bread. These guys even got the Library of Congress on board with their allegation, affirming their claim and calling Louis' Lunch a 'Connecticut Legacy'.

What began as a bun-less, immigrant-inspired Hamburg steak is now an indisputably juicy, towering symbol of American prosperity. Perhaps the real question is: who *wouldn't* want to lay claim to its invention? Whether the true creator was one of the five aforementioned, or perhaps even another undocumented (gasp!) innovator, we may never know. Unsolved mysteries aside, the hamburger and its many purveyors have established a satisfying global icon, here for the long haul.

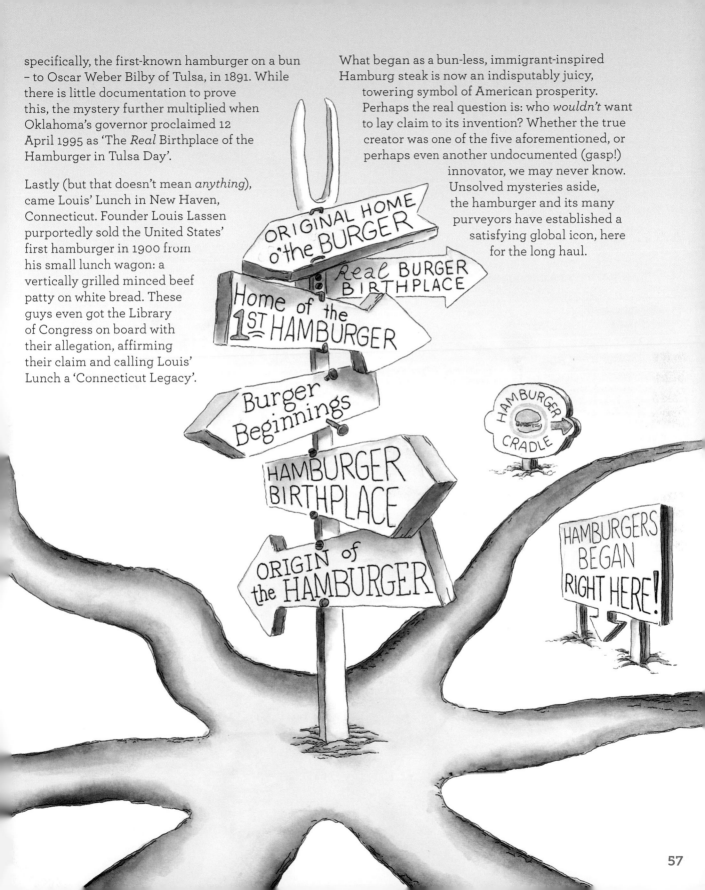

BURGERS

BACON PORTOBELLO CHEESEBURGERS

SERVES: **4** | PREP TIME: **30 MINUTES** | GRILLING TIME: **8-10 MINUTES**

BEEF

8 rashers thick-cut bacon
4 tablespoons extra-virgin
    olive oil
4 Portobello mushrooms,
    each about 10 cm/4 inches in
    diameter, stalks and gills
    removed, wiped clean
Freshly ground black pepper
700 g/1½ lb steak mince
    (80% lean)
½ teaspoon sea salt
4 thin slices Edam cheese
4 burger buns, split
Dijon mustard
4 lettuce leaves

1. In a frying pan over a medium heat, fry the bacon for 10–12 minutes until crisp, turning occasionally. Transfer the bacon to kitchen paper to drain. Reserve the bacon fat in the pan and add the oil. Brush the mushrooms with the bacon fat and oil mixture and season with pepper.

2. Mix the steak mince with the salt and ¼ teaspoon pepper, and then gently form four patties of equal size, each about 1.5 cm/¾ inch thick. With your thumb or the back of a spoon, make a shallow indentation about 2.5 cm/1 inch wide in the centre of the patties to prevent them from forming a dome as they cook. Refrigerate the patties until ready to grill.

3. Prepare the grill for direct cooking over medium-high heat (200–260°C/400–500°F).

4. Grill the mushrooms, gill side down first, and the patties over *direct medium-high heat* for 8–10 minutes, with the lid closed, until the mushrooms are tender and the patties are cooked to medium (70°C/160°F), turning once. During the last 30–60 seconds of grilling time, place a slice of cheese on each patty to melt, and toast the buns, cut side down, over direct heat.

5. Build each burger on a bun with mustard, a lettuce leaf, a patty, a mushroom and two rashers of bacon. Serve warm.

PANCETTA BEEF BURGERS WITH GARLIC-ROSEMARY MAYO

SERVES: **4** | PREP TIME: **15 MINUTES** | GRILLING TIME: **9–11 MINUTES**

PATTIES
600 g/1¼ lb steak mince
    (80% lean)
120 g/4 oz pancetta, finely diced
1½ tablespoons finely chopped
    fresh parsley leaves (optional)
2 garlic cloves, crushed

Sea salt
Freshly ground black pepper

MAYO
8 tablespoons mayonnaise
2 teaspoons extra-virgin olive oil
2 teaspoons fresh lemon juice
1½ teaspoons finely chopped
    fresh rosemary
1 large garlic clove, crushed

4 sesame seed buns, split
large handful rocket leaves

1. Mix the patty ingredients, including ½ teaspoon salt and ¼ teaspoon pepper, and then gently form four patties of equal size, each about 2.5 cm/1 inch thick. With your thumb or the back of a spoon, make a shallow indentation about 2.5 cm/1 inch wide in the centre of the patties to prevent them from forming a dome as they cook. Refrigerate the patties until ready to grill.

2. Prepare the grill for direct cooking over medium-high heat (200–260°C/400–500°F).

3. Combine the mayo ingredients, including ¼ teaspoon salt and ⅛ teaspoon pepper.

4. Lightly season the patties on both sides with salt and pepper, and then grill over *direct medium-high heat* for 9–11 minutes, with the lid closed, until cooked to medium (70°C/160°F), turning once. During the last 30–60 seconds of grilling time, toast the buns, cut side down, over direct heat.

5. Build each burger on a bun with rocket, a patty and a spoonful of garlic-rosemary mayo. Serve warm.

SMOKED MEATLOAF BURGERS WITH GRILLED ONION

SERVES: **4** | PREP TIME: **15 MINUTES** | GRILLING TIME: **8-10 MINUTES**
SPECIAL EQUIPMENT: **2 LARGE HANDFULS MESQUITE WOOD CHIPS**

BEEF

PATTIES

225 g/8 oz steak mince (80% lean)
225 g/8 oz veal mince
225 g/8 oz lean pork mince
2 large eggs, beaten
100 g/3½ oz dried Italian-seasoned breadcrumbs
4 tablespoons freshly grated Parmesan cheese
½ teaspoon sea salt
¼ teaspoon freshly ground black pepper

8 tablespoons tomato ketchup
1 canned chipotle chilli pepper in adobo sauce,
    finely diced
1 teaspoon adobo sauce (from the can)
1 red onion, cut crossways into 4 slices, each about
    1 cm/½ inch thick
2 teaspoons extra-virgin olive oil
8 slices sourdough bread, each
    about 1 cm/½ inch thick

1. Soak the wood chips in water for at least 30 minutes.

2. Mix the patty ingredients, and then gently form four patties of equal size, each about 1.5 cm/¾ inch thick. With your thumb or the back of a spoon, make a shallow indentation about 2.5 cm/1 inch wide in the centre of the patties to prevent them from forming a dome as they cook. Refrigerate the patties until ready to grill.

3. Whisk the tomato ketchup, chipotle chilli and adobo sauce.

4. Prepare the grill for direct cooking over medium-high heat (200–260°C/400–500°F).

5. Brush the onion slices with the oil. Drain and add the wood chips to the charcoal or to the smoker box of a gas grill, following manufacturer's instructions, and close the lid. When the wood begins to smoke, grill the patties and onion over *direct medium-high heat* for 8–10 minutes, with the lid closed, until the patties are cooked to medium (70°C/160°F), and the onion is tender. During the last minute of grilling time, toast the bread over direct heat, turning once.

6. Build each burger on a bread slice with a patty, chipotle tomato ketchup, a grilled onion slice and the remaining bread slice. Serve warm.

Meatloaf, America's quintessential comfort food, is also a whatever's-in-the-pantry wonder. No breadcrumbs? No problem! You can use anything from oats or cracker crumbs to rice or minced veggies as your meatloaf's obligatory binder.

BEEF BURGERS WITH CHARRED TOMATOES AND SMOKY MAYO

SERVES: **4** | PREP TIME: **20 MINUTES** | GRILLING TIME: **23–30 MINUTES** | SPECIAL EQUIPMENT: **CAST-IRON FRYING PAN**

PATTIES
700 g/1½ lb steak mince from grass-fed beef
   (90% lean)
1 large garlic clove, crushed
1 teaspoon sea salt
1 teaspoon freshly ground black pepper

450 g/1 lb ripe cherry tomatoes
1 tablespoon extra-virgin olive oil
½ teaspoon sea salt
½ teaspoon granulated sugar

MAYO
8 tablespoons mayonnaise
1–2 small canned chipotle chillies
   in adobo sauce, finely diced
¼ teaspoon paprika
¼ teaspoon sea salt

4 burger buns, split
2 large handfuls baby salad leaves

1. Mix the patty ingredients, and then gently form four patties of equal size, each about 1.5 cm/¾ inch thick. With your thumb or the back of a spoon, make a shallow indentation about 2.5 cm/1 inch wide in the centre of the patties to prevent them from forming a dome as they cook. Refrigerate the patties until ready to grill.

2. Prepare the grill for direct cooking over medium heat (180–230°C/350–450°F) and preheat a cast-iron frying pan.

3. Combine the tomatoes, oil, salt and sugar and turn to coat. Transfer to the hot cast-iron pan and cook over *direct medium heat* for 15–20 minutes, with the lid closed, until the tomatoes break down, stirring occasionally. Remove the pan from the grill and transfer the tomatoes to a bowl. Cool to room temperature.

4. Whisk the mayo ingredients.

5. Grill the patties over *direct medium heat* for 8–10 minutes, with the lid closed, until cooked to medium (70°C/160°F), turning once. During the last 30–60 seconds of grilling time, toast the buns, cut side down, over direct heat.

6. Build each burger on a bun with the smoky mayo, salad leaves, a patty and charred tomatoes. Serve immediately.

Grass-fed beef is leaner than grain-fed beef. Grilling at a slightly lower temperature will prevent grass-fed patties from drying out and will accentuate their flavour.

BEEF

BURGERS

OPEN-FACED SICILIAN BURGERS WITH SPINACH AND TOMATO SALAD

SERVES: **4** | PREP TIME: **25 MINUTES** | GRILLING TIME: **9–11 MINUTES**

BEEF

PATTIES
700 g/1½ lb steak mince
   (80% lean)
1 shallot, finely diced
2 tablespoons freshly grated
   Parmesan cheese
2 tablespoons roughly
   chopped pine nuts
2 garlic cloves, crushed
½ teaspoon dried oregano

Sea salt
Freshly ground black pepper

SALAD
1½ tablespoons extra-virgin
   olive oil
1½ teaspoons red wine vinegar
150 g/5 oz fresh baby spinach
150 g/5 oz ripe red and/or yellow
   cherry tomatoes, quartered
2 teaspoons pine nuts

4 slices Tuscan bread,
   each about 1 cm/½ inch thick

1. Mix the patty ingredients, including ½ teaspoon salt and ¼ teaspoon pepper, and then gently form four patties of equal size, each about 2.5 cm/1 inch thick. With your thumb or the back of a spoon, make a shallow indentation about 2.5 cm/1 inch wide in the centre of the patties to prevent them from forming a dome as they cook. Refrigerate the patties until ready to grill.

2. Prepare the grill for direct cooking over medium-high heat (200–260°C/400–500°F). Meanwhile, make the salad.

3. In a medium bowl whisk the oil, vinegar, ¼ teaspoon salt and ⅛ teaspoon pepper. Add the spinach, tomatoes and pine nuts. Do not toss.

4. Lightly season the patties on both sides with salt and pepper, and then grill over *direct medium-high heat* for 9–11 minutes, with the lid closed, until cooked to medium (70°C/160°F), turning once. During the last minute of grilling time, toast the bread over direct heat, turning once.

5. Toss the spinach and tomato salad. Top each bread slice with a patty and an equal amount of the salad. Serve immediately.

HUNGARIAN GOULASH BURGERS WITH GRILLED TOMATO AND SOUR CREAM

SERVES: **4** | PREP TIME: **15 MINUTES** | GRILLING TIME: **8–10 MINUTES**

PATTIES

700 g/1½ lb steak mince
   (80% lean)
2 tablespoons finely chopped
   onion
1 tablespoon sweet
   Hungarian paprika
1 tablespoon tomato purée
1 teaspoon caraway seeds
1 teaspoon dried marjoram

Sea salt
150 ml/¼ pint sour cream
2 tablespoons finely chopped
   fresh parsley leaves
1 large, ripe beefsteak tomato,
   cut crossways into 4 thick
   slices
2 teaspoons extra-virgin
   olive oil
Freshly ground black pepper
4 burger buns, split

1. Mix the patty ingredients, including ½ teaspoon salt, and then gently form four patties of equal size, each about 1.5 cm/ ¾ inch thick. With your thumb or the back of a spoon, make a shallow indentation about 2.5 cm/ 1 inch wide in the centre of the patties to prevent them from forming a dome as they cook. Refrigerate the patties until ready to grill.

2. Combine the sour cream and parsley. Cover and refrigerate until ready to use.

3. Prepare the grill for direct cooking over medium-high heat (200–260°C/400– 500°F).

4. Brush the tomato slices on both sides with oil and season evenly with salt and pepper. Grill the patties over *direct medium-high heat* for 8–10 minutes, with the lid closed, until cooked to medium (70°C/160°F), turning once. At the same time, grill the tomatoes over *direct medium-high heat* for about 5 minutes, until tender, turning once. During the last 30–60 seconds of grilling time, toast the buns, cut side down, over direct heat.

5. Build each burger on a bun with a patty, the sour cream mixture and a tomato slice. Serve warm.

Serving suggestion: Red Cabbage Slaw with Cider-Dill Vinaigrette (for recipe, see page 201).

CHILLI-BEEF BURGERS WITH QUICK KIMCHI

SERVES: **4** | PREP TIME: **40 MINUTES** | STANDING TIME: **2 HOURS** | GRILLING TIME: **9-11 MINUTES**

KIMCHI

1 small head savoy cabbage or Chinese leaves,
   about 375 g/12 oz, quartered and cored
6 spring onions, ends trimmed and finely chopped
1 tablespoon sea salt
1 small red pepper, finely chopped
1 tablespoon rice vinegar
2 teaspoons Asian fish sauce or soy sauce
1½ teaspoons crushed chilli flakes
   or hot pepper sauce
1½ teaspoons peeled, finely chopped fresh ginger
3 garlic cloves, crushed

PATTIES

700 g/1½ lb steak mince (80% lean)
1 small shallot, finely diced
1 Thai or serrano chilli, stemmed, seeded,
   deveined and finely chopped (about 2 teaspoons)
2 garlic cloves, crushed

Sea salt
Freshly ground black pepper
4 onion buns, split

1. Cut the cabbage or Chinese leaves crossways into thin strips, and then separate the strips by hand. In a colander toss the strips with the spring onions and salt. Leave to stand until the leaves wilt, about 2 hours, tossing occasionally. Squeeze as much liquid as you can out of the leaves. In a large bowl mix the remaining kimchi ingredients. Add the cabbage and spring onions and toss to combine.

2. Mix the patty ingredients, including ½ teaspoon salt and ¼ teaspoon pepper, and then gently form four patties of equal size, each about 2.5 cm/1 inch thick. With your thumb or the back of a spoon, make a shallow indentation about 2.5 cm/1 inch wide in the centre of the patties to prevent them from forming a dome as they cook. Refrigerate the patties until ready to grill.

3. Prepare the grill for direct cooking over medium-high heat (200-260°C/400-500°F).

4. Lightly season the patties on both sides with salt and pepper, and then grill over *direct medium-high heat* for 9-11 minutes, with the lid closed, until cooked to medium (70°C/160°F), turning once. During the last 30-60 seconds of grilling time, toast the buns, cut side down, over direct heat.

5. Build each burger on a bun with a patty and a spoonful or two of kimchi. Serve warm.

FUN FACT

Packed with vitamins, minerals and probiotics, kimchi (the national dish of Korea) is one of the world's five healthiest foods. Koreans even say 'kimchi' instead of 'cheese' when posing for photos. Now that's something to smile about!

SPICY GINGER SPRING ONION BURGERS WITH SESAME SPINACH

SERVES: **4** | PREP TIME: **30 MINUTES** | GRILLING TIME: **8–10 MINUTES**

PATTIES

375 g/12 oz steak mince (80% lean)

375 g/12 oz lean pork mince

5 spring onions, thinly sliced (white and light green parts only)

1 piece fresh ginger, about 5 cm/ 2 inches long, peeled and grated

1 tablespoon soy sauce

2 teaspoons toasted sesame oil

2 garlic cloves, crushed

½ teaspoon sea salt

½ teaspoon freshly ground black pepper

2 teaspoons vegetable oil

2 teaspoons toasted sesame oil

2 tablespoons plus 1 teaspoon hot chilli-garlic sauce

225 g/8 oz fresh baby spinach

1 tablespoon toasted sesame seeds

8 tablespoons tomato ketchup

4 sesame seed buns, split

1. Mix the patty ingredients, and then gently form four patties of equal size, each about 1.5 cm/ ¾ inch thick. With your thumb or the back of a spoon, make a shallow indentation about 2.5 cm/1 inch wide in the centre of the patties to prevent them from forming a dome as they cook. Refrigerate the patties until ready to grill.

2. Prepare the grill for direct cooking over medium-high heat (200–260°C/400–500°F).

3. In a large sauté pan over a medium heat, warm the vegetable oil, sesame oil and 1 teaspoon of the chilli-garlic sauce. Gradually add the spinach by the handful and stir for 2–3 minutes just until it begins to wilt. Remove from the heat and add the sesame seeds.

4. Combine the tomato ketchup with the remaining 2 tablespoons chilli-garlic sauce.

5. Grill the patties over *direct medium-high heat* for 8–10 minutes, with the lid closed, until cooked to medium (70°C/160°F), turning once. During the last 30–60 seconds of grilling time, toast the buns, cut side down, over direct heat.

6. Build each burger on a bun with chilli-garlic tomato ketchup, a patty and sesame spinach. Serve warm.

Serving suggestion: Corn and Black Bean Salad (for recipe, see page 219).

BOURBON BURGERS WITH CARAMELISED ONIONS AND HORSERADISH DIJON

SERVES: **4** | PREP TIME: **20 MINUTES, PLUS 20–22 MINUTES FOR THE ONIONS** | GRILLING TIME: **8–10 MINUTES**

BEEF

2 tablespoons extra-virgin
    olive oil
2 medium onions, each
    cut in half and thinly sliced
Sea salt
Freshly ground black pepper
1 teaspoon cider vinegar
½ teaspoon dark brown sugar
4 tablespoons Dijon mustard
1 tablespoon horseradish
700 g/1½ lb steak mince
    (80% lean)
1½ tablespoons bourbon
1 tablespoon
    Worcestershire sauce
4 burger buns, split
4 romaine lettuce leaves

1. In a large sauté pan over medium-high heat, warm the oil. Add the onions, ¼ teaspoon salt and ¼ teaspoon pepper and cook about 10 minutes until the onions begin to soften, stirring occasionally. Add the vinegar and brown sugar and continue cooking for 10–12 minutes more, until tender and golden, stirring often. Remove from the heat.

2. In a small bowl combine the mustard and horseradish.

3. Mix the steak mince, bourbon, Worcestershire sauce, ½ teaspoon salt and ¼ teaspoon pepper, and then gently form four patties of equal size, each about 1.5 cm/ ¾ inch thick. With your thumb or the back of a spoon, make a shallow indentation about 2.5 cm/1 inch wide in the centre of the patties to prevent them from forming a dome as they cook. Refrigerate the patties until ready to grill.

4. Prepare the grill for direct cooking over medium-high heat (200–260°C/400–500°F).

5. Grill the patties over *direct medium-high heat* for 8–10 minutes, with the lid closed, until cooked to medium (70°C/160°F), turning once. During the last 30–60 seconds of grilling time, toast the buns, cut side down, over direct heat.

6. Build each burger on a bun with horseradish mustard, a lettuce leaf, a patty and caramelised onions. Serve warm.

GAUCHO BURGERS WITH FRIED EGGS AND CHIMICHURRI

SERVES: **4** | PREP TIME: **20 MINUTES** | GRILLING TIME: **14–18 MINUTES** | SPECIAL EQUIPMENT: **CAST-IRON FRYING PAN**

PATTIES
450 g/1 lb steak mince (80% lean)
225 g/8 oz hot Italian sausages, meat removed
   from casings
1 shallot, finely diced
2 garlic cloves, crushed

Sea salt
Freshly ground black pepper

CHIMICHURRI
Large bunch fresh parsley, leaves and tender stems
4 garlic cloves, each quartered
2 tablespoons fresh oregano
120 ml/4 fl oz extra-virgin olive oil
¼ teaspoon crushed chilli flakes

4 slices French or Italian bread, each about
   1 cm/½ inch thick
Extra-virgin olive oil
15 g/½ oz unsalted butter
4 large eggs
3 tablespoons white or red wine vinegar

1. Mix the patty ingredients, including ½ teaspoon salt and ¼ teaspoon pepper, and then gently form four patties of equal size, each about 2.5 cm/1 inch thick. With your thumb or the back of a spoon, make a shallow indentation about 2.5 cm/1 inch wide in the centre of the patties to prevent them from forming a dome as they cook. Refrigerate the patties until ready to grill.

2. In a food processor fitted with a metal blade, finely chop the parsley, garlic and oregano. Transfer to a bowl and stir in the oil, chilli flakes, 1 teaspoon salt and 1 teaspoon black pepper.

3. Prepare the grill for direct cooking over medium-high heat (200–260°C/400–500°F).

4. Lightly season the patties on both sides with salt and pepper, and brush the bread slices on both sides with oil. Grill the patties over *direct medium-high heat* for 9–11 minutes, with the lid closed, until cooked to medium (70°C/160°F), turning once. Halfway into grilling time, place a cast-iron frying pan on the cooking grates or on a side burner set to medium-high to preheat. Remove the patties from the grill.

5. Add the butter to the frying pan. Fry the eggs sunny-side up for 4–6 minutes, with the lid open, until the whites are crisp and lacy on the edges and the yolks are partially runny. Toast the bread on the cooking grates over direct heat, about 1 minute, turning once.

6. Add the vinegar to the chimichurri. Mix well.

7. Top each bread slice with a patty, a fried egg and chimichurri. Serve immediately.

WHAT IS CHIMICHURRI?
Often called the 'tomato ketchup of Argentina', chimichurri is typically a green pesto-like condiment that's made from a blend of olive oil, lemon juice and chopped fresh herbs – usually Italian parsley and oregano – and seasoned with onion, garlic, vinegar and cayenne pepper. While chimichurri is traditionally served as a dipping sauce with grilled beef, it's also a bright, tangy flavour additive (either as a marinade or a sauce) for other meats and even grilled vegetables and tofu.

BEEF

BEEF AND VEAL PAPRIKASH BURGERS WITH ROASTED PEPPERS

SERVES: **4** | PREP TIME: **30 MINUTES, PLUS ABOUT 25 MINUTES FOR THE RELISH** | GRILLING TIME: **11–12 MINUTES**

PATTIES
225 g/8 oz steak mince (80% lean)
225 g/8 oz veal mince
1 tablespoon onion, finely diced
1 tablespoon finely chopped fresh parsley leaves
¾ teaspoon dried marjoram

Sea salt
Freshly ground black pepper

RELISH
2 tablespoons vegetable oil
2 large onions, each cut in half and thinly sliced
1 teaspoon paprika
½ teaspoon smoked paprika
½ teaspoon hot chilli powder
150 g/5 oz canned chopped tomatoes
15 g/½ oz unsalted butter, softened

2 large green peppers, each cut into 8 wedges
Vegetable oil
4 or 8 slices crusty bread, each about
    1 cm/½ inch thick
30 g/1 oz unsalted butter, softened
4 tablespoons sour cream

1. Mix the patty ingredients, including ½ teaspoon salt and ¼ teaspoon pepper, and then gently form four patties of equal size, each about 1.5 cm/¾ inch thick. With your thumb or the back of a spoon, make a shallow indentation about 2.5 cm/1 inch wide in the centre of the patties to prevent them from forming a dome as they cook. Refrigerate the patties until ready to grill.

2. In a large sauté pan over a medium-low heat, warm the oil. Add the onions and sauté for 18–20 minutes until golden brown, stirring often. Add the paprika, smoked paprika, chilli powder and ½ teaspoon salt and stir for 2 minutes. Add the tomatoes and continue cooking for 3–5 minutes until the sauce is very thick and deep red, stirring occasionally. Use the back of a wooden spoon to break up any large pieces of tomato. Remove from the heat and stir in the butter.

3. Prepare the grill for direct cooking over medium-high heat (200–260°C/400–500°F).

4. Lightly brush the pepper wedges with oil. Grill the peppers and patties over *direct medium-high heat* for 11–12 minutes, with the lid closed, until the peppers are charred and softened, and the patties are cooked to medium (70°C/160°F), turning once. During the last minute of grilling time, toast the bread over direct heat, turning once. Remove from the grill and butter each slice.

5. Top four bread slices each with a patty and relish. Serve warm with the pepper wedges, sour cream and another slice of bread, if liked.

Paprika, the intense red spice, has two common varieties: regular paprika has a relatively neutral flavour, whereas smoked paprika (called *pimentón* in Spain) has a rich, smoky flavour that's produced by slowly smoking red chillies over oak fires.

MINCING
YOUR OWN BURGER BLEND

Some things are best left to the professionals – think electrical wiring and cage fighting. But mincing your own meat? That's a simple and worthwhile DIY endeavour. Knowing exactly what cut of meat makes up your burger and how fresh it is will yield a tastier and juicier patty with no mystery add-ins.

WHICH MEAT?

We like chuck steak for its excellent flavour and ample amount of fat (around 20 per cent). Mincing chuck alone will give you better results than buying beef mince from the supermarket. To turn up the intensity of beefy taste, add some rump steak (for steak-like flavours) or boneless short ribs (for extra fat and juiciness) to the blend. Substituting thick-cut bacon for as much as one-quarter of all the beef will give your burgers a boost of smoke and tasty saltiness.

WEBER'S BURGER BLEND

SERVES: **6-8**
1 kg/2 lb chuck steak
450 g/1 lb rump steak or
    boneless short ribs

1. Trim off any tough gristle and remove any bones from the meat (or ask your butcher to prepare).

2. Cut the meat into 3.5 cm/1½ inch chunks and refrigerate them until ready to mince.

3. Mince the meat using one of the methods shown on the facing page.

Chuck   **Rump**   **Short ribs**

SELECT YOUR METHOD

Food mincer

Food processor

Don't worry, no huge meat mincer is required. You can use a mincer attachment for a stand mixer, or you can even mince the meat in a food processor fitted with a metal blade. Because mincing meat creates friction, which could warm the meat to the point where microbes start to grow, the first step is to put all the parts of your equipment in the freezer for at least 30 minutes.

(Top) If you are using a stand mixer, freeze the food mincer attachment, the mincing worm, mincing knife and coarse mincing plate.

(Bottom) If you are using a food processor, freeze the bowl, top and metal blade.

FOOD MINCER METHOD

Set up your mincer with the coarse mincing plate. This will give the meat a nice, loose texture. Turn on the mincer and add the chunks of meat one handful at a time. You want the beef to move through the mincer constantly in a smooth, steady way. If you add too much at once, the meat will probably get stuck and friction will start to build up, so take it slowly. Catch the minced meat in a bowl.

FOOD PROCESSOR METHOD

This method produces more of a chopped texture than a ground texture, but it still works well. To avoid warming up the meat, work in small batches, about 225 g/8 oz at a time, and pulse the chunks 8–10 times for a medium-fine mince. You will probably need to scrape down the side of the food processor bowl occasionally. Then transfer the meat to a bowl and process the next batch.

BISON CHEESEBURGERS WITH BALSAMIC MUSHROOMS

SERVES: **4** | PREP TIME: **30 MINUTES** | GRILLING TIME: **7–9 MINUTES**

MUSHROOMS

2 tablespoons extra-virgin
   olive oil
225 g/8 oz chestnut mushrooms,
   cleaned, stalks removed,
   and finely chopped
1 onion, finely chopped
3 large garlic cloves, crushed
2 tablespoons balsamic vinegar
2 tablespoons finely chopped
   fresh chives

Sea salt
Freshly ground black pepper
700 g/1½ lb minced bison meat
   (85–90% lean)
½ packet Philadelphia garlic and
   herb soft cheese,
   coarsely crumbled
4 burger buns, split
4 leaves romaine lettuce
1 large, ripe beefsteak tomato,
   cut crossways into 4 slices

1. In a large sauté pan over a medium-high heat, warm the oil. Add the mushrooms and onion and cook for 8–10 minutes, until the onion is deep golden brown, making sure that the mixture is still moist, stirring frequently. Add the garlic and cook for 2 minutes, stirring occasionally. Stir in the vinegar and season with ½ teaspoon salt and ¼ teaspoon pepper. Remove from the heat. Cool to room temperature, and then stir in the chives.

2. Mix the minced bison, 1 teaspoon salt and ½ teaspoon pepper, and then gently form four patties of equal size, each about 1.5 cm/ ¾ inch thick. With your thumb or the back of a spoon, make a shallow indentation about 2.5 cm/1 inch wide in the centre of the patties to prevent them from forming a dome as they cook. Refrigerate the patties until ready to grill.

3. Prepare the grill for direct cooking over medium heat (180–230°C/350–450°F).

4. Grill the patties over *direct medium heat* for 7–9 minutes, with the lid closed, until cooked to medium (70°C/160°F), turning once. During the last 30–60 seconds of grilling time, top each patty with an equal amount of cheese to melt slightly, and toast the buns, cut side down, over direct heat.

5. Build each burger on a bun with a lettuce leaf, a tomato slice, a patty and balsamic mushrooms. Serve immediately.

BISON BURGERS WITH BLUE CHEESE AND HOT WING SAUCE

SERVES: **6** | PREP TIME: **20 MINUTES** | GRILLING TIME: **7–9 MINUTES**

PATTIES

1 kg/2 lb minced bison meat
   (85–90% lean)
120 g/4 oz blue cheese, crumbled
1 onion, finely diced
2 garlic cloves, crushed
1 teaspoon celery seeds

40 g/1½ oz unsalted butter
4 tablespoons hot wing sauce
6 burger buns, split
6 leaves iceberg lettuce
12 slices ripe tomato
6 very thin slices red onion

1. Mix the patty ingredients, then gently form six patties of equal size, each about 1.5 cm/¾ inch thick. With your thumb or the back of a spoon, make a shallow indentation about 2.5 cm/1 inch wide in the centre of the patties to prevent them from forming a dome as they cook. Refrigerate the patties until ready to grill.

2. Prepare the grill for direct cooking over medium heat (180–230°C/350–450°F).

3. In a saucepan over a medium heat, melt the butter. Remove from the heat and stir in the hot wing sauce.

4. Grill the patties over *direct medium heat* for 7–9 minutes, with the lid closed, until cooked to medium (70°C/160°F), turning once. During the last 30–60 seconds of grilling time, toast the buns, cut side down, over direct heat. Remove the patties and the buns from the grill and immediately brush the patties on both sides with the hot wing sauce mixture.

5. Build each burger on a bun with a lettuce leaf, two tomato slices, an onion slice and a patty. Serve warm.

FUN FACT

Looking for a lean red meat alternative? Low in fat, low in cholesterol and always antibiotic- and hormone-free, bison meat contains 40 per cent more protein than beef.

JALAPEÑO LAMB BURGERS WITH GOATS' CHEESE AND SALSA

SERVES: **6** | PREP TIME: **30 MINUTES** | GRILLING TIME: **7–9 MINUTES**

LAMB

PATTIES

1 kg/2 lb lamb mince
4 tablespoons cold beer
3 medium jalapeño chillies, seeded and finely
  chopped
2 tablespoons tomato ketchup
¾ teaspoon sea salt
½ teaspoon freshly ground black pepper
2 garlic cloves, crushed

SALSA

1 large, ripe beefsteak tomato, cored, seeded and
  finely chopped
½ small onion, finely chopped
1 medium jalapeño chilli, seeded and finely chopped
1 tablespoon finely chopped fresh mint
2 teaspoons cider vinegar
Finely grated rind and juice of ½ lime
½ teaspoon sea salt
½ teaspoon granulated sugar
1 garlic clove, crushed

Extra-virgin olive oil
175 g/6 oz goats' cheese, crumbled
6 ciabatta or telera rolls, split

1. Mix the patty ingredients, and then gently form
six patties of equal size, each about 1.5 cm/¾ inch
thick. With your thumb or the back of a spoon, make
a shallow indentation about 2.5 cm/1 inch wide in the
centre of the patties to prevent them from forming a
dome as they cook. Refrigerate the patties until ready
to grill.

2. Prepare the grill for direct cooking over medium
heat (180–230°C/350–450°F).

3. In a serving bowl mix the salsa ingredients.

4. Lightly brush the patties on both sides with
oil, and then grill over *direct medium heat* for 7–9
minutes, with the lid closed, until cooked to medium
(70°C/160°F), turning once. During the last 30–60
seconds of grilling time, top the patties with the
cheese to soften, and toast the rolls, cut side down,
over direct heat.

5. Build each burger on a roll with a patty and a heaped
spoonful of salsa. Serve warm with any remaining
salsa on the side.

*Serving suggestion: Chilli-Spiced Fries
(for recipe, see page 223).*

SPICY LAMB BURGERS WITH ROASTED RED PEPPER MAYONNAISE

SERVES: **6** | PREP TIME: **20 MINUTES** | GRILLING TIME: **7-9 MINUTES**

200 g/7 oz chopped roasted red peppers
  (from a jar), patted dry
1 medium garlic clove
240 ml/8 fl oz mayonnaise
½ teaspoon freshly ground black pepper

PATTIES
1 tablespoon extra-virgin olive oil
100 g/3½ oz shallots, finely chopped
2 tablespoons finely chopped jalapeño chillies
2 garlic cloves, finely chopped
½ teaspoon dried basil
1 kg/2 lb lamb mince
1½ teaspoons sea salt
1 teaspoon ground cumin
¾ teaspoon ground coriander
½ teaspoon ground cayenne pepper

4 onion rolls, split
Large handful rocket leaves

1. In a food processor combine the red peppers and garlic and blend until very finely chopped. Transfer to a bowl and stir in the mayonnaise and pepper.

2. In a sauté pan over a medium heat, warm the oil. Add the shallot, jalapeños, garlic and basil, and sauté for 4–5 minutes until slightly softened, stirring occasionally. Remove from the heat and cool for 5 minutes. Transfer to a bowl and mix in the remaining patty ingredients. Gently form six patties of equal size, each about 1.5 cm/¾ inch thick. With your thumb or the back of a spoon, make a shallow indentation about 2.5 cm/1 inch wide in the centre of the patties to prevent them from forming a dome as they cook. Refrigerate the patties until ready to grill.

3. Prepare the grill for direct cooking over medium heat (180–230°C/350–450°F).

4. Grill the patties over *direct medium heat* for 7–9 minutes, with the lid closed, until cooked to medium (70°C/160°F), turning once. During the last 30–60 seconds of grilling time, toast the rolls, cut side down, over direct heat.

5. Build each burger on a roll with red pepper mayonnaise (you may not need all of it), a patty and rocket leaves. Serve warm.

Serving suggestion: Chopped Greek-Style Salad (for recipe, see page 209).

LAMB BURGERS WITH HERBED CHEESE AND RED WINE SAUCE

SERVES: **6** | PREP TIME: **20 MINUTES, PLUS 30–40 MINUTES TO REDUCE THE WINE**
GRILLING TIME: **19–21 MINUTES** | SPECIAL EQUIPMENT: **PERFORATED GRILL PAN**

1 bottle (750 ml) fruity red wine,
   such as cabernet sauvignon
180 ml/6 fl oz passata
2 tablespoons honey
Sea salt
Freshly ground black pepper
3 slices onion, each about 1 cm/½ inch thick
9 chestnut mushrooms, stalks removed
Extra-virgin olive oil
1 kg/2 lb lamb mince, preferably from
   the leg
2 tablespoons finely chopped fresh parsley leaves
2 tablespoons finely chopped fresh mint
2 garlic cloves, crushed
6 crusty or ciabatta rolls, split
6 tablespoons garlic and herb soft cheese

1. In a large saucepan over a medium-high heat, boil the wine until it is reduced to 4 tablespoons, 30–40 minutes (depending on the diameter of your pan). Pour off 2 tablespoons, set aside and allow to cool (you will use the cooled, reduced wine in the patty ingredients).

2. Add the passata to the saucepan with the remaining 2 tablespoons reduced wine and cook over a medium heat, simmering for about 5 minutes, until the mixture is thick enough to coat the back of a spoon. Stir in the honey, ½ teaspoon salt and ½ teaspoon pepper. Pour into a serving bowl and allow to cool.

3. Prepare the grill for direct cooking over medium-high heat (200–260°C/400–500°F) and preheat a perforated grill pan.

4. Brush the onion and mushrooms with oil, and then spread them in a single layer on the grill pan. Grill over *direct medium-high heat*, with the lid closed, until browned and tender, about 10 minutes for the onion and about 6 minutes for the mushrooms, turning once or twice. Remove from the grill and finely dice.

5. Mix the onion, mushrooms, the reserved and cooled reduced wine, the lamb, parsley, mint, garlic, ½ teaspoon salt and ¼ teaspoon pepper. Gently form six patties of equal size, each about 2.5 cm/1 inch thick. With your thumb or the back of a spoon, make a shallow indentation about 2.5 cm/1 inch wide in the centre of the patties to prevent them from forming a dome as they cook.

6. Lightly brush the patties on both sides with oil, and then grill over *direct medium-high heat* for 9–11 minutes, with the lid closed, until cooked to medium (70°C/160°F), turning once. During the last 30–60 seconds of grilling time, toast the rolls, cut side down, over direct heat.

7. Build each burger on a roll with 1 tablespoon of the cheese, a patty and some red wine sauce. Serve warm with the remaining sauce on the side.

The sauce is ready when you run your fingertip down the middle of the spoon and it makes a 'road'.

INDIAN LAMB BURGERS WITH MANGO CHUTNEY

SERVES: **4** | PREP TIME: **15 MINUTES** | GRILLING TIME: **7-9 MINUTES**

LAMB

PATTIES
700 g/1½ lb lamb mince
small bunch fresh
   coriander, chopped
small bunch fresh mint, chopped
1 jalapeño chilli, seeded and
   finely diced
2 teaspoons peeled,
   grated fresh ginger
2 teaspoons curry powder
1 teaspoon sea salt
¼ teaspoon freshly ground
   black pepper
1 garlic clove, crushed

4 soft Italian-style
   round rolls, split
2 tablespoons extra-virgin
   olive oil
8 tablespoons mango chutney
4 slices red onion

1. Mix the patty ingredients and then gently form four patties of equal size, each about 1.5 cm/ ¾ inch thick. With your thumb or the back of a spoon, make a shallow indentation about 2.5 cm/1 inch wide in the centre of the patties to prevent them from forming a dome as they cook. Refrigerate the patties until ready to grill.

2. Prepare the grill for direct cooking over medium heat (180–230°C/350–450°F).

3. Brush the cut side of the rolls with the oil. Grill the patties over *direct medium heat* for 7–9 minutes, with the lid closed, until cooked to medium (70°C/160°F), turning once. During the last 30–60 seconds of grilling time, toast the rolls, cut side down, over direct heat.

4. Build each burger on a roll with mango chutney, a patty and an onion slice. Serve warm.

Serving suggestion: Sour Cream Raita (for recipe, see page 234).

LAMB AND GRILLED ONION BURGERS

SERVES: **4** | PREP TIME: **15 MINUTES** | GRILLING TIME: **17–21 MINUTES**

PATTIES

4 slices onion, each about 5 mm/
  ¼ inch thick
1 tablespoon extra-virgin
  olive oil
425 g/14 oz lamb mince
175 g/6 oz lean pork mince
2 tablespoons chopped fresh mint
1 tablespoon Dijon mustard
1 teaspoon ground cumin
½ teaspoon sea salt
½ teaspoon freshly ground
  black pepper

SAUCE

90 g/3 oz feta cheese, crumbled
8 tablespoons natural Greek
  yogurt
1 tablespoon chopped fresh mint
1 teaspoon fresh lemon juice

4 crusty rolls or sesame
  buns, split
2 lemons, cut into wedges

1. Prepare the grill for direct cooking over medium-high heat (200–260°C/400–500°F).

2. Brush the onion slices with the oil, and then grill over *direct medium-high heat* for 8–10 minutes, with the lid closed, until golden brown and tender, turning once or twice. Remove from the grill and finely chop. Set aside to cool.

3. Mix the onion with the remaining patty ingredients, and then gently form four patties of equal size, each about 2.5 cm/1 inch thick. With your thumb or the back of a spoon, make a shallow indentation about 2.5 cm/1 inch wide in the centre of the patties to prevent them from forming a dome as they cook. Refrigerate the patties until ready to grill.

4. Combine the sauce ingredients. Cover and refrigerate until ready to serve.

5. Grill the patties over *direct medium-high heat* for 9–11 minutes, with the lid closed, until cooked to medium (70°C/160°F), turning once. During the last 30–60 seconds of grilling time, toast the rolls, cut side down, over direct heat.

6. Build each burger on a roll with a patty and as much sauce as you like. Serve warm with lemon wedges and any remaining sauce on the side.

SPICY JERK PORK AND BEEF BURGERS WITH PINEAPPLE SALSA

SERVES: **6** | PREP TIME: **20 MINUTES** | GRILLING TIME: **16–20 MINUTES** | SPECIAL EQUIPMENT: **RUBBER GLOVES**

PATTIES
1 habanero or Scotch bonnet chilli
450 g/1 lb lean pork mince
450 g/1 lb steak mince (80% lean)
4 spring onions, finely chopped
   (white and light green parts only)
2 tablespoons dark brown sugar
1 tablespoon fresh lime juice
1 tablespoon soy sauce
1½ teaspoons chopped fresh thyme
1½ teaspoons ground allspice
1 teaspoon sea salt
½ teaspoon ground cinnamon
1 garlic clove, crushed

SALSA
4 slices ripe, fresh pineapple, each about
   1 cm/½ inch thick, cored
1 small, ripe mango, peeled and roughly chopped
¼ red onion, roughly chopped
2 tablespoons fresh lime juice
2 tablespoons chopped fresh coriander
½ teaspoon sea salt

Freshly ground black pepper
6 brioche buns, split

1. Wearing rubber gloves (to avoid burning your skin), remove and discard the stem and seeds from the chilli. Finely dice the chilli and place in a large bowl. Add the remaining patty ingredients, and then gently form six patties of equal size, each about 2.5 cm/1 inch thick. With your thumb or the back of a spoon, make a shallow indentation about 2.5 cm/1 inch wide in the centre of the patties to prevent them from forming a dome as they cook. Refrigerate the patties until ready to grill.

2. Prepare the grill for direct cooking over medium heat (180–230°C/350–450°F).

3. Grill the pineapple slices over *direct medium heat* for 6–8 minutes, with the lid open, until marked and slightly softened, turning once. Roughly chop the pineapple, transfer to a food processor fitted with a metal blade, and add the remaining salsa ingredients. Pulse until the salsa is finely chopped. If it seems too wet, drain in a fine-mesh sieve.

4. Generously season the patties on both sides with pepper, and then grill over *direct medium heat* for 10–12 minutes, with the lid closed, until cooked to medium (70°C/160°F), turning once. During the last 30–60 seconds of grilling time, toast the buns, cut side down, over direct heat.

5. Build each burger on a bun with a patty and pineapple salsa. Serve immediately.

FUN FACT

The deceivingly small, lantern-shaped habanero chilli packs a hint of fruity flavour and a knockout in the heat department. Vivid orange when fully ripe, the habanero can be up to 40 times spicier than its more widely available chilli counterpart, the jalapeño.

PORK

FIVE-SPICE PORK BURGERS WITH SLAW

SERVES: **4** | PREP TIME: **30 MINUTES** | GRILLING TIME: **10–12 MINUTES**

PATTIES
700 g/1½ lb lean pork mince
2 spring onions, ends trimmed
   and finely chopped
1½ tablespoons chopped fresh
   coriander
4 garlic cloves, crushed
1 teaspoon Chinese five spice
   powder
½ teaspoon sea salt
¼ teaspoon freshly ground
   black pepper

SLAW
¼ green cabbage, finely shredded
¼ red pepper, cut into thin strips
1 small carrot, grated
2 teaspoons fresh lime
   juice or rice vinegar
1 teaspoon toasted sesame oil
⅛ teaspoon sea salt

Extra-virgin olive oil
5 tablespoons hoisin sauce
4 soft, slightly sweet rolls, split

Chinese five spice is an
ancient but still very popular
combination of ground star
anise, fennel seed, cinnamon,
cloves and Szechuan or
black peppercorns.

1. Mix the patty ingredients, then gently form four patties of equal size, each about 2.5 cm/1 inch thick. With your thumb or the back of a spoon, make a shallow indentation about 2.5 cm/1 inch wide in the centre of the patties to prevent them from forming a dome as they cook. Refrigerate the patties until ready to grill.

2. Combine the slaw ingredients.

3. Prepare the grill for direct cooking over medium heat (180–230°C/350–450°F).

4. Lightly brush the patties on both sides with olive oil, and then grill over *direct medium heat* for 10–12 minutes, with the lid closed, until cooked to medium (70°C/160°F), turning once and then brushing with the hoisin sauce. During the last 30–60 seconds of grilling time, toast the rolls, cut side down, over direct heat.

5. Build each burger on a roll with a patty and slaw. Serve immediately.

THAI PORK BURGERS IN LETTUCE LEAVES

SERVES: **4** | PREP TIME: **25 MINUTES** | GRILLING TIME: **10–12 MINUTES**

PATTIES

700 g/1½ lb lean pork mince
1 stalk lemongrass (pale inner
  heart only) or 2 spring onions,
  ends trimmed and finely diced
1 large shallot, finely diced
2 tablespoons fresh coriander
4 garlic cloves, crushed

Sea salt
Freshly ground black pepper
4 large leaves round lettuce
  or red leaf lettuce
Lime wedges (optional)

1. Mix the patty ingredients, including ½ teaspoon salt and ¼ teaspoon pepper, and then gently form four patties of equal size, each about 2.5 cm/1 inch thick. With your thumb or the back of a spoon, make a shallow indentation about 2.5 cm/1 inch wide in the centre of the patties to prevent them from forming a dome as they cook. Refrigerate the patties until ready to grill.

2. Prepare the grill for direct cooking over medium heat (180–230°C/350–450°F).

3. Lightly season the patties on both sides with salt and pepper, and then grill over *direct medium heat* for 10–12 minutes, with the lid closed, until cooked to medium (70°C/160°F), turning once.

4. Place each patty in a lettuce leaf cup. Garnish with lime wedges, if liked. Serve warm.

Serving suggestions: Easy Cold Noodle Salad with Peanut Sauce and Carrot (for recipe, see page 206) and Cucumber Relish (see page 234).

To get to the tender heart of lemongrass, chop off the bottom 5 cm/2 inches as well as the top 10–12 cm/4 5 inches of the stalk. Then peel away the outer leaves of the remaining stalk until it is about as thick as a spring onion. Cut the stalk in half lengthways and finely dice it for seasoning these burgers.

LITTLE ITALY PORK BURGERS

SERVES: **4** | PREP TIME: **20 MINUTES** | GRILLING TIME: **48–50 MINUTES**

PATTIES
700 g/1½ lb lean pork mince
2 tablespoons finely chopped fresh parsley leaves
1 teaspoon fennel seeds
1 teaspoon paprika
1 teaspoon crushed chilli flakes
½ teaspoon garlic granules
½ teaspoon dried oregano

Sea salt
Freshly ground black pepper
1 bulb garlic
Extra-virgin olive oil
8 tablespoons mayonnaise
1 medium red pepper, cut into thin strips
1 small onion, cut in half and thinly sliced
4 crusty rolls, split

1. Mix the patty ingredients, including 1 teaspoon salt and ¼ teaspoon pepper, and then gently form four patties of equal size, each about 1.5 cm/¾ inch thick. With your thumb or the back of a spoon, make a shallow indentation about 2.5 cm/1 inch wide in the centre of the patties to prevent them from forming a dome as they cook. Refrigerate until ready to grill.

2. Prepare the grill for direct and indirect cooking over medium-high heat (200–260°C/400–500°F).

3. Cut 1 cm/½ inch off the top of the bulb of garlic and discard. Place the garlic bulb on a small sheet of aluminium foil and drizzle 1 teaspoon oil over the exposed cloves. Bring the corners of the foil together and twist to completely cover the garlic, leaving a little room in the parcel for the expansion of steam. Place the garlic parcel over *indirect medium-high heat*, close the lid, and cook for about 40 minutes until the garlic is soft, fragrant and golden. When cool enough to handle, squeeze the cloves from their skins into a small bowl. Mash the garlic with a fork to form a paste. Stir in the mayonnaise, 1 teaspoon oil, ¼ teaspoon salt and ¼ teaspoon pepper to make an aioli.

4. In a sauté pan over a medium-high heat, warm 1 tablespoon oil. Add the pepper and onion and sauté for 7–8 minutes until softened, stirring occasionally. Season with ¼ teaspoon salt and ¼ teaspoon pepper and cook for 3 minutes more. Remove from the heat and keep warm.

5. Lightly brush the patties on both sides with oil, and then grill over *direct medium-high heat* for 8–10 minutes, with the lid closed, until cooked to medium (70°C/160°F), turning once. During the last 30–60 seconds of grilling time, toast the rolls, cut side down, over direct heat.

6. Build each burger on a roll with aioli, a patty and the pepper-onion mixture. Serve warm.

Roasting a bulb of garlic in foil over indirect heat for 40 minutes or so yields sweet golden cloves that you can squeeze right out of their papery skins. Mash the roasted garlic with mayonnaise for an unusually good aioli.

CHORIZO CHEESEBURGERS

SERVES: **4** | PREP TIME: **20 MINUTES** | GRILLING TIME: **8–10 MINUTES** | SPECIAL EQUIPMENT: **INSTANT-READ THERMOMETER**

PORK

PATTIES
450 g/1 lb lean pork mince
225 g/8 oz fresh Spanish
   chorizo sausage
4 garlic cloves, crushed
1 large shallot, finely diced
2 tablespoons finely chopped
   fresh parsley leaves
½ teaspoon smoked paprika
½ teaspoon dried thyme
½ teaspoon ground cumin

Sea salt
Freshly ground black pepper
4 sourdough rolls, split
Extra-virgin olive oil
4 slices manchego cheese,
   each about 30 g/1 oz
1 garlic clove, cut in half
8 thin slices ripe
   beefsteak tomato

The patties' centres will be slightly pink because of the chorizo. Have a thermometer on hand to be sure the pork is cooked to a safe temperature (70°C/160°F).

1. Mix the patty ingredients, including ½ teaspoon salt and ¼ teaspoon pepper, and then gently form four patties of equal size, each about 1.5 cm/¾ inch thick. With your thumb or the back of a spoon, make a shallow indentation about 2.5 cm/1 inch wide in the centre of the patties to prevent them from forming a dome as they cook. Refrigerate the patties until ready to grill.

2. Prepare the grill for direct cooking over medium-high heat (200–260°C/400–500°F).

3. Lightly season the patties on both sides with salt and pepper. Brush the cut side of the rolls with oil. Grill the patties over *direct medium-high heat* for 8–10 minutes, with the lid closed, until cooked to medium (70°C/160°F), turning once. During the last 30–60 seconds of grilling time, place a slice of cheese on each patty to melt, and toast the rolls, cut side down, over direct heat.

4. Rub the cut side of the toasted rolls with the cut side of the garlic half. Build each burger on a roll with two tomato slices and a patty. Serve warm.

CUBAN PORK BURGERS

SERVES: **4** | PREP TIME: **15 MINUTES** | GRILLING TIME: **10–14 MINUTES**
SPECIAL EQUIPMENT: **GRILL-PROOF GRIDDLE, ROASTING TRAY, 2 FOIL-WRAPPED BRICKS**

PATTIES

450 g/1 lb lean pork mince
1 teaspoon dried oregano
¾ teaspoon sea salt
½ teaspoon garlic granules
¼ teaspoon freshly ground
  black pepper

30 g/1 oz unsalted butter
3 garlic cloves, crushed
4 French sandwich rolls, each
  about 11 cm/4½ inches long,
  split
2 tablespoons Dijon mustard
8 slices Emmenthal cheese,
  each about 30 g/1 oz
8 slices Black Forest ham
Dill pickle slices

1. Prepare the grill for direct cooking over medium heat (180–230°C/350–450°F) and preheat a grill-proof griddle.

2. Mix the patty ingredients, and then gently form four oblong patties, each about 1.5 cm/¾ inch thick. With your thumb or the back of a spoon, make a shallow indentation about 2.5 cm/1 inch wide and 5 cm/2 inches long in the centre of the patties to prevent them from forming a dome as they cook. Refrigerate the patties until ready to grill.

3. In a small frying pan over a medium heat, melt the butter. Add the garlic and cook for 3–4 minutes until lightly browned, stirring occasionally. Remove from the heat.

4. Grill the patties over *direct medium heat* for 8–10 minutes, with the lid closed, until cooked to medium (70°C/160°F), turning once. Spread the cut side of the rolls with the mustard. Top the bottom half of each roll with a slice of cheese, two ham slices, a patty, pickle slices, one more slice of cheese and the top half of the roll. Brush the burgers on both sides with the garlic butter, place them on the griddle and put a roasting tray on top of the burgers, weighing it down with two foil-wrapped bricks. Grill over *direct medium heat* for 2–4 minutes, with the lid closed, until the rolls are toasted and the cheese is melted, turning once. Serve immediately.

Serving suggestion: Tropical Fruit Salad with Honey and Lime (for recipe, see page 217).

ITALIAN SAUSAGE SANDWICHES WITH BALSAMIC MAYO

〜〜〜〜〜〜〜〜〜〜〜〜〜〜〜〜〜〜〜〜〜〜〜〜〜〜

SERVES: **4** | PREP TIME: **20 MINUTES** | GRILLING TIME: **8-10 MINUTES**

PORK

MAYO

4 tablespoons mayonnaise
1 tablespoon Dijon mustard
2 teaspoons balsamic vinegar
¼ teaspoon sea salt
⅛ teaspoon freshly ground black pepper

PATTIES

1 tablespoon extra-virgin olive oil
2 onions, finely chopped
3 garlic cloves, crushed
450 g/1 lb Italian sausagemeat
225 g/8 oz beef mince (90% lean)
small bunch fresh parsley leaves, finely chopped

4 sourdough sandwich rolls, each 15–18 cm/
   6–7 inches long, split
4 golden pepperoncini (from a jar), sliced

1. Combine the mayo ingredients.

2. In a frying pan over a medium-high heat, warm the oil. Add the onion and garlic and cook for 2–3 minutes until they begin to soften, stirring often to prevent burning. Remove from the heat and cool for 5 minutes.

3. Mix the sausagemeat, minced beef, parsley and onion-garlic mixture, and then gently form four rectangular patties, each about 18 cm/7 inches long and 1.5 cm/¾ inch thick (to fit the rolls). With your thumb or the back of a spoon, make a shallow indentation about 2.5 cm/1 inch wide and 5 cm/2 inches long in the centre of the patties to prevent them from forming a dome as they cook. Refrigerate the patties until ready to grill.

4. Prepare the grill for direct cooking over medium-high heat (200–260°C/400–500°F).

5. Grill the patties over *direct medium-high heat* for 8–10 minutes, with the lid closed, until cooked to medium (70°C/160°F), turning once. During the last 30–60 seconds of grilling time, toast the rolls, cut side down, over direct heat.

6. Build each burger on a roll with balsamic mayo, a patty and pepperoncini. Serve warm.

LUAU PORK BURGERS WITH GRILLED PINEAPPLE AND SWEET PEPPERS

SERVES: **6** | PREP TIME: **25 MINUTES** | GRILLING TIME: **8–10 MINUTES** | SPECIAL EQUIPMENT: **PERFORATED GRILL PAN**

GLAZE

150 g/5 oz dark brown sugar
6 tablespoons soy sauce
3 tablespoons tomato ketchup
1½ tablespoons sherry vinegar
1½ teaspoons crushed black or Szechwan
   peppercorns
1½ teaspoons aniseed
1½ teaspoons sea salt

1 kg/2 lb lean pork mince
6 slices ripe, fresh pineapple, each about 8 mm/
   ⅓ inch thick
3 peppers, 1 red, 1 yellow, 1 green, each cut into
   8-mm/⅓-inch strips
6 burger buns, split

1. In a saucepan whisk the glaze ingredients. Bring to
a simmer over a medium heat, stirring for 3–4 minutes
until the sugar dissolves. Remove from the heat and
leave to cool. Pour 6 tablespoons of the glaze into a
large bowl and pour 4 tablespoons into a medium
bowl. Reserve the remaining glaze in the saucepan.

2. To the large bowl with the glaze add the pork and
mix. Gently form six patties of equal size, each about

1.5 cm/¾ inch thick. With your thumb or the back of a
spoon, make a shallow indentation about 2.5 cm/1 inch
wide in the centre of the patties to prevent them from
forming a dome as they cook. Refrigerate the patties
until ready to grill.

3. Prepare the grill for direct cooking over medium-high
heat (200–260°C/400–500°F) and preheat a perforated
grill pan.

4. To the medium bowl with the 4 tablespoons glaze
add the pineapple and peppers and turn to coat evenly.

5. Spread the pineapple and peppers in a single
layer on the grill pan and place the patties on the
cooking grates. Grill over *direct medium-high heat* for
8–10 minutes, with the lid closed, until the pineapple
and peppers are tender and the patties are cooked to
medium (70°C/160°F), turning the patties once and
the pineapple and peppers occasionally. During the
last 30–60 seconds of grilling time, toast the buns, cut
side down, over direct heat. Remove from the grill and
generously brush the patties with the remaining glaze
in the saucepan. Build each burger on a bun with a
patty and the pineapple-pepper mixture.

THREE-PORK BURGERS STUFFED WITH FETA

SERVES: **4** | PREP TIME: **30 MINUTES** | GRILLING TIME: **10–12 MINUTES**

PATTIES

375 g/12 oz lean pork mince
300 g/10 oz hot or mild Italian sausages, removed from their casings
60 g/2 oz Parma ham, finely diced
1 large shallot, finely diced
2 teaspoons chopped fresh oregano or ½ teaspoon dried oregano
4 garlic cloves, crushed
½ teaspoon sea salt
¼ teaspoon freshly ground black pepper

120 g/4 oz cold feta cheese, drained and cut into 4 squares
4 or 8 slices Italian or French bread, each about 1 cm/½ inch thick
Extra-virgin olive oil
1 garlic clove, cut in half
Large handful fresh spinach leaves

1. Mix the patty ingredients, and then gently form eight patties of equal size, each about 1 cm/½ inch thick. Place four of the patties on a work surface. Cut each feta square in half horizontally, creating two thinner blocks. Centre two blocks of the feta side by side on the top of each of the four patties. Centre the remaining four patties over the top and press down until each double patty is about 2.5 cm/1 inch thick. Pinch the edges together to seal in the cheese. Refrigerate the patties until ready to grill.

2. Prepare the grill for direct cooking over medium heat (180–230°C/350–450°F).

3. Brush the bread on both sides with oil. Grill the patties over *direct medium heat* for 10–12 minutes, with the lid closed, until cooked to medium (70°C/160°F), turning once. During the last minute of grilling time, toast the bread over direct heat, turning once. Remove the patties and bread from the grill and allow the patties to rest for 2–3 minutes. Rub the bread with the cut side of the garlic half.

4. Top four bread slices with half of the spinach, a patty and the remaining spinach. Serve warm, open-faced or with a second piece of bread.

CAROLINA BARBECUE PORK BURGERS

SERVES: **6** | PREP TIME: **20 MINUTES** | GRILLING TIME: **8–10 MINUTES**

MOP
125 ml/4 fl oz cider vinegar
2 tablespoons spicy brown mustard
2 tablespoons light brown sugar
2 teaspoons paprika
2 teaspoons hot pepper sauce
1 teaspoon sea salt
½ teaspoon freshly ground black pepper
¼ teaspoon ground allspice

COLESLAW
225 g/8 oz shredded coleslaw mix
3 tablespoons mayonnaise
2 tablespoons mop (from the recipe above)
1 teaspoon sweet orange marmalade

PATTIES
1 kg/2 lb lean pork mince
½ onion, grated
¼ teaspoon sea salt
¼ teaspoon freshly ground black pepper

6 burger buns, split

1. Whisk the mop ingredients.

2. Combine the coleslaw ingredients.

3. Mix the patty ingredients, then gently form six patties of equal size, each about 1.5 cm/¾ inch thick. With your thumb or the back of a spoon, make a shallow indentation about 2.5 cm/1 inch wide in the centre of the patties to prevent them from forming a dome as they cook. Refrigerate the patties until ready to grill.

4. Prepare the grill for direct cooking over medium-high heat (200–260°C/400–500°F).

5. Grill the patties over *direct medium-high heat* for 8–10 minutes, with the lid closed, until cooked to medium (70°C/160°F), turning once. During the last 30–60 seconds of grilling time, toast the buns, cut side down, over direct heat. Remove the patties and the buns from the grill and generously brush the patties with the remaining mop.

6. Build each burger on a bun with a patty and coleslaw. Serve warm.

Serving suggestion: Pickled Okra (for recipe, see page 234).

95

BURGER GEOGRAPHY

From sea to shining sea, the burger is America's culinary calling card. Just as dramatic as the changes in landscape are the regional preferences for the classic beef patty. While this list is by no means exhaustive, it does give us a taste (ahem) of the collective creativity between the bun. Behold, America the Burgerful.

CALIFORNIA BURGER

California

Californians are a lucky group: they've got the weather, the landscape and all those avocados. So when in the Golden State of mind, do as the locals do, and throw a couple of slices of ripe avocado on your burger right before serving. A dollop of citrusy-spicy guacamole qualifies, too.

PASTRAMI BURGER

Salt Lake City, Utah

When a standard burger simply isn't meaty enough, Utah doubles down. Slices of pastrami, the brined and smoked deli staple, are piled on top of a beef patty with a special Thousand Island–esque sauce, American cheese, shredded lettuce, tomato and onions, all on a sesame seed bun. Vegetarians, look away.

GREEN CHILLI CHEESEBURGER

Santa Fe, New Mexico

The South-west is known for its heat, both out of doors and on the plate. New Mexicans pile their beloved green chillies, roasted, fried, or whirred into salsa, on top of cheeseburgers to scorching effect. The cheese is a must, since dairy can help to cool torched tastebuds.

BEAN BURGER

San Antonio, Texas

Forget the Alamo – remember the bean burger. The original version combines some of America's more eclectic culinary traditions, all with a Tex-Mex twist: a beef patty topped with diced onions, refried beans, crushed corn chips and, yep, processed cheese sauce.

THETA BURGER

Oklahoma

You've got to love college kids and their ingenuity. Rumour has it that a late-night food order made by a University of Oklahoma sorority to a nearby restaurant inspired this saucy creation. A patty is topped with thick grated Cheddar, mayo, dill pickle slices, and barbecue or 'hickory' sauce on a sesame bun.

JUCY LUCY

Minneapolis, Minnesota

It's what's inside that counts, which is why some crafty Minnesotans put cheese in the burger rather than on it. (Maybe they took the 'i' out of 'juicy' to make room for more cheese.) A slice of American is laid between two thin burger patties, which are then pinched shut and grilled.

GUBERBURGER

Sedalia, Missouri

Opposites attract, and this burger's ingredients are gooey proof. First peddled at a drive-in nearly 100 miles south-east of Kansas City, the Guberburger is comprised of a thin chuck patty topped with lettuce, tomato, mayo and – get this – creamy melted peanut butter. Grab extra napkins.

SLUGBURGER

North-east Mississippi

Stretching a dollar is a tasty endeavour in Mississippi, where we found this Depression-era holdout. Minced beef is mixed with flour, grits, crackers or soya meal; formed into patties; and cooked on a griddle. They got their name because you could once buy one for a nickel, known as a 'slug' way back when.

PIMENTO CHEESE BURGER

Columbia, South Carolina

Pardon our drool, but we like our burgers with a drawl. Pimento cheese is grated Cheddar that is mixed with mayonnaise, diced pimento (or pimiento) peppers, salt and pepper until chunky and spreadable. It's yummy, period, but when zapped with a little radiant heat from a piping-hot burger, the flavours come alive.

TURKEY BURGERS WITH BRIE AND CRANBERRY MAYO

SERVES: **4** | PREP TIME: **20 MINUTES** | GRILLING TIME: **8–10 MINUTES**

PATTIES

700 g/1½ lb turkey mince, preferably thigh meat
1 tablespoon chopped fresh sage
1 tablespoon chopped fresh rosemary
2 teaspoons chopped fresh thyme
2 teaspoons finely chopped garlic

Sea salt
Freshly ground black pepper
4 tablespoons mayonnaise
4 tablespoons whole-berry cranberry sauce
Extra-virgin olive oil
½ teaspoon fresh lemon juice
2 full leaves Swiss chard or kale
   (remove tough stems before cutting),
   cut crossways into 5-mm/¼-inch strips
225 g/8 oz Brie cheese, cut into 8 slices
4 crusty rolls, split

1. Mix the patty ingredients, including 1 teaspoon salt and ½ teaspoon pepper, and then gently form four patties of equal size, each about 1.5 cm/¾ inch thick. With your thumb or the back of a spoon, make a shallow indentation about 2.5 cm/1 inch wide in the centre of the patties to prevent them from forming a dome as they cook. Refrigerate the patties until ready to grill.

2. Prepare the grill for direct cooking over medium-high heat (200–260°C/400–500°F).

3. Combine the mayonnaise, cranberry sauce, ¼ teaspoon salt and ¼ teaspoon pepper.

4. Whisk 2 teaspoons oil, the lemon juice and a pinch of salt and pepper. Add the Swiss chard and toss to combine.

5. Brush the patties on both sides with oil, and then grill over *direct medium-high heat* for 8–10 minutes, with the lid closed, until fully cooked (74°C/165°F), turning once. During the last 30–60 seconds of grilling time, place two slices of cheese on each patty to soften, and toast the buns, cut side down, over direct heat.

6. Build each burger on a bun with a patty, cranberry mayo and dressed Swiss chard.

LEMON AND DILL TURKEY BURGERS

SERVES: **4** | PREP TIME: **20 MINUTES** | GRILLING TIME: **11–13 MINUTES**

PATTIES
2 tablespoons extra-virgin
  olive oil
1 small onion, finely chopped
1 garlic clove, crushed
700 g/1½ lb turkey mince,
  preferably thigh meat
2 tablespoons chopped fresh dill
Finely grated rind of 1 lemon
1 tablespoon fresh lemon juice
1 teaspoon sea salt
¼ teaspoon freshly ground
  black pepper

Extra-virgin olive oil
4 burger buns, split
4 tablespoons mayonnaise
4 leaves round lettuce
2 roasted red peppers
  (from a jar), each cut in half

1. In a medium frying pan over a medium heat, warm the oil. Add the onion and garlic and sauté for about 5 minutes, until tender, stirring occasionally. Remove from the heat and allow to cool for at least 5 minutes. Combine the onion and garlic with the remaining patty ingredients, and then gently form four patties of equal size, each about 2.5 cm/1 inch thick. With your thumb or the back of a spoon, make a shallow indentation about 2.5 cm/1 inch wide in the centre of the patties to prevent them from forming a dome as they cook. Refrigerate the patties until ready to grill.

2. Prepare the grill for direct cooking over medium heat (180–230°C/350–450°F).

3. Brush the patties on both sides with oil, and then grill over *direct medium heat* for 11–13 minutes, with the lid closed, until fully cooked (74°C/165°F), turning once. During the last 30–60 seconds of grilling time, toast the buns, cut side down, over direct heat.

4. Build each burger on a bun with mayonnaise, a lettuce leaf, a roasted pepper half and a patty. Serve immediately.

CURRIED TURKEY BURGERS WITH APPLE CHUTNEY

SERVES: **4** | PREP TIME: **20 MINUTES, PLUS 20–25 MINUTES FOR THE CHUTNEY** | GRILLING TIME: **11–13 MINUTES**

PATTIES
700 g/1½ lb turkey mince, preferably thigh meat
2 tablespoons finely chopped onion
2 teaspoons curry powder
1½ teaspoons Worcestershire sauce
1 teaspoon sea salt
¼ teaspoon freshly ground black pepper

CHUTNEY
2 Granny Smith apples, peeled, cored and diced
225 g/8 oz sultanas
100 g/3½ oz roughly chopped walnuts
120 ml/4 oz white wine vinegar
60 g/2 oz granulated sugar
4 tablespoons fresh orange juice
1 cinnamon stick
¼ teaspoon sea salt

Extra-virgin olive oil
4 wholemeal buns, split

1. Mix the patty ingredients, then gently form four patties of equal size, each about 2.5 cm/1 inch thick. With your thumb or the back of a spoon, make a shallow indentation about 2.5 cm/1 inch wide in the centre of the patties to prevent them from forming a dome as they cook. Refrigerate the patties until ready to grill.

2. In a heavy saucepan combine the chutney ingredients and stir until the sugar is dissolved. Bring to a simmer over a medium heat and cook, uncovered, for 20–25 minutes, until most of the liquid is gone. Transfer to a bowl and allow to cool slightly. Discard the cinnamon stick.

3. Prepare the grill for direct cooking over medium heat (180–230°C/350–450°F).

4. Brush the patties on both sides with oil, and then grill over *direct medium heat* for 11–13 minutes, with the lid closed, until fully cooked (74°C/165°F), turning once. During the last 30–60 seconds of grilling time, toast the buns, cut side down, over direct heat.

5. Build each burger on a bun with a patty and apple chutney. Serve warm.

GREEK TURKEY BURGERS WITH TOMATO VINAIGRETTE

SERVES: **6** | PREP TIME: **20 MINUTES** | GRILLING TIME: **8–10 MINUTES**

PATTIES

1 tablespoon extra-virgin olive oil
300 g/10 oz frozen chopped spinach, thawed and
    squeezed dry
1 garlic clove, crushed
6 kalamata olives, coarsely chopped
1 kg/2 lb turkey mince, preferably thigh meat
120 g/4 oz feta cheese, crumbled
2 tablespoons apple butter
½ teaspoon poultry seasoning
½ teaspoon sea salt
¼ teaspoon freshly ground black pepper

VINAIGRETTE

240 ml/8 fl oz passata
4 tablespoons extra-virgin olive oil
2 tablespoons red wine vinegar
1 tablespoon finely chopped fresh oregano
1 tablespoon finely chopped fresh parsley leaves
½ teaspoon sea salt
¼ teaspoon freshly ground black pepper

Extra-virgin olive oil
6 burger buns, split

1. In a large sauté pan over a medium heat, warm the oil. Add the spinach and garlic and cook until the spinach is dry, stirring occasionally. Remove from the heat and stir in the olives. Allow to cool.

2. Combine the spinach mixture with the remaining patty ingredients, and then gently form six patties of equal size, each about 1.5 cm/¾ inch thick. With your thumb or the back of a spoon, make a shallow indentation about 2.5 cm/1 inch wide in the centre of the patties to prevent them from forming a dome as they cook. Refrigerate the patties until ready to grill.

3. Prepare the grill for direct cooking over medium-high heat (200–260°C/400–500°F).

4. Whisk the vinaigrette ingredients.

5. Brush the patties on both sides with oil, and then grill over *direct medium-high heat* for 8–10 minutes, with the lid closed, until fully cooked (74°C/165°F), turning once. During the last 30–60 seconds of grilling time, toast the buns, cut side down, over direct heat.

6. Build each burger on a bun with a patty and as much tomato vinaigrette as you like. Serve warm with any remaining vinaigrette on the side.

Minced turkey is often bland and dry. It needs help to become a succulent burger, which is why turkey burgers usually have a lot more ingredients in them than burgers made from beef or pork. The secret to this one is apple butter, which gives the turkey a darker colour and adds spices that make the meat taste much richer.

TURKEY CHEESEBURGERS

SERVES: **4** | PREP TIME: **20 MINUTES** | GRILLING TIME: **8–10 MINUTES**

PATTIES

700 g/1½ lb turkey mince, preferably thigh meat
2 spring onions, ends trimmed and finely chopped
1 stick celery, ends trimmed and finely chopped
2 teaspoons hot pepper sauce
1 teaspoon finely chopped garlic
1 teaspoon sea salt
½ teaspoon freshly ground black pepper

Extra-virgin olive oil
4 slices Edam cheese, each about 30 g/1 oz
4 brioche buns, split
4 leaves crisp lettuce
8 slices ripe tomato

1. Mix the patty ingredients, then gently form four patties of equal size, each about 1.5 cm/¾ inch thick. With your thumb or the back of a spoon, make a shallow indentation about 2.5 cm/1 inch wide in the centre of the patties to prevent them from forming a dome as they cook. Refrigerate the patties until ready to grill.

2. Prepare the grill for direct cooking over medium-high heat (200–260°C/400–500°F).

3. Brush the patties on both sides with oil, and then grill over *direct medium-high heat* for 8-10 minutes, with the lid closed, until fully cooked (74°C/165°F), turning once. During the last 30–60 seconds of grilling time, place a slice of cheese on each patty to melt, and toast the buns, cut side down, over direct heat.

4. Build each burger on a bun with a patty, a lettuce leaf and two tomato slices. Serve warm.

Serving suggestion: Weber's Secret Sauce (for recipe, see page 237).

PEPPER JACK TURKEY BURGERS WITH JALAPEÑO MAYO

SERVES: **4** | PREP TIME: **25 MINUTES** | GRILLING TIME: **11–13 MINUTES**

PATTIES

700 g/1½ lb turkey mince,
  preferably thigh meat
¼ small green pepper,
  finely chopped
¼ small red pepper,
  finely chopped
½ onion, finely chopped
2 tablespoons fresh coriander
2 garlic cloves, crushed
½ teaspoon dried oregano
½ teaspoon hot chilli powder

Sea salt
Freshly ground black pepper
Ground cumin

MAYO

8 tablespoons mayonnaise
1 jalapeño chilli, seeded and
  finely diced
1 tablespoon finely grated
  lime rind
1 tablespoon fresh lime juice
1 garlic clove, crushed

Extra-virgin olive oil
4 thick slices pepper jack or
  Cheddar cheese
4 crusty rolls, split
4 leaves crisp lettuce

1. Mix the patty ingredients, including 1 teaspoon salt, ½ teaspoon pepper and ¼ teaspoon cumin, and then gently form four patties of equal size, each about 2.5 cm/1 inch thick. With your thumb or the back of a spoon, make a shallow indentation about 2.5 cm/1 inch wide in the centre of each patty to prevent them from forming a dome as they cook. Refrigerate the patties until ready to grill.

2. Prepare the grill for direct cooking over medium heat (180–230°C/350–450°F).

3. In a small bowl whisk the mayo ingredients, including ¼ teaspoon salt, ¼ teaspoon pepper and ¼ teaspoon cumin.

4. Brush the patties on both sides with oil, and then grill over *direct medium heat* for 11–13 minutes, with the lid closed, until fully cooked (74°C/165°F), turning once. During the last 30–60 seconds of grilling time, place a slice of cheese on each patty to melt, and toast the rolls, cut side down, over direct heat.

5. Build each burger on a roll with jalapeño mayo, a patty and a lettuce leaf. Serve warm.

TURKEY BURGERS WITH CORN AND PEPPER RELISH

SERVES: **4** | PREP TIME: **15 MINUTES** | GRILLING TIME: **21–28 MINUTES**

POULTRY

PATTIES
700 g/1½ lb turkey mince, preferably thigh meat
1½ teaspoons Worcestershire sauce
3 garlic cloves, crushed
1 teaspoon hot chilli powder
1 teaspoon dried oregano
½ teaspoon ground cumin

Sea salt

RELISH
2 corn cobs, outer leaves and silk removed
2 tablespoons extra-virgin olive oil
1½ teaspoons white wine vinegar
½ teaspoon Dijon mustard
½ teaspoon finely grated lime rind
1 tablespoon fresh lime juice
½ small red pepper, cut into 5-mm/¼-inch dice
4 spring onions (white and light green parts only),
   thinly sliced
¼ teaspoon paprika

Extra-virgin olive oil
Freshly ground black pepper
4 wholemeal buns, split

1. Mix the patty ingredients, including 1 teaspoon salt, and then gently form four patties of equal size, each about 2.5 cm/1 inch thick. With your thumb or the back of a spoon, make a shallow indentation about 2.5 cm/1 inch wide in the centre of the patties to prevent them from forming a dome as they cook. Refrigerate the patties until ready to grill.

2. Prepare the grill for direct cooking over medium heat (180–230°C/350–450°F).

3. Grill the corn cobs over *direct medium heat for 10–15 minutes*, with the lid closed, until browned in spots and tender, turning occasionally. When cool enough to handle, cut the kernels off the cobs. In a medium bowl whisk 2 tablespoons oil, the vinegar, mustard, lime rind and lime juice. Add the corn kernels and the remaining relish ingredients. Season with ¼ teaspoon salt. Toss to coat.

4. Brush the patties on both sides with oil and lightly season with salt and pepper. Grill the patties over *direct medium heat* for 11–13 minutes, with the lid closed, until fully cooked (74°C/165°F), turning once. During the last 30–60 seconds of grilling time, toast the buns, cut side down, over direct heat.

5. Build each burger on a bun with a patty and corn and pepper relish. Serve warm.

Serving suggestion: Grilled Avocado and Jalapeño Guacamole (for recipe, see page 230).

CHICKEN POPEYE SLIDERS WITH MOZZARELLA AND PESTO

SERVES: **6** | PREP TIME: **20 MINUTES** | GRILLING TIME: **18-22 MINUTES**

PATTIES

700 g/1½ lb chicken mince
300 g/10 oz frozen chopped spinach,
   thawed and squeezed dry
120 g/4 oz mozzarella cheese, grated
4 tablespoons dried breadcrumbs
½ onion, finely chopped
2 tablespoons balsamic vinegar
1 teaspoon sea salt
2 garlic cloves, crushed
½ teaspoon freshly ground black pepper

2 medium red peppers
Extra-virgin olive oil
12 slices mozzarella cheese, trimmed to
   roughly the size of the sliders
12 slider buns, split
Shop-bought pesto

1. Mix the patty ingredients, and then gently form 12 patties of equal size, each about 1 cm/½ inch thick (roughly the size of the buns). Refrigerate the patties until ready to grill.

2. Prepare the grill for direct cooking over medium heat (180–230°C/350–450°F).

3. Grill the peppers over *direct medium heat* for 10–12 minutes, with the lid closed, until blackened and blistered all over, turning occasionally. Place the peppers in a bowl and cover with clingfilm to trap the steam. Allow to stand for about 10 minutes. Remove and discard the charred skin, stalk and seeds, and cut each pepper into six strips.

4. Brush the patties on both sides with oil, and then grill over *direct medium heat* for 8–10 minutes, with the lid closed, until fully cooked (74°C/165°F), turning once. During the last 30–60 seconds of grilling time, place a slice of cheese on each patty to melt, and toast the buns, cut side down, over direct heat.

5. Build each slider on a bun with a thin layer of pesto, a pepper strip and a patty. Serve immediately.

FUN FACT

In the 1930s, Popeye, the lovable, roughneck comic strip and cartoon character, was best known for consuming massive amounts of canned spinach, which gave him superhuman strength and instantaneous talents. During this time, spinach growers credited the sailor man with increasing American spinach consumption by more than a third – even briefly slotting spinach as the third most popular kids' food, after ice cream and turkey.

SPICY CHICKEN SLIDERS WITH BLUE CHEESE DRESSING

SERVES: **4** | PREP TIME: **15 MINUTES** | GRILLING TIME: **8-10 MINUTES**

DRESSING

60 g/2 oz blue cheese, crumbled
4 tablespoons sour cream
4 tablespoons mayonnaise
2 teaspoons white wine vinegar
¼ teaspoon sea salt
⅛ teaspoon freshly ground
   black pepper
2 sticks celery, finely chopped

PATTIES

700 g/1½ lb chicken mince, thigh
   or mixed thigh and breast meat
8 tablespoons dried breadcrumbs
1-2 tablespoons hot pepper sauce
1 teaspoon chilli powder
¾ teaspoon smoked paprika
¼ teaspoon ground cayenne
   pepper
½ teaspoon sea salt

30 g/1 oz unsalted butter, melted
8 slider buns, split

1. Combine all the dressing ingredients except for the celery and mash well with a fork. Stir in the celery.

2. Mix the patty ingredients, and then gently form eight patties of equal size, each about 1 cm/½ inch thick (roughly the size of the buns). Refrigerate the patties until ready to grill.

3. Prepare the grill for direct cooking over medium heat (180-230°C/350-450°F).

4. Brush the patties on both sides with the butter, and then grill over *direct medium heat* for 8-10 minutes, with the lid closed, until fully cooked (74°C/165°F), turning once. During the last 30-60 seconds of grilling time, toast the buns, cut side down, over direct heat.

5. Build each slider on a bun with a patty and blue cheese dressing. Serve warm.

Serving suggestion: Classic Creamy Slaw (for recipe, see page 200).

FUN FACT

The term 'sliders' probably originated in the US Navy in the 1930s or '40s, when it referred to hamburgers so greasy that they slid across the galley grill during heavy seas – though some sailors say the term refers to the way those burgers slid right down your gullet. Now chefs use the term to describe small burgers of any kind that are slipped inside little buns.

CHICKEN BURGERS WITH GRILLED PINEAPPLE AND HULI HULI SAUCE

SERVES: **4** | PREP TIME: **20 MINUTES, PLUS ABOUT 15 MINUTES FOR THE SAUCE** | GRILLING TIME: **8–10 MINUTES**

SAUCE

8 tablespoons tomato ketchup
75 g/2½ oz dark brown sugar
4 tablespoons soy sauce
2 tablespoons sherry vinegar
1 teaspoon peeled, grated
    fresh ginger
2 garlic cloves, crushed

600 g/1¼ lb chicken mince,
    preferably thigh meat
8 tablespoons panko
    breadcrumbs
4 slices ripe, fresh pineapple,
    each about 8 mm/⅓ inch
    thick, cored
4 burger buns, split
4 lettuce leaves
4 thin slices red onion

1. In a saucepan combine the sauce ingredients. Bring to the boil over a medium-high heat, and then reduce the heat to medium. Simmer gently for about 15 minutes, until the sauce is thickened, stirring frequently. Remove from the heat and cool to room temperature.

2. Combine 5 tablespoons of the sauce with the chicken mince and breadcrumbs, and then gently form four patties of equal size, each about 1.5 cm/¾ inch thick. With your thumb or the back of a spoon, make a shallow indentation about 2.5 cm/1 inch wide in the centre of the patties to prevent them from forming a dome as they cook. Refrigerate the patties until ready to grill.

3. Prepare the grill for direct cooking over medium-high heat (200–260°C/400–500°F).

4. Grill the patties and pineapple slices over *direct medium-high heat*, with the lid closed, until the patties are fully cooked (74°C/165°F), 8–10 minutes, and the pineapple slices are well marked, 4–6 minutes, turning once. During the last 2–3 minutes of grilling time, brush the patties and pineapple slices with the remaining sauce. During the last 30–60 seconds of grilling time, toast the buns, cut side down, over direct heat.

5. Build each burger on a bun with a lettuce leaf, an onion slice, a patty and a pineapple slice. Serve warm.

CHEESE, IF YOU PLEASE

AMERICAN

This no-frills standby is the best for pleasing a crowd. Many of us were reared on these individual slices of cheese ease.

PROS: Good melter; inexpensive; easy to find; mild flavour; will please the pickiest eaters

CONS: Can taste metallic or synthetic; lacks depth and nuance; can be melty to the point of messy

BEST USES: With all-American (that's no coincidence) burgers and hot dogs to be served at large gatherings

CHEDDAR

The only thing sharper than a good mature Cheddar is the knife you'll need to cut it. This reliable cheese is frequently our first choice to top a burger.

PROS: Easy to find; universally liked; versatile; a great grater

CONS: The generic stuff can be waxy and flavourless; overheating or reheating makes it rubbery

BEST USES: With beef burgers; with any items that have Latin or Southwestern undertones

EMMENTHAL

Nutty and sophisticated, this holey favourite is mild enough to delight the masses.

PROS: Great when baked or grilled; affordable; widely available; tones down big flavours; a nice alternative to American and Cheddar

CONS: Some mass-produced types are flavourless; can be stubborn melters

BEST USES: With pork, poultry or lamb burgers; with German-influenced hot dog and sausage varieties

MOZZARELLA

Don't you get fresh … unless we're talking mozzarella. Mild and chewy, it's unmatched in its ability to melt.

PROS: The authentic stuff is a delicacy worth the price tag; melts beautifully; grated varieties are easy to find

CONS: The mass-produced stuff is flavourless and chalky, as are low-fat versions; the real deal is expensive

BEST USES: With anything Italian; with tomatoes or tomato sauce; alongside bold flavours

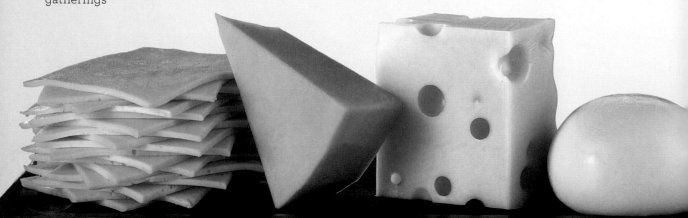

Now here's a topic that really makes us melt. A little dose of dairy can make beef taste beefier, spice tamer and lean meats more luxurious. As with much in life, you get what you pay for, so shelling out a little bit more for quality leads to superior results. There are really no bad cheese choices in our book, but below are a few of our favourites.

PROVOLONE

This Italian *formaggio* can take the heat, and likes it. Aged varieties can be quite sharp, while supermarket styles are much milder.

PROS: Soft and subtle flavours; great complement to bold meats and spices

CON: Can taste bland and forgettable

BEST USES: With dried Italian sausages; anything with 'pizza' flavours (it's a good change-up from the typical mozzarella choice)

PEPPER JACK

Is it hot in here, or is it just the cheese? Studded with hot pepper flakes, the assertive, spicy pepper jack melts in an instant.

PROS: Packs a flavour punch; good melter

CON: May overpower subtler flavours

BEST USES: With any burger or sausage under the Mexican influence; with leaner poultry burgers that lack flavour on their own

BLUE CHEESE

Pungent and piquant, this mould-injected variety can get the party started, or clear a room.

PROS: Loaded with flavour; varieties vary from sweet to knock-you-on-your-behind strong; complex, creamy, crumbly and a darling of cheese aficionados

CONS: Can be over-powering; the good stuff is pricey; doesn't melt well

BEST USE: With beef burgers

BRIE

This wheel of creamy dreaminess is as indulgent as it gets for cheese lovers. The French long ago dubbed it 'King of Cheeses'.

PROS: An instant statement-maker; mild and approachable, but still flavourful; very soft and melts with little effort

CONS: Difficult to slice; usually needs the rind left on to hold its shape, which might be unappealing to some; a little too ooey-gooey at times

BEST USES: On veggie burgers with walnuts; on poultry patties topped with a compote or chutney

CHICKEN PATTY MELTS

SERVES: **4** | PREP TIME: **30 MINUTES** | GRILLING TIME: **10–14 MINUTES**

2 tablespoons extra-virgin olive oil
450 g/1 lb onions, cut in half and thinly sliced
½ teaspoon dried thyme
¼ teaspoon sea salt
⅛ teaspoon freshly ground black pepper

PATTIES

700 g/1½ lb chicken mince, preferably thigh meat
5 tablespoons dried breadcrumbs
1 teaspoon ground cumin
1 teaspoon sea salt
½ teaspoon freshly ground black pepper

40 g/1½ oz unsalted butter, softened
8 slices rye bread, each about 1 cm/1½ inch thick
8 slices mature Cheddar cheese, each about
   30 g/1 oz
Tomato ketchup

1. In a large sauté pan over a medium-high heat, warm the oil. Add the onions, thyme, salt and pepper, and cook for about 20 minutes, until the onions are tender and golden, stirring often. Remove from the heat.

2. Mix the patty ingredients, and then gently form four patties, each slightly larger than the bread slices and about 1.5 cm/¾ inch thick. With your thumb or the back of a spoon, make a shallow indentation about 2.5 cm/1 inch wide in the centre of the patties to prevent them from forming a dome as they cook. Refrigerate the patties until ready to grill.

3. Prepare the grill for direct cooking over medium-high heat (200–260°C/400–500°F).

4. Butter one side of each bread slice. Place four slices on a work surface, buttered side down, and top each with one slice of cheese and one-quarter of the onions.

5. Grill the patties over *direct medium-high heat* for 8–10 minutes, with the lid closed, until fully cooked (74°C/165°F), turning once. Transfer the patties to the prepared bread on top of the onions. Top the patties with the remaining cheese and bread slices, buttered side up. Grill the patty melts over *direct medium-high heat* for 2–4 minutes, with the lid closed, until the bread is toasted and the cheese is melted, carefully turning once. Serve hot with tomato ketchup.

Everyday brown-skinned onions have a nice balance of astringency and sweetness – and they get even sweeter and nuttier as they cook, making them excellent for recipes like this one. White-skinned onions are sharper and more astringent. We like them in bold-tasting salsas, though we often rinse the chopped onions in a fine-mesh sieve under cold water to take off some of their harshness.

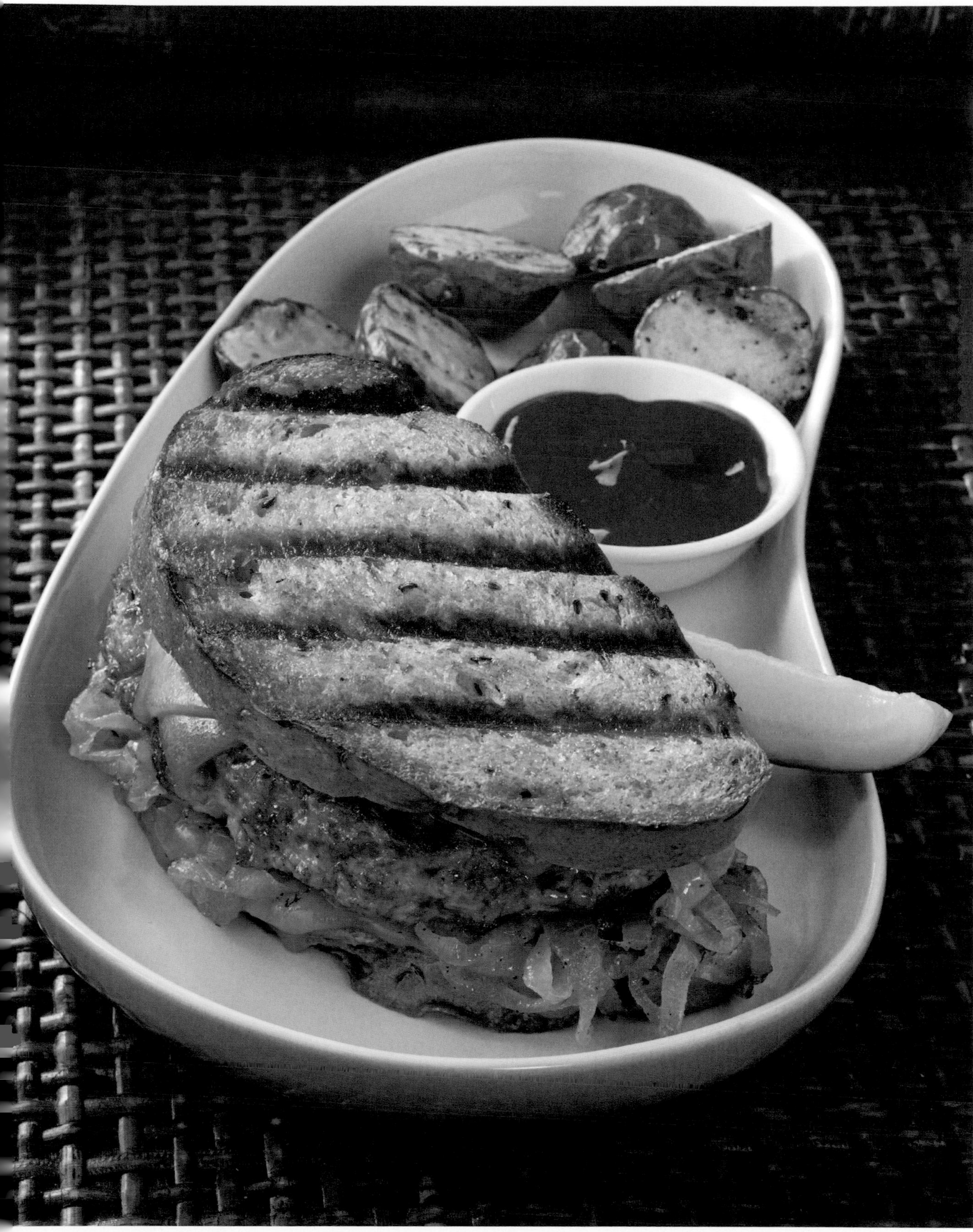

POULTRY

CHICKEN BURGERS WITH GUACAMOLE

SERVES: **4** | PREP TIME: **20 MINUTES** | GRILLING TIME: **11–13 MINUTES**

PATTIES
700 g/1½ lb chicken mince, preferably thigh meat
1½ teaspoons Worcestershire sauce
1½ teaspoons garlic, finely chopped
1 teaspoon sea salt
½ teaspoon hot pepper sauce
½ teaspoon dried oregano

GUACAMOLE
1 large or 2 small ripe avocados, diced
1 tablespoon red onion, finely diced
1 tablespoon chopped fresh coriander
1 tablespoon fresh lime juice, or to taste
¼ teaspoon hot pepper sauce, or to taste

Sea salt
Freshly ground black pepper
Extra-virgin olive oil
4 wholemeal buns, split
4 thick slices ripe tomato
4 thin slices red onion

1. Mix the patty ingredients, and then gently form four patties of equal size, each about 2.5 cm/1 inch thick. With your thumb or the back of a spoon, make a shallow indentation about 2.5 cm/1 inch wide in the centre of the patties to prevent them from forming a dome as they cook. Refrigerate the patties until ready to grill.

2. Prepare the grill for direct cooking over medium heat (180–230°C/350–450°F).

3. Mash the guacamole ingredients and season with salt and pepper.

4. Brush the patties on both sides with oil and lightly season with salt and pepper. Grill the patties over *direct medium heat* for 11–13 minutes, with the lid closed, until fully cooked (74°C/165°F), turning once. During the last 30–60 seconds of grilling time, toast the buns, cut side down, over direct heat.

5. Build each burger on a bun with a tomato slice, an onion slice, a patty and a mound of guacamole. Serve warm.

CHICKEN-APPLE BURGERS WITH CELERY SALAD

SERVES: **4** | PREP TIME: **20 MINUTES** | GRILLING TIME: **11–13 MINUTES**

PATTIES
700 g/1½ lb chicken mince, preferably thigh meat
1 large Granny Smith apple, peeled and finely diced
1 large shallot, finely diced
¾ teaspoon ground cumin

Sea salt
Freshly ground black pepper

SALAD
4 tablespoons mayonnaise
1 tablespoon fresh lemon juice
6 sticks celery, preferably from the heart,
   trimmed and cut into thin slices
5 tablespoons roughly chopped walnuts
1½ tablespoons finely chopped red onion
1 tablespoon finely chopped fresh parsley leaves
½ teaspoon horseradish

Extra-virgin olive oil
8 slices walnut bread, each about 1 cm/½ inch thick
   or 4 wholemeal buns, split
4 teaspoons Dijon mustard

1. Mix the patty ingredients, including 1 teaspoon salt and ½ teaspoon pepper, and then gently form four patties of equal size, each about 2.5 cm/1 inch thick. With your thumb or the back of a spoon, make a shallow indentation about 2.5 cm/1 inch wide in the centre of the patties to prevent them from forming a dome as they cook. Refrigerate the patties until ready to grill.

2. Prepare the grill for direct cooking over medium heat (180–230°C/350–450°F).

3. Whisk the mayonnaise and lemon juice, and then fold in the remaining salad ingredients. Season with ½ teaspoon salt and ¼ teaspoon pepper.

4. Brush the patties on both sides with oil and lightly season with salt and pepper. Grill the patties over *direct medium heat* for 11–13 minutes, with the lid closed, until fully cooked (74°C/165°F), turning once. During the last minute of grilling time, toast the bread over direct heat, turning once.

5. Build each burger on a bread slice with mustard, a patty, a spoonful of celery salad and the remaining bread slice. Serve immediately.

117

SMOKED CHICKEN BURGERS WITH BACON AND BLUE CHEESE

SERVES: **4** | PREP TIME: **25 MINUTES** | GRILLING TIME: **8–10 MINUTES**
SPECIAL EQUIPMENT: **2 LARGE HANDFULS HICKORY WOOD CHIPS**

PATTIES

4 rashers streaky bacon
½ medium onion, finely chopped
½ teaspoon fresh thyme leaves, finely chopped
600 g/1¼ lb chicken mince, preferably thigh meat
½ teaspoon sea salt
¼ teaspoon freshly ground black pepper

SAUCE

8 tablespoons mayonnaise
1 tablespoon cider vinegar
1 teaspoon horseradish
½ teaspoon granulated sugar
¼ teaspoon sea salt
¼ teaspoon freshly ground black pepper

4 burger buns, split
120 g/4 oz blue cheese, crumbled
12 sweet pickle slices

1. Soak the wood chips in water for at least 30 minutes.

2. In a frying pan over a medium heat for 10–12 minutes, fry the bacon until crisp, turning occasionally. Transfer the bacon to kitchen paper to drain. Pour off all but 1 tablespoon of bacon fat. Return the pan to medium heat and add the onion and thyme. Cook for 2–3 minutes until the onion starts to soften, stirring occasionally. Crumble the bacon. Mix the bacon, onion mixture, chicken mince, salt and pepper, and then gently form four patties of equal size, each about 1.5 cm/¾ inch thick. With your thumb or the back of a spoon, make a shallow indentation about 2.5 cm/1 inch wide in the centre of the patties to prevent them from forming a dome as they cook. Refrigerate the patties until ready to grill.

3. Prepare the grill for direct cooking over medium-high heat (200–260°C/400–500°F).

4. Whisk the sauce ingredients.

5. Drain and add the wood chips to the charcoal or to the smoker box of a gas grill, following manufacturer's instructions, and close the lid. When smoke appears, grill the patties for 8–10 minutes, with the lid closed, until fully cooked (74°C/165°F), turning once. During the last 30–60 seconds of grilling time, toast the buns, cut side down, over direct heat.

6. Build each burger on a bun with sauce, a patty, blue cheese and pickle slices. Serve warm.

FUN FACT

Did you know that the bluish-green veins running through the white, crumbly wheels and wedges of blue cheese are actually mould? But it's not just any old mould – it's a harmless, pungent, mouthwatering mould, said to have been gleefully discovered by early cheese makers who aged their cheeses in the naturally dark, damp, cool environment of caves.

SURF AND TURF BURGERS WITH PESTO

SERVES: **4** | PREP TIME: **15 MINUTES** | CHILLING TIME: **30 MINUTES–2 HOURS**
GRILLING TIME: **8–9 MINUTES** | SPECIAL EQUIPMENT: **PERFORATED GRILL PAN**

SEAFOOD

PATTIES

350 g/12 oz prawns, peeled and deveined
350 g/12 oz chicken mince, preferably thigh meat
6–8 tablespoons panko breadcrumbs
3 tablespoons finely chopped red pepper
1 large egg, lightly beaten
1 tablespoon Dijon mustard
1 tablespoon mayonnaise
½ teaspoon garlic granules
½ teaspoon hot chilli powder
¼ teaspoon sea salt
¼ teaspoon freshly ground black pepper

8 teaspoons shop-bought pesto
Extra-virgin olive oil
4 wholemeal buns, split
4 leaves round lettuce
8 thin slices ripe tomato

1. Wrap the prawns in kitchen paper and squeeze out the excess moisture. Roughly chop the prawns into chunks of 5 mm/¼ inch or less. Mix the prawns with the remaining patty ingredients, starting with 6 tablespoons of panko. Gently squeeze a bit of the mixture to see if it clumps; if not, add up to 2 additional tablespoons of panko. Freeze for 5 minutes. Form eight patties of equal size, each about 1 cm/½ inch thick.

2. Place four patties on a work surface and spread 2 teaspoons of pesto on top of each, leaving a 1-cm/½-inch border. Centre the remaining four patties over the tops, and press down until each double patty is about 2.5 cm/1 inch thick. Pinch the edges together tightly, sealing in the pesto. Cover

and refrigerate for 30 minutes to 2 hours.

3. Prepare the grill for direct cooking over high heat (230–290°C/450–550°F) and preheat a perforated grill pan.

4. Brush the patties with oil, place on the grill pan over *direct high heat*, close the lid, and grill for 4 minutes (do not move the patties). Turn the patties over and continue cooking for 4–5 minutes more, until golden and firm. During the last 30–60 seconds of grilling time, toast the buns on the cooking grates, cut side down, over direct heat.

5. Build each burger on a bun with a lettuce leaf, two tomato slices and a patty. Serve warm.

After you fill the patties with pesto, making sure that it doesn't spill out of the sides, refrigerate the patties for at least 30 minutes to make them firmer and easier to handle on the grill.

PRAWN AND SPRING ONION BURGERS WITH CRISPY PANCETTA

SERVES: **4** | PREP TIME: **30 MINUTES** | CHILLING TIME: **30 MINUTES–2 HOURS**
GRILLING TIME: **12–16 MINUTES** | SPECIAL EQUIPMENT: **GRILL-PROOF GRIDDLE**

MAYONNAISE

4 tablespoons mayonnaise
Finely grated rind of 1 lemon
1 teaspoon fresh lemon juice
1 teaspoon horseradish
⅛ teaspoon sea salt

PATTIES

600 g/1¼ lb prawns,
   peeled and deveined
6–8 tablespoons panko
   breadcrumbs
3 spring onions, ends trimmed
   and finely chopped
1 large egg, lightly beaten
1 tablespoon Dijon mustard
1 tablespoon mayonnaise
Finely grated rind of 1 lemon
½ teaspoon sea salt
⅛ teaspoon freshly ground
   black pepper

8 thin slices pancetta
Extra-virgin olive oil
4 English muffins, split
2 tablespoons finely chopped
   spring onion tops

Squeezing water out of the raw prawns is an important first step; otherwise, the patties will be too wet and will steam rather than char on the grill. You must have *some* moisture in the patties, which should come from ingredients like mayonnaise and mustard (they taste a lot better than prawn water).

1. Mix the mayonnaise ingredients. Refrigerate until ready to use.

2. Wrap the prawns in kitchen paper and squeeze out the excess moisture. In a food processor fitted with a metal blade, pulse the prawns until roughly chopped. Mix the prawns with the remaining patty ingredients, starting with 6 tablespoons of panko. Gently squeeze a bit of the mixture to see if it clumps; if not, add up to 2 additional tablespoons of panko. Freeze for 5 minutes. Form four patties of equal size, each about 1.5 cm/¾ inch thick. Cover and refrigerate for 30 minutes–2 hours.

3. Prepare the grill for direct cooking over medium heat (180–230°C/350–450°F) and preheat a grill-proof griddle.

4. Cook the pancetta on the griddle for 6–8 minutes, until crisp, turning occasionally. Drain on kitchen paper. Increase the temperature of the grill to high heat (230–290°C/450–550°F). Keep the griddle on the cooking grates.

5. Brush the patties on both sides with oil. Place the patties on the griddle and cook over *direct high heat* for 6–8 minutes, with the lid closed, until golden and firm. During the last 30–60 seconds of grilling time, toast the English muffins on the cooking grates, cut side down, over direct heat.

6. Build each burger on an English muffin with a patty, lemon mayonnaise, pancetta and chopped spring onions. Serve warm.

121

SEAFOOD

PRAWN BURGERS WITH RÉMOULADE

SERVES: **4** | PREP TIME: **30 MINUTES** | CHILLING TIME: **30 MINUTES–2 HOURS**
GRILLING TIME: **6–8 MINUTES** | SPECIAL EQUIPMENT: **GRILL-PROOF GRIDDLE**

RÉMOULADE

4 tablespoons mayonnaise
3 spring onions, ends trimmed and finely chopped
2 tablespoons chopped fresh parsley leaves
1½ tablespoons fresh lemon juice
1½ tablespoons finely chopped celery heart
1 tablespoon wholegrain mustard
1 tablespoon tomato ketchup
1 tablespoon horseradish
¾ teaspoon Worcestershire sauce
1 garlic clove, crushed
¼ teaspoon paprika
⅛ teaspoon hot pepper sauce, or to taste

Sea salt
Freshly ground black pepper

PATTIES

600 g/1¼ lb prawns, peeled and deveined
6–8 tablespoons panko breadcrumbs
1 large egg, lightly beaten
3 spring onions, ends trimmed and finely chopped
2 tablespoons chopped celery heart
1 tablespoon mayonnaise
Finely grated rind of 1 lemon

Extra-virgin olive oil
30 g/1 oz unsalted butter, softened
4 slices challah, each about 1 cm/½ inch thick

1. Whisk the rémoulade ingredients until smooth, including ¼ teaspoon salt and ⅛ teaspoon pepper. Cover and refrigerate until ready to serve.

2. Wrap the prawns in kitchen paper and squeeze out the excess moisture. Put the prawns in a food processor fitted with a metal blade, and pulse about six times until roughly chopped (pieces should be about 5 mm/¼ inch or less). Combine the prawns, 6 tablespoons panko, the egg, spring onions, celery, mayonnaise, lemon rind, ½ teaspoon salt and ¼ teaspoon pepper. Blend well with a fork. Gently squeeze a bit of the mixture to see if it clumps; if not, add up to 2 additional tablespoons panko. Freeze for 5 minutes. Form four patties of equal size, each about 1.5 cm/¾ inch thick. Cover and refrigerate for 30 minutes to 2 hours.

3. Prepare the grill for direct cooking over medium heat (180–230°C/350–450°F) and preheat a grill-proof griddle.

4. Lightly brush the patties on both sides with oil. Spread the butter on both sides of the challah. Place the patties on the griddle and cook over *direct medium heat* for 6–8 minutes, with the lid closed, until golden and firm, carefully turning once. During the last minute of grilling time, toast the challah on the cooking grates over direct heat, turning once.

5. Place a patty on a slice of challah and top with rémoulade. Serve warm.

To grill prawn prawn patties without sticking problems, make sure the grill is hot and the food is cold. It also helps to have a grill-proof griddle and the patience to wait until the patties have browned on the first side before trying to turn them.

SMOKED SALMON BURGERS WITH FRIED EGGS AND SPRING ONION CREAM CHEESE

SERVES: **6** | PREP TIME: **30 MINUTES** | CHILLING TIME: **1 HOUR**
GRILLING TIME: **6–8 MINUTES** | SPECIAL EQUIPMENT: **GRILL-PROOF GRIDDLE**

PATTIES

700 g/1½ lb skinless salmon fillets, pin bones
   removed, cut into 2.5-cm/1-inch pieces
225 g/8 oz lox-style smoked salmon, finely chopped
8 tablespoons panko breadcrumbs
3 tablespoons finely chopped onion
3 tablespoons finely chopped fresh chives
1 tablespoon finely chopped garlic
1 teaspoon sea salt

Freshly ground black pepper
90 g/3 oz cream cheese, softened
3 spring onions (white and light green parts only),
   finely chopped
1 tablespoon extra-virgin olive oil
6 English muffins, split
15 g/½ oz unsalted butter
6 large eggs
Microgreens or sprouts

1. In a food processor fitted with a metal blade, pulse the salmon fillet pieces 8–10 times until coarsely chopped but not paste-like; transfer to a bowl. Add the remaining patty ingredients to the bowl, including ¼ teaspoon pepper, and stir gently to combine. Form six patties of equal size, each about 1.5 cm/¾ inch thick. Cover and refrigerate the patties for 1 hour.

2. Prepare the grill for direct cooking over medium heat (180–230°C/350–450°F) and preheat a grill-proof griddle.

3. Mix the cream cheese and spring onions until well blended. Refrigerate until ready to grill the patties.

4. Brush the patties on both sides with the oil. Place the patties on the griddle and cook over *direct medium heat* for 6–8 minutes, with the lid closed, until fully cooked but still juicy, carefully turning once. During the last 30–60 seconds of grilling time, toast the English muffins on the cooking grates, cut side down, over direct heat.

5. In a frying pan over a medium-high heat, melt the butter. Fry the eggs until the whites are set to your desired doneness.

6. Spread the spring onion cream cheese on both toasted sides of the English muffins. Place a patty on each muffin bottom, and top with an egg and a small handful of microgreens. Season with pepper. Serve warm with the muffin tops on the side.

Serving suggestion: Tropical Fruit Salad with Honey and Lime (for recipe, see page 217).

One key to great salmon burgers is evenly chopped fish, which is easy to get with a big food processor. However, if the bowl of your processor has a diameter of less than 18 cm/7 inches, process the fish in two batches with quick pulses until you get a coarsely chopped consistency in each batch.

LEMON-CAPER SALMON BURGERS WITH PESTO MAYO

SERVES: **4** | PREP TIME: **20 MINUTES** | CHILLING TIME: **1 HOUR** | GRILLING TIME: **6–8 MINUTES**

SEAFOOD

PATTIES

700 g/1½ lb skinless salmon
   fillets, pin bones removed,
   cut into 2.5-cm/1-inch pieces
1 shallot, finely diced
4 tablespoons chopped fresh
   parsley leaves
1 large egg, beaten
Finely grated rind of 1 lemon
1 tablespoon fresh lemon juice
8 tablespoons fresh white
   breadcrumbs
1½ tablespoons capers,
   drained and chopped
¾ teaspoon sea salt
½ teaspoon freshly ground
   black pepper

5 tablespoons shop-bought pesto
4 tablespoons mayonnaise
Extra-virgin olive oil
2 or 4 focaccia squares, each
   about 11 cm/4½ inches, split
8 slices ripe tomato
4 leaves round lettuce

1. In a food processor fitted with a metal blade, pulse the salmon pieces 8–10 times until coarsely chopped but not paste-like. Add the shallot, parsley, egg, lemon rind and juice. Pulse a few times until just blended, being careful to leave some texture. Transfer to a bowl and gently stir in the remaining patty ingredients. Form four patties of equal size, each about 1.5 cm/ ¾ inch thick. Cover and refrigerate for 1 hour.

2. Combine the pesto and mayonnaise. Cover and refrigerate until ready to use.

3. Prepare the grill for direct cooking over medium heat (180–230°C/350–450°F).

4. Brush the patties on both sides with oil and then grill over *direct medium heat* for 6–8 minutes, with the lid closed, until fully cooked but still juicy, carefully turning once. During the last 30–60 seconds of grilling time, toast the focaccia, cut side down, over direct heat.

5. Top four focaccia halves with pesto mayo, two tomato slices, a lettuce leaf and a patty. Serve warm topped with another focaccia half, if liked.

OPEN-FACED SALMON BURGERS WITH PINEAPPLE-GINGER SALSA

SERVES: **6** | PREP TIME: **45 MINUTES** | CHILLING TIME: **1 HOUR** | GRILLING TIME: **16–18 MINUTES**

PATTIES

1 kg/2 lb skinless salmon
  fillets, pin bones removed,
  cut into 2.5-cm/1-inch pieces
8 tablespoons panko
  breadcrumbs
1 spring onion (white and green
  parts only), finely chopped
Finely grated rind and
  juice of 1 lime
2 tablespoons soy sauce
½ teaspoon hot pepper sauce
¼ teaspoon freshly ground
  black pepper

SALSA

100 g/3½ oz ripe, fresh pineapple,
  finely chopped
150 g/5 oz ripe tomatoes, finely
  chopped
2 teaspoons peeled, grated
  fresh ginger
½ small jalapeño chilli,
  seeded and finely diced
½ teaspoon sea salt
⅛ teaspoon freshly ground
  black pepper
1 large sweet onion, cut
  crossways into 8-mm/⅓-inch
  slices

Vegetable oil
6 slices sourdough bread,
  each about 8 mm/⅓ inch thick
6 tablespoons mayonnaise
6 leaves baby lettuce

1. In a food processor fitted with a metal blade, pulse the salmon pieces 8–10 times until coarsely chopped but not paste-like; transfer to a bowl. Add the remaining patty ingredients to the bowl and stir gently to combine. Form six patties of equal size, each about 1.5 cm/ ¾ inch thick. Cover and refrigerate for 1 hour.

2. Prepare the grill for direct cooking over medium heat (180–230°C/350–450°F).

3. Combine all the salsa ingredients except for the onion. Brush the onion slices on both sides with oil and then grill over *direct medium heat* for about 10 minutes, with the lid closed, until well marked and tender, turning once or twice. Finely chop the onion and add it to the salsa. Mix well.

4. Brush the patties on both sides with oil, and then grill over *direct medium heat* for 6–8 minutes, with the lid closed, until fully cooked but still juicy, carefully turning once. During the last minute of grilling time, toast the bread over direct heat, turning once.

5. Spread a tablespoon of mayonnaise on each bread slice and top with a lettuce leaf, a patty and pineapple-ginger salsa. Serve warm.

CEDAR-PLANKED SALMON BURGERS WITH MAPLE MUSTARD

SERVES: **4** | PREP TIME: **25 MINUTES** | CHILLING TIME: **1 HOUR** | GRILLING TIME: **12–14 MINUTES**
SPECIAL EQUIPMENT: **1 UNTREATED CEDAR PLANK, 30–37 CM/12–15 INCHES LONG AND ABOUT 18 CM/7 INCHES WIDE**

SEAFOOD

PATTIES

700 g/1½ lb skinless salmon fillets, pin bones
   removed, cut into 2.5-cm/1-inch pieces
8 tablespoons panko breadcrumbs
2 spring onions, finely chopped
   (white and light green parts only)
1 large egg, beaten
2 tablespoons chopped fresh parsley leaves
2 teaspoons Dijon mustard
1 teaspoon hot pepper sauce
1 teaspoon sea salt
½ teaspoon freshly ground black pepper

MUSTARD

3 tablespoons Dijon mustard
1½ tablespoons maple syrup
¼ teaspoon sea salt
¼ teaspoon freshly ground black pepper

1 tablespoon extra-virgin olive oil
4 ciabatta rolls, split
1 small red onion, thinly sliced
Large handful baby salad leaves

1. Soak the cedar plank in water for at least 1 hour.

2. In a food processor fitted with a metal blade, pulse the salmon pieces 8–10 times until coarsely chopped but not paste-like; transfer to a bowl. Add the remaining patty ingredients to the bowl and stir gently to combine. Form four patties of equal size, each about 1.5 cm/¾ inch thick. Cover and refrigerate for 1 hour.

3. Whisk the mustard ingredients.

4. Prepare the grill for direct cooking over medium heat (180–230°C/350–450°F).

5. Lightly brush the patties on both sides with the oil. Place the soaked cedar plank over *direct medium heat* and close the lid. After 5–10 minutes, when the plank begins to smoke and char, turn the plank over. Place the patties in a single layer on the plank. Grill over *direct medium heat* for 12–14 minutes, with the lid closed, until the patties are fully cooked but still juicy, carefully turning once. During the last 30–60 seconds of grilling time, toast the rolls on the cooking grates, cut side down, over direct heat.

6. Build each burger on a roll with a patty, maple mustard, onion and baby salad leaves. Serve warm.

Char one side of the plank over direct heat before turning it over and placing the salmon patties on top. In other words, the plank should be smoking before you start cooking the patties.

SEAFOOD

SALMON BURGERS WITH LEMON SALSA VERDE

~~~~~~

SERVES: **4** | PREP TIME: **20 MINUTES**
CHILLING TIME: **1 HOUR** | GRILLING TIME: **6–8 MINUTES**

PATTIES
600 g/1¼ lb skinless salmon fillets, pin bones
   removed, cut into 2.5-cm/1-inch pieces
8 tablespoons panko breadcrumbs
4 tablespoons mayonnaise
1 large shallot, finely chopped
2 tablespoons finely chopped fresh basil

Sea salt
Freshly ground black pepper

SALSA
4 tablespoons extra-virgin olive oil
4 tablespoons finely chopped fresh basil
1½ tablespoons capers, drained and finely chopped
Finely grated rind of 1 lemon
1 tablespoon fresh lemon juice

Extra-virgin olive oil
4 burger buns, split
4 lettuce leaves
8 slices ripe plum tomato

1. In a food processor fitted with a metal blade, pulse
the salmon pieces 8–10 times until coarsely chopped
but not paste-like; transfer to a bowl. Add the
remaining patty ingredients to the bowl, including
½ teaspoon salt and ¼ teaspoon pepper, and stir gently
to combine. Form four patties of equal size, each about
1.5 cm/¾ inch thick. Cover and refrigerate for 1 hour.

2. Mix the salsa ingredients and season with salt and
pepper. Set aside at room temperature.

3. Prepare the grill for direct cooking over medium
heat (180–230°C/350–450°F).

4. Brush the patties on both sides with oil, and then
grill over *direct medium heat* for 6–8 minutes, with the
lid closed, until fully cooked but still juicy, carefully
turning once. During the last 30–60 seconds of
grilling time, toast the buns, cut side down, over
direct heat.

5. Build each burger on a bun with a lettuce leaf,
two tomato slices, a patty and lemon salsa verde.
Serve warm.

YELLOWTAIL BURGERS WITH WASABI MAYO AND PICKLED VEGETABLES

SERVES: **6** | PREP TIME: **30 MINUTES** | CHILLING TIME: **AT LEAST 30 MINUTES**
GRILLING TIME: **6-8 MINUTES** | SPECIAL EQUIPMENT: **PERFORATED GRILL PAN**

PATTIES

1 kg/2 lb boneless, skinless yellowtail or tuna fillet
4 spring onions, finely chopped
   (white and light green parts only)
8 tablespoons panko breadcrumbs
3 tablespoons chopped pickled sushi ginger
2 tablespoons rapeseed oil
1½ tablespoons soy sauce
2 teaspoons toasted sesame oil
1 teaspoon wasabi paste
2 garlic cloves, crushed
½ teaspoon sea salt
¼ teaspoon freshly ground black pepper

2 medium, ripe avocados, finely diced
3 red radishes, finely diced
2 tablespoons rice vinegar
1 tablespoon mirin (sweet rice wine)
2 teaspoons toasted sesame oil
5 tablespoons mayonnaise
1 teaspoon wasabi paste
Vegetable oil
6 ciabatta rolls, split

1. Cut the fish into small pieces, and place in a food processor. Pulse 8–10 times until coarsely chopped but not paste-like; transfer to a bowl. Add the remaining patty ingredients and stir gently to combine. Form six patties of equal size, each about 1.5 cm/¾ inch thick. Cover and refrigerate the patties for at least 30 minutes.

2. In a bowl combine the avocados, radishes, vinegar, mirin and 1 teaspoon of the sesame oil.

3. In another bowl whisk the mayonnaise, wasabi and the remaining 1 teaspoon sesame oil.

4. Prepare the grill for direct cooking over medium heat (180–230°C/350–450°F) and preheat a perforated grill pan.

5. Brush the patties on both sides with vegetable oil. Grill the patties on the grill pan over *direct medium heat* for 6–8 minutes, with the lid closed, until fully cooked but still juicy, turning once. During the last 30–60 seconds of grilling time, toast the rolls on the cooking grates, cut side down, over direct heat.

6. Build each burger on a roll with wasabi mayo, a patty and pickled vegetables. Serve warm.

TUNA PATTIES WITH CREAMY GINGER SLAW

SERVES: **4** | PREP TIME: **40 MINUTES** | FREEZING TIME: **2 HOURS** | CHILLING TIME: **1–2 HOURS**
GRILLING TIME: **5–6 MINUTES** | SPECIAL EQUIPMENT: **GRILL-PROOF GRIDDLE**

PATTIES

3 skinless tuna steaks, each
   about 175 g/6 oz and 2.5 cm/1 inch thick
6–8 tablespoons panko breadcrumbs
3 tablespoons cottage cheese
1 large egg
2 large egg yolks
1 medium shallot, finely diced
2 teaspoons peeled, grated fresh ginger
Finely grated rind of 1 lime
½ teaspoon sea salt
⅛ teaspoon freshly ground black pepper

DRESSING

4 tablespoons mayonnaise
4 tablespoons pickled sushi ginger, drained
2½ tablespoons rice vinegar
2 tablespoons toasted sesame oil
1 small shallot, thinly sliced
1½ tablespoons mirin (sweet rice wine) (optional)
6–7 fresh basil leaves
1 tablespoon soy sauce
1 tablespoon granulated sugar
2 large garlic cloves, thinly sliced

1 small head savoy cabbage, cored
   and very thinly sliced
1 fennel bulb, trimmed, quartered, cored,
   and very thinly sliced
3 spring onions, ends trimmed and finely chopped
Extra-virgin olive oil
4 small, ripe tomatoes, each cut in half
2 tablespoons finely chopped fresh parsley leaves

1. Freeze the tuna steaks for 2 hours (this will make it easier to chop them).

2. Finely chop the tuna. Pat dry. Combine all of the patty ingredients, starting with 6 tablespoons of panko. Blend well with a fork. Gently squeeze a bit of the mixture to see if it clumps; if not, add up to 2 additional tablespoons of panko. Form four patties of equal size, each about 2.5 cm/1 inch thick. Cover and refrigerate for 1–2 hours. Leave the patties in the refrigerator until just before grilling.

3. Prepare the grill for direct cooking over high heat (230–290°C/450–550°F) and preheat a grill-proof griddle.

4. Meanwhile, in a food processor fitted with a metal blade, combine the dressing ingredients and process until smooth. In a large bowl toss the cabbage and fennel with the dressing. Just before serving, fold in the spring onions.

5. Brush the patties on both sides with oil. Grill the patties on the griddle over *direct high heat* for 5–6 minutes, with the lid closed, until firm but still pink in the centre, carefully turning once after 4 minutes. During the last minute of grilling time, warm the tomato halves on the cooking grates, cut side down, over direct heat.

6. Serve the patties warm with creamy ginger slaw and tomato halves. Garnish with parsley.

Panko breadcrumbs are the preferred binder for all kinds of seafood burgers, because they have a coarser texture than traditional breadcrumbs. In fact, they are more like jagged flakes than crumbs, meaning that they don't soak up as much moisture and turn dense. They maintain a certain airiness that makes the burgers themselves wonderfully light.

WHAT'S THE DILL?

Consider their longevity: Aristotle praised pickles' healing powers, Cleopatra credited them as a beauty aid, and George Washington was such a fan that he had a collection of more than 400 varieties. From Biblical and Shakespearean references to a hitched ride on Christopher Columbus's voyages, the humble cured cuke sure has gotten a lot of press. But it doesn't stop there.

Today's modern pickle is more popular than ever. According to Pickle Packers International, Inc., Americans consume more than 20 billion pickles each year – that's about 4.5 kg (9 lb) of pickles per person. It makes sense, then, that half of the United States' cucumber crop is specifically grown for pickle production.

You may be thinking: *There's no way that I eat 9 lb of pickles each year ... oh wait. You mean fried pickles, too? Yep, make that 10 lb.* These crisp, tangy, easy-to-eat little treats are delicious fresh or fried, on burgers and sandwiches, in salads and dips, and, of course, on their own. Plus, pickles are fat free and low in calories – when served in their original form.

From chips to spears to sandwich slices, dill to half-sour to sweet, and relish to salad cubes to pickled peppers, there are literally hundreds of pickle varieties. It only seems fair to begin with the daddy of them all, the world's most popular pickle: the Grand Dillmeister. Even within the dill division, you'll find dozens of types, including genuine, overnight and kosher, to name a few. Highly acidic, and some say sour, genuine dills are processed and fermented slowly with dill weed; whereas, the crunchy, bright green overnight dills are brined quickly and are *always* refrigerated. Robust and flavourful, kosher dills, while not always truly 'kosher' by rabbinic standards, are fermented and distinctly garlic-flavoured.

Occupying the opposite end of the pickle spectrum, sweet pickles are classically packed in sugar, spices and vinegar. Sweet and slightly tangy, the perennial favourite bread-and-butter pickle supposedly got its name in the 1920s from a man whose family had fallen on hard times. His solution? Selling cucumbers pickled with onions and peppers on the street corner. His quick pickle fix was successful enough to put bread and butter on his own table – and his bread-and-butter brainchildren on relish trays throughout the United States.

But what about the brine? For many, pickle brine is both a curative and culinary commodity. Some athletes swear by drinking pickle juice for its scientifically proven, electrolyte-restoring prowess in preventing post-workout muscle cramps. It's hailed by others as a hangover remedy (and prevention) and a heartburn cure. And with its complex flavour it's a tasty addition to salad dressings and soups, marinades and Bloody Marys. Plus, pickle juice is a great weed killer. Cramp-free, pickle cocktail in hand, overlooking a picture-perfect lawn – who's laughing now?

We're now in a bit of a pickle renaissance, with boutique brands made from locally sourced traditional cucumber varieties popping up at markets regularly. Are pickles the next big thing in food, or are they just getting their due? Definitely the latter. Pickles are the real dill.

MAHI MAHI BURGERS WITH MISO MAYO

SERVES: **4** | PREP TIME: **20 MINUTES** | CHILLING TIME: **6–8 HOURS**
GRILLING TIME: **6–8 MINUTES** | SPECIAL EQUIPMENT: **GRILL-PROOF GRIDDLE**

SEAFOOD

600 g/1¼ lb skinless mahi mahi fillets, pin bones removed, patted dry and cut into 2.5-cm/1-inch pieces
1 large egg, beaten
3 tablespoons white miso paste
¼ teaspoon toasted sesame oil
5 tablespoons panko breadcrumbs, toasted in a dry pan
1 tablespoon sesame seeds, toasted in a dry pan
¼ teaspoon sea salt
8 tablespoons mayonnaise
1 tablespoon vegetable oil
4 sesame seed buns, split
1 medium, ripe beefsteak tomato, cut crossways into 4 slices
½ cucumber, thinly sliced

Most seafood patties are so delicate that it is best to cook them on a grill-proof griddle.

1. In a food processor fitted with a metal blade, pulse the mahi mahi pieces 8–10 times until coarsely chopped but not paste-like. Add the egg, 1 tablespoon of the miso paste and the sesame oil. Pulse a few times until just blended, and leave some texture. Transfer to a bowl and gently stir in the panko, sesame seeds and salt. Form four patties of equal size, each about 1.5 cm/¾ inch thick. Cover and refrigerate for 6–8 hours.

2. Prepare the grill for direct cooking over medium heat (180–230°C/350–450°F) and preheat a grill-proof griddle.

3. Whisk the mayonnaise and the remaining 2 tablespoons miso paste. Cover and refrigerate until ready to use.

4. Drizzle the vegetable oil on the griddle. Place the patties on the griddle and cook over *direct medium heat* for 6–8 minutes, with the lid closed, until fully cooked but still moist, turning once. During the last 30–60 seconds of grilling time, toast the buns on the cooking grates, cut side down, over direct heat.

5. Build each burger on a bun with miso mayo, a patty, a tomato slice and cucumber slices. Serve immediately.

RED BEAN AND MUSHROOM BURGERS WITH CHILLI MAYO

SERVES: **4** | PREP TIME: **20 MINUTES** | CHILLING TIME: **30 MINUTES**
GRILLING TIME: **6–8 MINUTES** | SPECIAL EQUIPMENT: **GRILL-PROOF GRIDDLE**

PATTIES

2 tablespoons extra-virgin olive oil
120 g/4 oz button or chestnut mushrooms, cleaned,
   stalks removed and finely chopped
2 tablespoons finely diced jalapeño chilli
   (without seeds)
2 garlic cloves, crushed
1 can (400 g/13 oz) pinto beans, rinsed and drained
8 tablespoons panko breadcrumbs
1 large egg, beaten
¾ teaspoon sea salt
½ teaspoon ground cumin

5 tablespoons mayonnaise
1½ teaspoons finely diced canned chipotle chillis
   in adobo sauce
Extra-virgin olive oil
4 burger buns, split
4 large leaves crisp lettuce
8 slices ripe tomato

1. In a sauté pan over a medium-high heat, warm the oil. Add the mushrooms and cook for about 3 minutes, until tender, stirring occasionally. Add the jalapeño and garlic and cook for 2–3 minutes, until lightly browned. Transfer to a food processor fitted with a metal blade, add the remaining patty ingredients, and pulse several times until coarsely chopped. Form four patties of equal size, each about 1 cm/½ inch thick. Refrigerate the patties for 30 minutes.

2. Prepare the grill for direct cooking over medium heat (180–230°C/350–450°F) and preheat a grill-proof griddle.

3. Combine the mayonnaise and chipotle chillis.

4. Generously brush the patties on both sides with oil. Place the patties on the griddle and cook over *direct medium heat* for 6-8 minutes, with the lid closed, until browned, turning once. During the last 30–60 seconds of grilling time, toast the buns on the cooking grates, cut side down, over direct heat.

5. Build each burger on a bun with chilli mayo, a lettuce leaf, two tomato slices and a patty. Serve immediately.

BLACK BEAN CHEESEBURGERS WITH AVOCADO

SERVES: **4** | PREP TIME: **20 MINUTES** | CHILLING TIME: **1–4 HOURS**
GRILLING TIME: **6–8 MINUTES** | SPECIAL EQUIPMENT: **PERFORATED GRILL PAN**

VEGETARIAN

1 can (400 g/13 oz) black beans,
    rinsed and drained
4 tablespoons fresh coriander or
    parsley leaves
1 shallot, thinly sliced
2 garlic cloves, thinly sliced
¾ teaspoon hot chilli powder
½ teaspoon dried oregano
Extra-virgin olive oil
Sea salt
Freshly ground black pepper
1 large egg
1 large egg white
100 g/3½ oz panko breadcrumbs
4 thin slices pepper jack cheese
4 wholemeal buns, split
4 tablespoons mayonnaise
4 leaves romaine lettuce
2 small, ripe avocados,
    cut into thin slices

Bean burgers lend themselves
to lots of variations. Use
chickpeas or kidney beans
instead. Choose different herbs.
Substitute a cooked grain like
quinoa or brown rice for an
equal amount of the beans. But
always pay special attention to
the texture: it should be moist
(yet not wet) when you shape
the patties.

1. In a food processor fitted with a metal blade, combine the beans, coriander, shallot, garlic, chilli powder, oregano, 1 tablespoon oil, ½ teaspoon salt and ¼ teaspoon pepper and pulse 15–20 times to form a thick, slightly chunky paste. Transfer to a large bowl. In a small bowl whisk the egg and egg white until blended. Add the eggs and panko to the large bowl and combine thoroughly. The mixture should be quite thick. Form four compact patties of equal size, each about 1.5 cm/¾ inch thick. Cover and refrigerate the patties for 1–4 hours.

2. Prepare the grill for direct cooking over medium-high heat (200–260°C/400–500°F) and preheat a perforated grill pan.

3. Brush the patties on both sides with oil and season evenly with salt and pepper. Place the patties on the grill pan and cook over *direct medium-high heat* for 6–8 minutes, with the lid closed, until browned and warm throughout, carefully turning once. During the last 30–60 seconds of grilling time, place a slice of cheese on each patty to melt, and toast the buns on the cooking grates, cut side down, over direct heat.

4. Build each burger on a bun with mayonnaise, a lettuce leaf, a patty and avocado slices. Serve warm.

CURRIED RED LENTIL BURGERS WITH MANGO CHUTNEY

SERVES: **4** | PREP TIME: **25 MINUTES** | CHILLING TIME: **2–4 HOURS**
GRILLING TIME: **5–7 MINUTES** | SPECIAL EQUIPMENT: **GRILL-PROOF GRIDDLE**

VEGETARIAN

100 g/3½ oz red lentils, picked over, rinsed in a fine-mesh sieve and drained
480 ml/16 fl oz water
1 can (400 g/13 oz) chickpeas, rinsed and drained
175 g/6 oz roasted, salted peanuts
2 teaspoons curry powder
2 teaspoons ground cumin
½ teaspoon sea salt
¼ teaspoon freshly ground black pepper
8 tablespoons panko breadcrumbs
8 tablespoons natural Greek yogurt
2 large eggs, beaten
2 tablespoons chopped fresh coriander
1 tablespoon vegetable oil
4 large pitta breads
1 baby lettuce, shredded
½ cucumber, thinly sliced
8 tablespoons mango chutney

1. In a saucepan combine the lentils and water. Bring to the boil. Skim off any foam that rises to the top. Reduce the heat to medium-low and simmer for 10–20 minutes, until tender. Drain well, rinse briefly, and allow to cool.

2. In a food processor fitted with a metal blade, pulse the lentils, chickpeas, peanuts, curry powder, cumin, salt and pepper to form a thick, slightly chunky paste. Transfer to a bowl and fold in the panko, yogurt, eggs and coriander until combined. Form four gently packed patties, each about 1.5 cm/¾ inch thick. The patties will be quite wet. Cover and refrigerate the patties for 2–4 hours.

3. Prepare the grill for direct cooking over medium-high heat (200–260°C/400–500°F) and preheat a grill-proof griddle.

4. Coat the griddle lightly with the oil. Place the patties on the griddle and cook over *direct medium-high heat* for 5–7 minutes, with the lid closed, until firm and nicely marked, carefully turning once. During the last minute of grilling time, warm the pittas on the cooking grates over direct heat, turning once.

5. Cut the pittas and patties in half. Place a patty half inside each pitta half. Divide the lettuce, cucumber and mango chutney among the pittas, tucking the ingredients inside. Serve immediately.

CHICKPEA PATTIES WITH LEMON PICKLED ONION

SERVES: **6** | PREP TIME: **45 MINUTES** | CHILLING TIME: **3-4 HOURS**
GRILLING TIME: **6-8 MINUTES** | SPECIAL EQUIPMENT: **GRILL-PROOF GRIDDLE**

VEGETARIAN

2 cans (each 400 g/13 oz) chickpeas, rinsed and
   drained
2 garlic cloves, chopped
1 large egg, lightly beaten
4 tablespoons tahini
120 ml/4 fl oz fresh lemon juice
1 teaspoon ground cumin
1 teaspoon ground coriander
½ teaspoon freshly ground black pepper
¼ teaspoon ground cayenne pepper
Sea salt
120 ml/4 fl oz full-fat natural Greek yogurt
8 tablespoons panko breadcrumbs
4 tablespoons finely chopped fresh coriander
2 tablespoons finely diced red jalapeño chilli
   (without seeds)
1 medium red onion, cut in half and thinly sliced
½ teaspoon granulated sugar

SAUCE
180 ml/6 fl oz full-fat natural Greek yogurt
2 tablespoons fresh lemon juice
1 tablespoon tahini
2 teaspoons harissa or hot pepper sauce
⅛ teaspoon granulated sugar

Extra-virgin olive oil
1 tablespoon finely chopped fresh
   parsley leaves
1 tablespoon finely chopped fresh mint
Chopped ripe tomato
Harissa or hot pepper sauce

1. Place half of the chickpeas in a food processor
fitted with a metal blade. Add the garlic, egg, tahini,
4 tablespoons of the lemon juice, the cumin, ground
coriander, black pepper, cayenne pepper and
1 teaspoon salt. Process to blend. Add the remaining
chickpeas, the yogurt, panko, fresh coriander and
jalapeño. Pulse for 10–15 one-second bursts to

coarsely blend. Gently form six patties, each about
1.5 cm/¾ inch thick. Place on a roasting tray lined with
greaseproof paper. Cover and refrigerate the patties
for 3-4 hours. Meanwhile, prepare the pickled onion.

2. Place the onion in a heatproof bowl. Pour in boiling
water to cover the onion and allow to stand for
5 minutes. Rinse under cold water and drain. Blot dry.
In a medium bowl whisk the remaining lemon juice,
sugar and ¼ teaspoon salt until the sugar and salt are
dissolved. Add the onion and toss to combine. Set aside
at room temperature for 1 hour, stirring once or twice.

3. Prepare the grill for direct cooking over medium
heat (180–230°C/350–450°F) and preheat a
grill-proof griddle.

4. Whisk the sauce ingredients together, including
½ teaspoon salt.

5. Brush the tops of the patties with oil. Place the
patties on the griddle, oiled side down, and remove
the greaseproof paper. Cook over *direct medium heat*
for 3-4 minutes, with the lid closed. Oil the tops of the
patties, turn them over, and continue cooking until
browned and heated through, 3-4 minutes more.

6. Add the parsley and mint to the pickled onion.
Top the patties with sauce, pickled onion, tomato
and harissa. Serve warm.

To lift fragile patties, cut
the greaseproof paper
underneath them, and
use the paper to support
the patties as you take
them to the grill.

QUINOA AND PINTO BEAN BURGERS WITH YOGURT SAUCE

SERVES: **6** | PREP TIME: **50 MINUTES** | CHILLING TIME: **1–3 HOURS**
GRILLING TIME: **8–10 MINUTES** | SPECIAL EQUIPMENT: **GRILL-PROOF GRIDDLE**

SAUCE

8 tablespoons natural Greek yogurt
3 tablespoons finely chopped fresh coriander
1 garlic clove, crushed

Sea salt
Freshly ground black pepper

PATTIES

90 g/3 oz yellow or red quinoa, rinsed in a
   fine-mesh sieve, drained
240 ml/8 fl oz water
Extra-virgin olive oil
½ red onion, finely chopped
½ red pepper, finely chopped
2 garlic cloves, crushed
1 can (400 g/13 oz) pinto beans, rinsed and drained
1 small (198 g/7 oz) can sweetcorn, drained
225 g/8 oz panko breadcrumbs
1 large egg, lightly beaten
3 tablespoons natural Greek yogurt
3 tablespoons coarsely chopped fresh coriander
1 teaspoon finely grated lime rind
1 tablespoon fresh lime juice
½ teaspoon hot chilli-garlic sauce

6 burger buns, split
Large handful rocket leaves
2 medium, ripe plum tomatoes, each cut crossways
   into 6 slices

1. Mix the sauce ingredients and season with salt and pepper. Refrigerate until ready to use.

2. In a saucepan over a medium-high heat, bring the quinoa, water and 1 teaspoon salt to the boil. Cover the saucepan and reduce the heat to low. Simmer for 18–20 minutes until the quinoa is tender and the water is almost absorbed. Remove from the heat, keep covered, and let stand for 5 minutes. Drain the quinoa in a fine-mesh sieve to remove any excess water. Let cool completely.

3. In a sauté pan over a medium heat, warm 1 tablespoon oil. Add the onion, pepper and garlic. Cook for about 8 minutes, until tender, stirring occasionally. Remove from the heat and cool completely.

4. In a food processor fitted with a metal blade, combine the quinoa, the onion mixture and the remaining patty ingredients, including 1 teaspoon salt. Pulse until well combined and the sweetcorn is coarsely chopped.

5. Generously oil a rimmed roasting tray. Transfer one-sixth of the quinoa mixture to the roasting tray and form into a 7-cm/3-inch patty, 1–1.5 cm/½–¾ inch thick. Repeat with the remaining quinoa mixture. Cover and refrigerate the patties for 1–3 hours.

6. Prepare the grill for direct cooking over medium heat (180–230°C/350–450°F) and preheat a grill-proof griddle.

7. Brush the tops of the patties with oil and drizzle 1 tablespoon oil on the griddle. Place the patties on the griddle, oiled side down, and cook over *direct medium heat* for 4–5 minutes, with the lid closed, until the undersides are golden brown. Brush the tops of the patties with oil, turn them over, and continue cooking until the other side is golden brown, 4–5 minutes more. During the last 30–60 seconds of grilling time, toast the buns on the cooking grates, cut side down, over direct heat.

8. Build each burger on a bun with rocket, two tomato slices, a patty and a dollop of yogurt sauce. Serve immediately.

FARRO AND CANNELLINI BURGERS WITH GRILLED RADICCHIO SLAW

SERVES: **4** | PREP TIME: **35 MINUTES, PLUS 20–25 MINUTES FOR THE FARRO** | CHILLING TIME: **1–3 HOURS**
GRILLING TIME: **12–16 MINUTES** | SPECIAL EQUIPMENT: **GRILL-PROOF GRIDDLE**

PATTIES

300 ml/½ pint water
120 g/4 oz semi-pearled or pearled farro
1½ teaspoons sea salt
2 spring onions (white and light green parts only)
2 garlic cloves, roughly chopped
½ teaspoon crushed chilli flakes
1 can (400 g/13 oz) cannellini beans, rinsed
   and drained
2 large eggs
8 tablespoons fresh breadcrumbs
8 tablespoons freshly grated Parmesan cheese
2 tablespoons chopped fresh basil
1 tablespoon red wine vinegar

Extra-virgin olive oil

SLAW

1 small head radicchio, 200 g/7 oz,
   cut lengthways in half
1 head romaine lettuce, thinly sliced
4 tablespoons torn fresh basil
1 teaspoon balsamic vinegar
½ teaspoon sea salt
¼ teaspoon freshly ground black pepper

8 slices crusty Italian bread, each about
   5 mm/¼ inch thick
5 tablespoons mayonnaise

1. In a saucepan over a medium heat, bring the water, farro and ½ teaspoon of the salt to the boil. Cover and reduce the heat to medium-low. Simmer for 20–25 minutes, until the farro is tender and almost all of the water is absorbed. Drain, rinse under cold water and drain again. Cool completely.

2. In a food processor fitted with a metal blade, first add the spring onions, garlic and chilli flakes, then add the farro, the remaining 1 teaspoon salt, the beans, eggs, breadcrumbs, cheese, basil and vinegar. Pulse until the mixture is combined and the farro is coarsely chopped.

3. Generously oil a roasting tray. Transfer one-quarter of the farro mixture to the roasting tray and, with oiled hands, form into a 7-cm/3-inch oval patty (to fit the bread slices). Repeat with the remaining farro mixture. Cover and refrigerate the patties for 1–3 hours.

4. Prepare the grill for direct cooking over medium heat (180–230°C/350–450°F) and preheat a grill-proof griddle.

5. Brush the radicchio halves with oil, place them on the cooking grates, and grill over *direct medium heat* for 4–6 minutes, with the lid closed, until lightly browned on the outside but still raw inside, turning once. Remove from the grill and allow to cool. Cut out the core, and cut the radicchio crossways into 5-mm/¼-inch strips. In a bowl toss the radicchio, lettuce and basil with 1 tablespoon oil and the vinegar. Season with the salt and pepper.

6. Brush the patties on both sides with oil and drizzle 1 tablespoon oil on the griddle. Place the patties on the griddle and cook over *direct medium heat* for 8–10 minutes, with the lid closed, until golden brown, carefully turning once. During the last 30 seconds of grilling time, toast the bread slices on the cooking grates over direct heat, one side only.

7. Brush the ungrilled side of four slices of the bread with mayonnaise, and top with the patties, radicchio slaw and the remaining bread slices. Serve immediately.

Serving suggestion: Tomato and Avocado Salad with Lemon-Caper Vinaigrette (for recipe, see page 208).

Shaping these patties directly on an oiled roasting tray is the simplest way to handle the sticky farro-and-bean mixture.

GREEK AUBERGINE SLIDERS WITH CREAMY FETA SAUCE

SERVES: **6–8 (MAKES 12 SLIDERS)** | PREP TIME: **30 MINUTES** | CHILLING TIME: **30 MINUTES**
GRILLING TIME: **13–15 MINUTES** | SPECIAL EQUIPMENT: **GRILL-PROOF GRIDDLE**

VEGETARIAN

SAUCE

120 g/4 oz feta cheese, crumbled
4 tablespoons natural Greek yogurt
1 tablespoon mayonnaise
1 tablespoon fresh lemon juice
½ teaspoon paprika

Freshly ground black pepper

PATTIES

1.25 kg/2½ lb aubergines, ends trimmed, cut
   crossways into 1-cm/½-inch slices
Extra-virgin olive oil
Sea salt
200 g/7 oz panko breadcrumbs
120 g/4 oz Asiago or Parmesan cheese, finely grated
1 large egg, lightly beaten
½ onion, finely chopped
4 tablespoons finely chopped fresh parsley leaves
½ teaspoon dried oregano
2 garlic cloves, crushed
¼ teaspoon ground cayenne pepper

12 slider buns, split
24 large fresh basil leaves
12 thin slices red onion

1. In a food processor fitted with a metal blade, combine the sauce ingredients, including ½ teaspoon pepper, and process until smooth. Transfer to a small bowl.

2. Prepare the grill for direct cooking over medium heat (180–230°C/350–450°F).

3. Brush the aubergine slices on both sides with oil and season evenly with ¾ teaspoon salt. Grill over *direct medium heat* for 8–10 minutes, with the lid closed, until charred and soft, turning once or twice. Remove from the grill and cool slightly, and then cut each slice into quarters. Place the aubergine in the food processor and pulse 8–10 times until blended but not completely smooth. Transfer to a large bowl. Add the remaining patty ingredients, including 1 teaspoon salt and ½ teaspoon pepper, and stir to combine. Gently form 12 patties of equal size, each about 1 cm/½ inch thick. Cover and refrigerate the patties for 30 minutes.

4. Preheat a grill-proof griddle over *direct medium heat*. Add 2 tablespoons oil to the griddle. Place the patties on the griddle and cook over *direct medium heat* for about 5 minutes, with the lid closed, until browned on both sides and heated through, turning once. During the last 30–60 seconds of grilling time, toast the buns on the cooking grates, cut side down, over direct heat.

5. Build each slider on a bun with creamy feta sauce, a patty, two basil leaves and an onion slice. Serve warm.

Aubergine sliders are at their best when their texture is a little chunky, not completely smooth. Grill the slices first and then pulse them just until coarsely chopped.

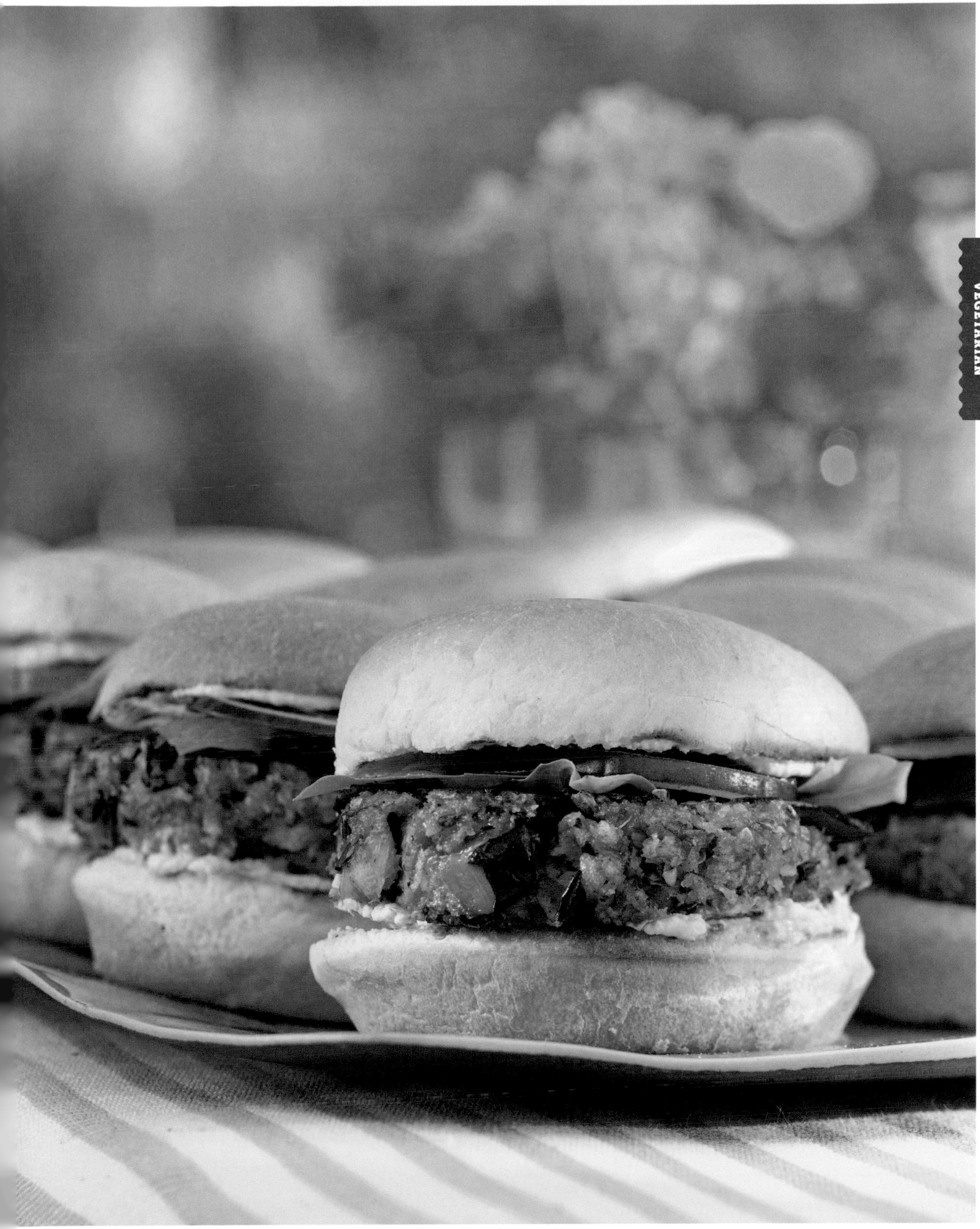

CAPRESE BURGERS

SERVES: **4** | PREP TIME: **20 MINUTES** | GRILLING TIME: **11–15 MINUTES**

PESTO

1 garlic clove
3 tablespoons toasted pine nuts
Large bunch basil
5 tablespoons extra-virgin
   olive oil
5 tablespoons freshly grated
   Parmesan cheese
¼ teaspoon sea salt
⅛ teaspoon freshly ground
   black pepper

1 large red onion, cut crossways
   into four 1-cm/½-inch slices
1 ripe beefsteak tomato, cut
   crossways into four 1-cm/
   ½-inch slices
2 tablespoons extra-virgin
   olive oil
½ teaspoon sea salt
¼ teaspoon freshly ground
   black pepper
4 focaccia squares, each about
   11 cm/4½ inches, split
2 tablespoons balsamic vinegar
225 g/8 oz fresh mozzarella
   cheese, cut into 8 slices,
   at room temperature

To toast pine nuts, heat them
in a preheated frying pan over
medium heat until light golden,
about 3 minutes, shaking the
frying pan occasionally and
watching to prevent burning.

1. Prepare the grill for direct and indirect cooking over medium heat (180–230°C/350–450°F).

2. In a food processor fitted with a metal blade, purée the garlic. Add the pine nuts and pulse until finely chopped. Add the basil and process to a coarse purée. With the motor running, add the oil through the feed tube and process until almost smooth. Add the cheese, salt and pepper and process until just combined. Transfer to a bowl.

3. Brush the onion and tomato slices with the oil and season evenly with the salt and pepper. Grill the vegetables over *direct medium heat*, with the lid closed, until tender and nicely marked, turning once. The onion will take 8–12 minutes, and the tomato will

take 2–4 minutes. During the last 30–60 seconds of grilling time, toast the focaccia, cut side down, over direct heat.

4. Brush the toasted side of the focaccia with the vinegar. Top each bottom half with one onion slice, one tomato slice and two mozzarella slices. Spread the top halves of the focaccia with the pesto (you may not need all of it) and place, pesto side down, on top of the mozzarella. Grill the burgers over *indirect medium heat* for 3–5 minutes, with the lid closed, until the cheese melts slightly and the bread is hot (do not turn). Serve immediately.

PORTOBELLO BURGERS WITH CHEDDAR AND GRILLED RED PEPPERS

SERVES: **4** | PREP TIME: **25 MINUTES** | MARINATING TIME: **20 MINUTES** | GRILLING TIME: **8–12 MINUTES**

MARINADE

6 tablespoons extra-virgin
    olive oil
2 tablespoons balsamic vinegar
1 shallot, finely chopped
1 tablespoon soy sauce
½ tablespoon honey
1 teaspoon Dijon mustard
1 garlic clove, crushed

4 large Portobello mushrooms,
    each 10–12 cm/4–5 inches
    in diameter, stalks and gills
    removed, wiped clean
1 red onion, cut crossways into
    1-cm/½-inch slices
2 medium red peppers,
    each cut into 4 planks
¾ teaspoon sea salt
¼ teaspoon freshly ground
    black pepper
4 slices mild Cheddar cheese
4 burger buns, split
20 small fresh basil leaves

1. Whisk the marinade ingredients. Reserve 5 tablespoons of the marinade in a separate bowl for basting the mushrooms and brushing the buns.

2. Prepare the grill for direct cooking over medium heat (180–230°C/350–450°F).

3. Generously brush the mushrooms and onion slices with the remaining marinade. Allow to stand at room temperature for 20 minutes.

4. Season the vegetables evenly with the salt and pepper. Grill the mushrooms, gill side down first, over *direct medium heat* for 8–12 minutes, with the lid closed, until tender when pierced with the tip of a knife, basting with half of the reserved marinade and turning occasionally. At the same time, grill the peppers and onion over *direct medium heat* for 8–12 minutes, until tender, turning occasionally. During the last 30–60 seconds of grilling time, place one slice of cheese on the gill side of each mushroom to melt, and toast the buns, cut side down, over direct heat.

5. Brush the cut side of the buns with the remaining reserved marinade. Build each burger on a bun with two pepper planks, one mushroom, onion slices and five basil leaves. Serve immediately.

149

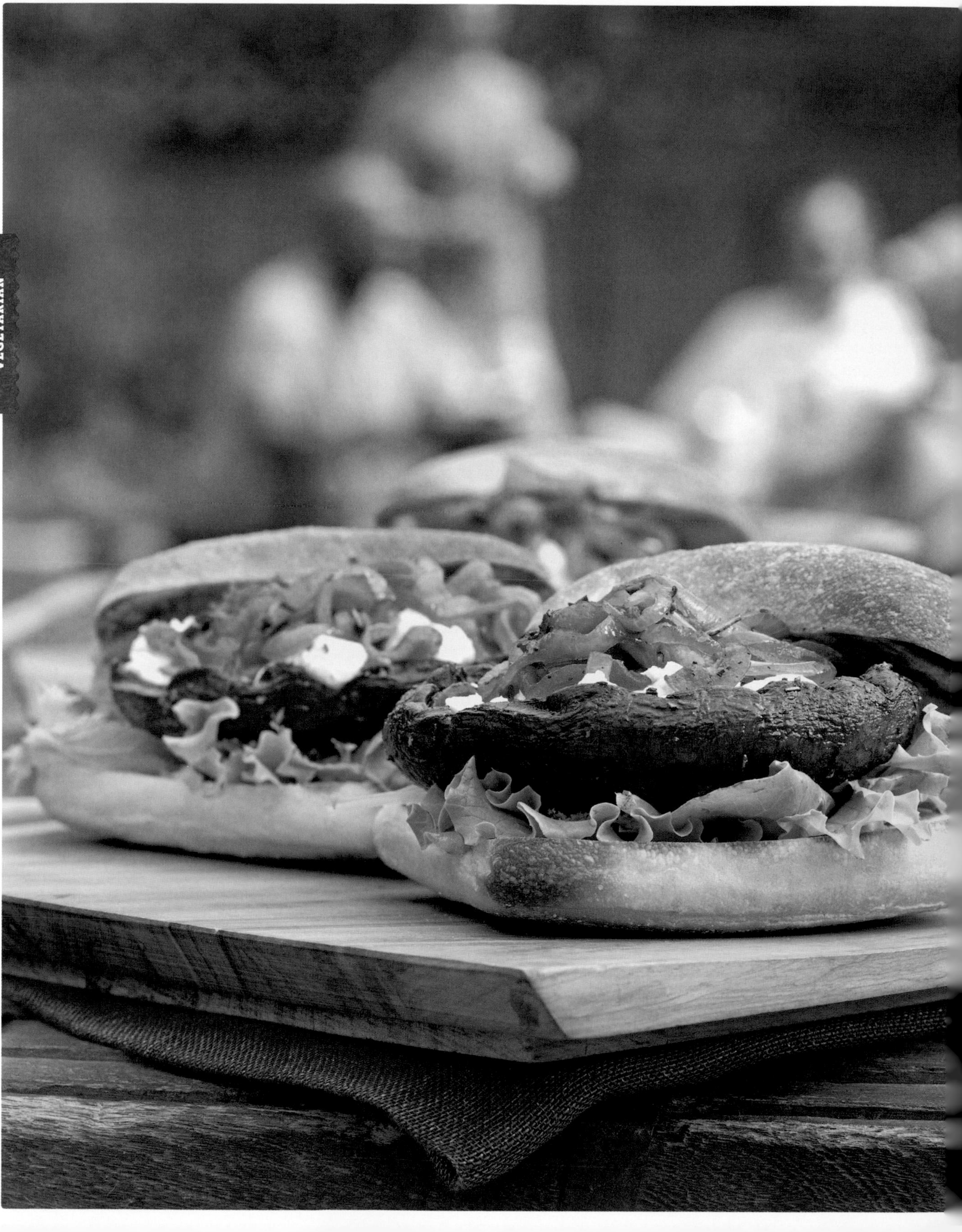

WINE COUNTRY MUSHROOM BURGERS WITH GOATS' CHEESE

SERVES: **4** | PREP TIME: **20 MINUTES** | MARINATING TIME: **30 MINUTES–1 HOUR** | GRILLING TIME: **10–12 MINUTES**

VEGETARIAN

MARINADE
4 tablespoons full-bodied red wine
1 tablespoon chopped fresh rosemary leaves
2 garlic cloves, crushed
1 teaspoon sea salt
½ teaspoon freshly ground black pepper
5 tablespoons extra-virgin olive oil

4 large Portobello mushrooms, each 10–12 cm/
   4–5 inches in diameter, stalks and gills
   removed, wiped clean

ONIONS
1 tablespoon extra-virgin olive oil
2 large onions, thinly sliced
1 tablespoon finely chopped fresh rosemary leaves
½ teaspoon sea salt
¼ teaspoon granulated sugar
2 tablespoons full-bodied red wine
¼ teaspoon freshly ground black pepper

120 g/4 oz goats' cheese, crumbled
4 ciabatta rolls, halved
2 large handfuls mixed salad leaves

1. Whisk the wine, rosemary, garlic, salt and pepper. Add the oil in a steady stream, whisking constantly to emulsify. Arrange the mushrooms in a single layer on a rimmed roasting tray. Liberally brush the mushrooms on all sides with the marinade, and marinate at room temperature for 30 minutes to 1 hour. Meanwhile, prepare the onions.

2. In a sauté pan over a medium heat, warm the oil. Add the onions, rosemary, salt and sugar. Cook for about 20 minutes, until the onions turn golden brown, stirring occasionally. Add the wine and cook for about 2 minutes, until the liquid evaporates, stirring once or twice. Remove from the heat and season with the pepper.

3. Prepare the grill for direct cooking over medium heat (180–230°C/350–450°F).

4. Grill the mushrooms, gill side down first, over *direct medium heat* for 10–12 minutes, with the lid closed, until juicy and tender, turning once or twice and basting with any juices from the roasting tray. During the last 2 minutes of grilling time, turn the mushrooms to remove any collected juice in their caps, arrange them gill side up, and sprinkle the cavities with an equal amount of the cheese. During the last 30–60 seconds of grilling time, toast the rolls, cut side down, over direct heat.

5. Build each burger on a roll with salad leaves, a mushroom and onions. Serve immediately.

Mushrooms dry out quickly, so brush them with the leftover marinade once or twice in order to keep them moist.

HOT DOGS,
SAUSAGES
& BRATS

HOT DOG GEOGRAPHY

If you want to know where someone is from, listen to how they talk. If you *really* want to know where they're from, listen to them talk about their hot dogs. About as big a source of regional pride (and competitiveness) as their sports allegiances, Americans' take on hot dogs is as inventive and diverse as they are. Whether in a cart, drenched in chilli or doused in cheese, they are passionately linked to their links. Take a taste of some regional traditions.

SEATTLE DOG

Seattle, Washington

For those who like a schmear: hear, hear. Inside a toasted bun lined with cream cheese lies a hot dog or Polish sausage that is grilled, split and topped with grilled onions and cabbage, jalapeños and any variety of other toppings and sauces.

SONORAN DOG

Arizona

This meaty number comprises a bacon-wrapped hot dog tucked into a soft Mexican *bolillo* roll and topped with chopped tomatoes and onions, pinto beans, jalapeño salsa, mustard and mayonnaise. *Ay, caramba!* (For recipe, see page 160.)

REUBEN DOG

Kansas City, Missouri

This is the frank of choice at Kauffman Stadium, where the Royals play. Here, hot dogs are done the deli way: with melted Swiss cheese, sauerkraut, caraway seeds and Thousand Island dressing. Is there such a thing as a rye bun? There ought to be.

CHICAGO-STYLE HOT DOG

Chicago, Illinois

Purists demand an all-beef frank on a poppy seed bun, and toppings *must* include the following: diced onions, sliced tomatoes, super green sweet pickle relish, spicy pickled green chillies, a dill pickle spear, yellow mustard and a dusting of celery salt – no substitutions, and *never* tomato ketchup. (For recipe, see page 159.)

DETROIT CONEY DOG

Detroit, Michigan

This petite hot dog in a steamed bun is topped with no-bean chilli, mustard, onions and – if you ask for it 'loaded' – grated Cheddar. Did we mention the chilli ought to be made with beef heart? Don't say we didn't warn you.

SLAW DOG

West Virginia

Here we've got a three-course meal on a steamed bun, and a common sight on menus all over the South. A frank is blanketed in spicy chilli and capped with mayo-based coleslaw, creating that hot-spicy-cool-crunchy-creamy sensation that can really only be found when chilli and slaw meet on a hot dog.

NEW YORK DOG

New York, New York

Visualise a quick lunch for a harried New Yorker: an all-beef frank is plucked from a warm water bath in a street cart, dressed with a couple of squirts of brown mustard, sauerkraut or onions stewed in tomato purée, and eaten tie-over-shoulder while heading to a power meeting. Or so we imagine. (For recipe, see page 166.)

ITALIAN DOG

Newark, New Jersey

How to make a hot dog more indulgent in three easy steps: (1) deep-fry your frank; (2) stuff it into a half-moon of pizza bread or an Italian roll; and (3) top with fried or grilled onions, peppers and fried potatoes. All that is left to do is *mangia*, New Jersey-style.

NEW YORK SYSTEM HOT WIENER

Providence, Rhode Island

And you may ask yourself, why 'New York' if this is Rhode Island? Supposedly, the creators were New Yorkers before heading to the Ocean State. Small, griddled 'wieners' in natural casings are topped with minced beef sauce, mustard, diced onions and a dash of celery salt. Skilled purveyors can line up a dozen on the inside of a forearm for easy serving.

CALIFORNIA HOT DOGS WITH AVOCADO, ROCKET AND BASIL CREMA

SERVES: **4** | PREP TIME: **20 MINUTES** | GRILLING TIME: **4-5 MINUTES**

CREMA
120 ml/4 fl oz sour cream
4 tablespoons roughly chopped fresh basil leaves
1 spring onion, trimmed and roughly chopped
½ teaspoon fresh lemon juice
¼ teaspoon sea salt
1 small garlic clove, chopped
⅛ teaspoon hot pepper sauce, or to taste

4 best-quality all-beef hot dogs
4 hot dog buns, split
1 large, ripe avocado, cut into thin slices
Small handful rocket, roughly chopped
1 carrot, grated
¼ cucumber, diced
4 tablespoons canned sweetcorn, drained

1. Prepare the grill for direct cooking over medium heat (180-230°C/350-450°F).

2. In a food processor fitted with a metal blade, combine the crema ingredients and process until smooth.

3. Cut a few shallow slashes in each hot dog. Grill the hot dogs over *direct medium heat* for 4-5 minutes, with the lid closed, until hot all the way to the centre, turning occasionally. During the last 30-60 seconds of grilling time, toast the buns, cut side down, over direct heat.

4. Place each hot dog in a bun and top with avocado, rocket, carrot, cucumber, sweetcorn and basil crema. Serve immediately.

HOT DOGS

FUN FACT

Did you know that avocados don't ripen on the tree? They must be picked to initiate ripening, which is why many times the supermarket shelves are piled high with this rock-hard fruit. To speed up the ripening process, place your avocado in a paper bag with an apple or a banana; these fruits emit ethylene gas, which will soften the avocado in just a few days.

CHILLI DOGS WITH CRUMBLED CORN CHIPS

SERVES: **6-8** | PREP TIME: **15 MINUTES, PLUS ABOUT 1 HOUR FOR THE CHILLI** | GRILLING TIME: **4-5 MINUTES**

CHILLI
1 tablespoon extra-virgin olive oil
225 g/8 oz steak mince (80% lean)
1 small onion, finely chopped
1 can (400 g/13 oz) chopped tomatoes in juice
240 ml/8 fl oz tomato juice
1½ teaspoons ground cumin
1 teaspoon ancho chilli powder
1 teaspoon dried oregano
½ teaspoon hot pepper sauce, or to taste
¼ teaspoon sea salt
¼ teaspoon freshly ground black pepper
1 can (400 g/13 oz) red kidney beans, drained

6-8 best-quality all-beef hot dogs
6-8 hot dog buns, split
175 g/6 oz Cheddar cheese, grated
Handful corn chips, crumbled

1. In a medium sauté pan over a medium-high heat, warm the oil. Add the mince and onion and sauté for 4-6 minutes, stirring occasionally and breaking up the meat with a spoon. Stir in the chopped tomatoes, tomato juice, cumin, chilli powder, oregano, hot pepper sauce, salt and pepper and bring to a strong simmer. Simmer over a medium heat, partially covered, for about 20 minutes, until very thick, stirring occasionally to keep the mixture from scorching. Stir in the beans and cook for 10 minutes more. Remove from the heat and set aside for up to 30 minutes; rewarm before serving.

2. Prepare the grill for direct cooking over medium heat (180–230°C/350–450°F).

3. Cut a few shallow slashes in each hot dog, and then grill over *direct medium heat* for 4-5 minutes, with the lid closed, until hot all the way to the centre, turning occasionally. During the last 30–60 seconds of grilling time, toast the buns, cut side down, over direct heat.

4. Place each hot dog in a bun and top with warm chilli, cheese and corn chips.

CHICAGO-STYLE HOT DOGS

SERVES: **8** | PREP TIME: **10 MINUTES** | GRILLING TIME: **4–5 MINUTES**

8 slices ripe tomato, each about 5 mm/¼ inch thick
8 best-quality all-beef hot dogs with natural casings (slightly longer than the buns)
8 poppy seed hot dog buns, split
16 pickled jalapeño chillies
2 dill pickles, each cut into 4 spears
1 white onion, finely chopped and rinsed in a fine mesh sieve under cold water
8 tablespoons super green sweet pickle relish
Yellow mustard
Celery salt

1. Prepare the grill for direct cooking over medium heat (180–230°C/350–450°F).

2. Cut each tomato slice in half to make half-moons.

3. Cut a few shallow slashes in each hot dog, and then grill over *direct medium heat* for 4–5 minutes, with the lid closed, until hot all the way to the centre, turning occasionally.

4. Place each hot dog in a bun and add two tomato half-moons, two chillies, one pickle spear, onion and relish. Add mustard to taste and finish with a dash of celery salt. Serve warm.

WHERE DID THE WORD 'FRANKFURTER' COME FROM?

Who's the father of this … frankfurter? While Germany may seem like the obvious answer, as 'frankfurter' means 'of Frankfurt', there are always two sides to every story – even behind the birth of our beloved frank. The Germans claim to have first created the Frankfurter Würstchen (its official name), even enacting a law to reserve the term 'frankfurter' for sausages actually made in or around the city of Frankfurt. The second story credits the Austrians: Johann Georg Lahner, a Frankfurt-area butcher, allegedly moved to Vienna, Austria and sold sausages, which he called the 'frankfurter'. Hmm … so, Germany or a German emigrant? Either way you spin it, it seems that, sorry, Austria: you are not the father.

SONORAN HOT DOGS

SERVES: **4** | PREP TIME: **15 MINUTES** | GRILLING TIME: **ABOUT 8 MINUTES**

HOT DOGS

4 best-quality all-beef hot dogs
4 rashers bacon (not thick-cut)
4 torpedo rolls, split
   (don't cut all the way through)
4 tablespoons mayonnaise
175 g/6 oz Monterey Jack or
   Cheddar cheese, grated
225 g/8 oz canned pinto beans,
   rinsed and drained
1 large, ripe tomato, cored,
   seeded and roughly chopped
Crisp lettuce, roughly chopped
1 small, ripe avocado, diced
5 tablespoons sliced pickled
   jalapeño chillies (from a jar),
   well drained

1. Prepare the grill for direct cooking over low heat (130–180°C/250–350°F).

2. Wrap each hot dog with a slice of bacon, winding it around in a spiral. Open the rolls and spread the cut side evenly with the mayonnaise.

3. Grill the hot dogs over *direct low heat* for about 8 minutes, with the lid closed, until the bacon is nicely browned and crispy on the outside and the hot dogs are hot all the way to the centre, turning three times. During the last 30–60 seconds of grilling time, toast the buns, mayo side down, over direct heat.

4. Place each hot dog in a bun and top with cheese, beans, tomato, lettuce, avocado and pickled jalapeños. Serve immediately.

SPICY BUFFALO HOT DOGS WITH CELERY RELISH AND BLUE CHEESE

SERVES: **4** | PREP TIME: **20 MINUTES** | GRILLING TIME: **4–5 MINUTES**

RELISH

2 shallots, finely chopped
1 tablespoon white wine vinegar
4 sticks celery, ends trimmed and
  cut into small dice
½ cucumber, diced
2 tablespoons extra-virgin
  olive oil
1 tablespoon mayonnaise
1 tablespoon finely chopped
  fresh dill
½ teaspoon sea salt
¼ teaspoon freshly ground
  black pepper
¼ teaspoon celery salt

4 best-quality all-beef hot dogs
4 poppy seed hot dog buns, split
120 g/4 oz blue cheese, crumbled
Hot wing sauce

1. In a bowl combine the shallots and vinegar and allow to stand for 20 minutes. Place the diced celery in a fine-mesh sieve and bring 750 ml/1¼ pints water to the boil. Holding the sieve over the sink, pour the water slowly over the celery; drain thoroughly. Add the celery and the remaining relish ingredients to the bowl and fold until evenly blended.

2. Prepare the grill for direct cooking over medium heat (180–230°C/350–450°F).

3. Cut a few shallow slashes in each hot dog, and then grill over *direct medium heat* for 4–5 minutes, with the lid closed, until hot all the way to the centre, turning occasionally. During the last 30–60 seconds of grilling time, toast the buns, cut side down, over direct heat.

4. Spread an even layer of celery relish on the bottom half of each bun (you may not need all of it), and top each with a hot dog, blue cheese and hot wing sauce. Serve immediately.

HOT DOGS

FUN FACT

Few can resist the fiery orange goodness of buffalo wing sauce: hence, its sweeping adoption in non-wing dishes like buffalo chicken salads and dips, and meatless dishes like buffalo fries and even devilled eggs. In this recipe, we continue to expand the saucy trend to dress up the all-American hot dog.

THE NEW ENGLAND-STYLE TOP-LOADING
WONDER BUN

Does your hot dog suffer from soggy bun syndrome? Does your bun split before you even get a chance to take that first bite, causing an awkward wiener-wrangling moment? Do your condiments weep and run off to the side, making for a less-than-desirable presentation? If the answer is 'yes' to any of these questions, then we're here to tell you: there is life outside the basic side-split bun.

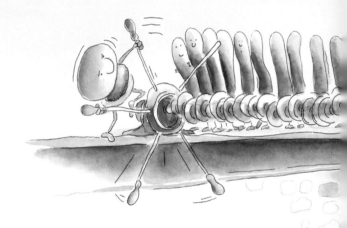

Enter the New England-style hot dog bun – also known as the 'top-sliced', 'top-loading' or 'frankfurter' roll. This Texas toast-like north-eastern summertime staple, prized as much for its satisfying crunch as for its form and function, has flat, crustless sides that make the perfect surface for buttering and toasting on the grill. And unlike the two-piece rounded rolls that are common across most of the country, this V-shaped bun's flat bottom provides a stable seat and a neat presentation for everything from hot dogs to lobster salad. No more runny condiments: this guy can stand up (literally) to its standard side-split competition any day.

Developed in Massachusetts in the mid- to late 1940s, the New England-style bun came about thanks to America's first franchised restaurant chain: Howard Johnson's. The orange-roofed landmark's owners had originally approached Maine's J.J. Nissen Baking Company about creating a special bun for its fried clam strip sandwich. The restaurant chain specifically wanted top-sliced rolls that would stand upright and, thus, would be easier to assemble, serve and devour. And so, the quintessential 'New England-style' bun was born.

This top-loading wonder bun remains true to its namesake, rarely available anywhere outside of the North-east. From fish shacks to backyard barbecues, the New England–style bun is also a home-team concessions staple at America's oldest ballpark. Cubs fans have their Chicago-Style Hot Dogs in poppy seed buns and Milwaukee fans their Brewers Bratwurst served in crusty rolls, but Red Sox rooters enjoy a favourite found exclusively at Boston's famed Fenway Park – the Fenway Frank, a slightly smoky, garlicky hot dog, traditionally topped with mustard, onions and relish, then tucked into the classic top-sliced bun.

For those of you New Englanders who have fled the coop and lust for your beloved split-top rolls but can't find them in your regional supermarkets or restaurants, consider getting crafty and creating your own out of a basic hot dog bun. To make your own top-loaders, start with fresh, unsliced hot dog buns from your local bakery. Simply slice each bun vertically from the top, trim off the sides to create two flat surfaces for grilling, toast them up, stuff with creamy lobster salad or sizzling sausage, and let the nostalgia begin.

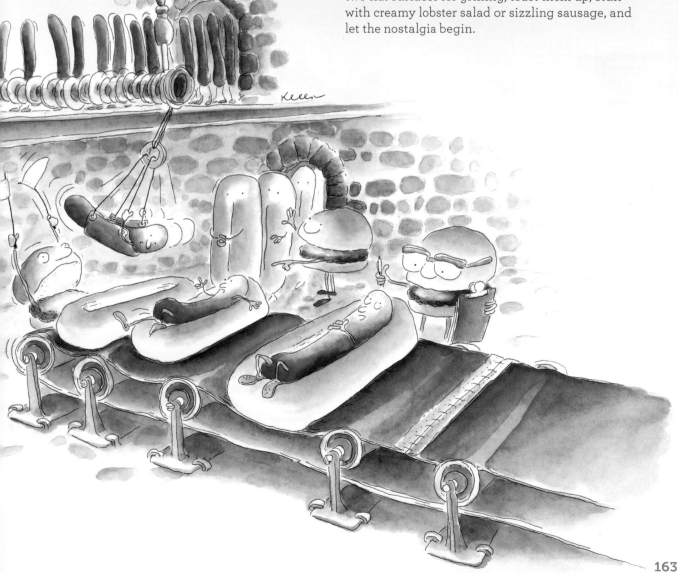

WARM AND CHEESY FRANKS

SERVES: **4** | PREP TIME: **5 MINUTES** | GRILLING TIME: **5–7 MINUTES**

HOT DOGS

4 top-split New England-style hot dog buns
120 g/4 oz Cheddar cheese, finely grated
4 best-quality all-beef hot dogs
4 tablespoons tomato ketchup
4 tablespoons yellow mustard
4 tablespoons sweet pickle relish

1. Prepare the grill for direct and indirect cooking over medium heat (180–230°C/350–450°F).

2. Gently open the buns a little bit to make room for the cheese. Sprinkle an equal amount of the cheese inside each bun. Cut a few shallow slashes in each hot dog.

3. Grill the cheese-filled buns over *indirect medium heat* for 5–7 minutes, with the lid closed, until the cheese is melted and the buns are lightly toasted. At the same time, grill the hot dogs over *direct medium heat* for 4–5 minutes, until hot all the way to the centre, turning occasionally.

4. Place each hot dog in a bun, being careful to keep the two halves of each bun in one piece, and top with your choice of tomato ketchup, mustard and/or relish. Serve immediately.

PATAGONIAN HOT DOGS WITH AVOCADO MAYO

SERVES: **4–8** | PREP TIME: **20 MINUTES** | GRILLING TIME: **4–5 MINUTES**

MAYO
1 ripe avocado, roughly chopped
5 tablespoons mayonnaise
½ jalapeño chilli, seeded and chopped
1 tablespoon chopped shallot
1 tablespoon fresh lemon juice
1 garlic clove, crushed
¼ teaspoon sea salt
¼ teaspoon freshly ground black pepper

8 best-quality all-beef hot dogs
8 hot dog buns, split
1 jar or bag (450 g/1 lb) sauerkraut, drained
450 g/1 lb ripe tomatoes, cored, seeded and chopped
Small bunch fresh coriander, roughly chopped
¼ red onion, finely chopped

1. In a food processor fitted with a metal blade, combine the mayo ingredients and purée until smooth.

2. Prepare the grill for direct cooking over medium heat (180–230°C/350–450°F).

3. Cut a few shallow slashes in each hot dog, and then grill over *direct medium heat* for 4–5 minutes, with the lid closed, until hot all the way to the centre, turning occasionally. During the last 30–60 seconds of grilling time, toast the buns, cut side down, over direct heat.

4. Generously spread the avocado mayo inside each bun (you will not need all of it). Then add a hot dog, sauerkraut, tomatoes, coriander and onion. Serve warm.

At the southern end of South America, hot dog fanatics in Patagonia, Argentina, like a colourful variation that involves copious amounts of sauerkraut, chopped tomatoes and a creamy avocado mayo.

NEW YORK HOT DOGS WITH SWEET ONIONS

SERVES: **4** | PREP TIME: **20 MINUTES, PLUS ABOUT 40 MINUTES FOR THE ONIONS** | GRILLING TIME: **4–5 MINUTES**

HOT DOGS

ONIONS

150 ml/¼ pint water
1 teaspoon cornflour
1 tablespoon shop-bought barbecue sauce
1 tablespoon tomato purée
1 tablespoon balsamic vinegar
1 teaspoon Dijon mustard
1 teaspoon light brown sugar
1 teaspoon caraway seeds
½ teaspoon hot pepper sauce
2 tablespoons vegetable oil
2 large red onions, each cut in half and
   thinly sliced
¼ teaspoon sea salt
1 teaspoon crushed garlic

4 best-quality all-beef hot dogs
4 soft hot dog buns, split
Spicy brown mustard
Dill pickle spears

1. Combine the water and cornflour and whisk until smooth. Whisk in the barbecue sauce, tomato purée, vinegar, mustard, brown sugar, caraway seeds and hot pepper sauce.

2. In a medium saucepan over a medium heat, warm the oil. Add the onions and salt, partially cover the pan and cook for 10–12 minutes, until the onions are softened but not at all brown, stirring occasionally. Add the garlic and cook for 1 minute more. Add the cornflour mixture and stir to blend. Adjust the heat to low, cover the pan and cook for 20–25 minutes, until the onions are juicy and glossy but not wet, stirring occasionally and checking to make sure the onions don't scorch. Add another tablespoon of water, if needed. Remove from the heat.

3. Prepare the grill for direct cooking over medium heat (180–230°C/350–450°F).

4. Cut a few shallow slashes in each hot dog, and then grill over *direct medium heat* for 4–5 minutes, with the lid closed, until hot all the way to the centre, turning occasionally. During the last 30–60 seconds of grilling time, toast the buns, cut side down, over direct heat.

5. Spread a little mustard on each bun, add a hot dog, and top with plenty of onions. Serve with the pickles.

DELUXE HOT DOGS WITH PARMA HAM AND RED ONION RELISH

SERVES: **4** | PREP TIME: **20 MINUTES, PLUS 20–24 MINUTES FOR THE RELISH** | GRILLING TIME: **3–4 MINUTES**

RELISH
2 tablespoons extra-virgin olive oil
2 large red onions, finely chopped
250 ml/8 fl oz fruity red wine
2 tablespoons red wine vinegar
1 tablespoon brown sugar
60 g/2 oz Parma ham, trimmed of perimeter fat,
    finely chopped
2 tablespoons finely chopped fresh basil leaves
½ teaspoon sea salt
¼ teaspoon freshly ground black pepper

4 best-quality all-beef hot dogs, each cut lengthways
    in half (don't cut all the way through)
4 rectangles focaccia bread, each about 2.5 cm/1
    inch thick and 6 cm/2½ inches wide, split
Extra-virgin olive oil
2 tablespoons wholegrain mustard

1. In a medium saucepan over a medium heat, warm the oil. Add the onions and sauté until very tender, 10–12 minutes, stirring occasionally. Add the wine, vinegar and brown sugar and continue cooking until most of the liquid is absorbed but the mixture is still juicy, 10–12 minutes more, stirring occasionally. Remover from the heat and stir in the Parma ham, basil, salt and pepper.

2. Prepare the grill for direct cooking over medium heat (180–230°C/350–450°F).

3. Cut a few shallow slashes in each hot dog. Lightly brush the cut side of the focaccia with oil. Grill the hot dogs over *direct medium heat*, with the lid closed until hot, 3–4 minutes, turning once. During the last 30–60 seconds of grilling time, toast the focaccia, cut side down, over direct heat, until lightly golden but still soft.

4. Spread the focaccia generously with mustard and top with a hot dog and a mound of relish. Serve immediately.

CHORIZO QUESADILLAS WITH MANGO SALSA

SERVES: **4; 8–10 AS AN APPETISER** | PREP TIME: **20 MINUTES** | GRILLING TIME: **30–38 MINUTES**

SALSA
1 large, ripe mango, peeled and finely chopped
1 small red pepper, finely chopped
¼ red onion, finely chopped
2 tablespoons finely chopped fresh coriander
1 tablespoon fresh lime juice
¼ teaspoon sea salt

4 serrano chillies
450 g/1 lb fresh chorizo sausages, pierced several
   times with a fork
2 ripe avocados, diced
2 teaspoons fresh lime juice
8 flour tortillas (20 cm/8 inches)
600 g/1¼ lb Monterey Jack or Cheddar cheese,
   grated
Sour cream

1. Prepare the grill for direct and indirect cooking over medium heat (180–230°C/350–450°F).

2. Mix the salsa ingredients.

3. Grill the chillies over *direct medium heat* for 6–7 minutes, with the lid closed, until blackened and blistered, turning occasionally. Transfer to a bowl and cover with clingfilm to trap the steam. Allow to stand for about 10 minutes.

4. Grill the sausages over *indirect medium heat* for 20–25 minutes, with the lid closed, until fully cooked (70°C/160°F), turning occasionally. Remove from the grill and cut the sausages at an angle into 1-cm/ ½-inch slices.

5. Decrease the temperature of the grill to low heat (130–180°C/250–350°F).

6. Remove the chillies from the bowl and peel away and discard the skin, seeds and stems. Finely chop the chillies and place them in a bowl. Add the avocados and lime juice, and then mash with a fork until the mixture is fairly smooth.

7. Assemble the quesadillas by spreading the avocado mixture evenly over one half of each tortilla, then one-sixteenth of the cheese, an equal amount of sausage slices and another sixteenth of cheese. Fold the empty side of the tortillas over the filling.

8. Grill the quesadillas over *direct low heat* for 4–6 minutes, with the lid closed, until golden on both sides, turning once. Cut the quesadillas into wedges and serve warm with mango salsa and sour cream.

Don't be afraid to blacken the chillies' skins.
You will scrape away most of the skin later,
leaving the tender flesh for spicing up the
avocado filling of these fabulous quesadillas.

GARLIC SAUSAGE BRUSCHETTA WITH SWEETCORN AND WATERCRESS

SERVES: **8 AS AN APPETISER** | PREP TIME: **15 MINUTES** | GRILLING TIME: **9–11 MINUTES**

SAUSAGES

1 bunch watercress, thick stems removed and leaves roughly chopped
1 can (325 g/11 oz) sweetcorn, drained
1 large shallot, finely diced
Finely grated rind of 1 lemon
1½ tablespoons fresh lemon juice
1 teaspoon finely chopped garlic
1 teaspoon Dijon mustard
Extra-virgin olive oil
Sea salt
Freshly ground black pepper
8 slices French or sourdough bread, each about 7 by 12 cm/ 3 by 5 inches and 1 cm/½ inch thick
450 g/1 lb pre-cooked garlic sausages, each cut lengthways in half

1. Prepare the grill for direct cooking over medium heat (180–230°C/350–450°F).

2. Combine the watercress, sweetcorn, shallot, lemon rind and juice, garlic, mustard, ½ teaspoon salt, 5 tablespoons oil, and ¼ teaspoon pepper. Toss to blend. Lightly coat the bread slices with oil and season with a little salt and pepper.

3. Grill the sausages over *direct medium heat* for 8–10 minutes, with the lid closed, until nicely browned and heated through, turning once. Remove from the grill and cut crossways into 1-cm/½-inch slices. Add the sausage slices to the large bowl with the sweetcorn mixture and toss to blend.

4. Grill the bread slices over *direct medium heat* until golden and crusty on the outside, but not crisp, about 1 minute, turning once. Place a slice of bread on each plate and top evenly with the sausage-corn mixture. Serve warm.

POLENTA CROSTINI WITH SAUSAGE-TOMATO RAGOUT

SERVES: **4–6; 8–10 AS AN APPETISER**
PREP TIME: **20 MINUTES, PLUS ABOUT 25 MINUTES FOR THE RAGOUT** | GRILLING TIME: **4–6 MINUTES**

RAGOUT
225 g/8 oz fresh Italian sausages, hot or mild, casings removed
Extra-virgin olive oil
½ small onion, finely chopped
2 large garlic cloves, finely chopped
1 can (400 g/13 oz) chopped plum tomatoes in juice
Sea salt
Freshly ground black pepper
4 tablespoons chopped fresh basil

2 packs (each 450 g/1 lb) pre-cooked polenta, ends trimmed, cut into 1-cm/½-inch slices
120 g/4 oz Parmesan cheese, at room temperature, shaved into pieces with a vegetable peeler

Polenta tends to stick to the cooking grates unless you brush the rounds generously with oil and use high heat. Then you should be able to turn them easily.

1. Prepare the grill for direct cooking over high heat (230–290°C/450–550°F).

2. Warm a frying pan over a medium heat. Add the sausages and cook for 5–8 minutes, until no trace of pink remains, stirring and breaking up the meat with a spoon. Tip the pan, and spoon off all but about 1 tablespoon of the fat, if necessary. If there is no liquid fat in the pan, add 1 tablespoon oil. Add the onion and garlic and sauté until softened, about 5 minutes. Add the tomatoes, ½ teaspoon salt and ¼ teaspoon pepper, and bring to a simmer. Cook for about 10 minutes, until the liquid is evaporated and the mixture is quite thick, stirring occasionally. Stir in half of the basil and keep the ragout warm while you grill the polenta.

3. Generously brush the polenta slices on both sides with oil, season with salt and pepper, and grill over *direct high heat* for 4–6 minutes, with the lid closed, until nicely marked by the grill, turning once. Transfer to a serving plate and immediately top each slice with a little cheese and a spoonful of ragout. Garnish with the remaining basil and serve immediately.

WHITE WINE-STEAMED CLAMS WITH CHORIZO

SERVES: **4** | PREP TIME: **15 MINUTES** | GRILLING TIME: **ABOUT 30 MINUTES**
SPECIAL EQUIPMENT: **GRILL-PROOF CAST-IRON CASSEROLE OR LARGE CAST-IRON FRYING PAN**

375 g/12 oz fully cooked Spanish chorizo sausage
1 baguette, about 40 cm/16 inches long, cut on a
   diagonal into 32 slices
Extra-virgin olive oil
40 g/1½ oz unsalted butter
1 medium onion, finely chopped
6 garlic cloves, thinly sliced
1 tablespoon finely chopped fresh oregano leaves
2 teaspoons finely chopped fresh thyme leaves
250 ml/8 fl oz dry white wine
36 clams, scrubbed under cold running water
   (discard any clams that won't close)
1 large garlic clove, cut in half

1. Prepare the grill for direct cooking over medium heat (180–230°C/350–450°F).

2. Grill the sausage over *direct medium heat* for about 8 minutes, with the lid closed, until browned, turning occasionally. Cut each sausage lengthways in half, and then cut the halves crossways into 1-cm/½-inch pieces.

3. Lightly brush the baguette slices on both sides with oil.

4. Place a grill-proof cast-iron casserole or a large cast-iron frying pan over *direct medium heat* and preheat for 10 minutes. To the pan add 2 tablespoons oil and the butter. When the butter is melted and begins to foam, add the onion, sliced garlic, oregano and thyme. Continue cooking until the onion softens, about 5 minutes, stirring occasionally. Pour in the wine, bring to the boil, close the grill lid, and cook for 2 minutes more.

5. Arrange the clams and sausage pieces in the pan and cover with the lid. Cook over *direct medium heat* for 10 minutes, with the grill lid closed. Carefully lift the lid off the pan and check to see if the clams are open. If not, replace the lid and cook for 3–5 minutes more. Wearing insulated barbecue mitts or oven gloves, carefully remove the pan from the grill. Discard any unopened clams.

6. Grill the baguette slices over *direct medium heat* for about 1 minute, with the lid open, until lightly toasted, turning once or twice. Remove from the grill and rub the bread with the cut side of the garlic clove.

7. Spoon equal amounts of sausage, clams and juice into deep bowls. Serve with the bread for dipping.

FUN FACT

Much like a tree, you can tell a clam's age by counting the rings on its shell. In 2007, scientists pulled an adult littleneck clam from the icy Arctic waters off Iceland's northern coast that reportedly had 507 annual growth rings – now known as the world's oldest animal.

SAUSAGES

MERGUEZ SAUSAGE PIZZAS WITH MOZZARELLA, PEPPERS AND FETA

SERVES: **4** | PREP TIME: **25 MINUTES** | GRILLING TIME: **24–35 MINUTES**

4 spring onions, ends trimmed
Extra-virgin olive oil
1 medium red pepper, cut into 4 planks
225 g/8 oz fresh merguez sausage
450 g/1 lb prepared pizza dough, at room
  temperature
450 g/1 lb fresh mozzarella cheese, grated
150 g/5 oz feta cheese, crumbled
3 tablespoons finely chopped fresh mint
3 tablespoons thinly sliced fresh basil

1. Prepare the grill for direct cooking over medium heat (180–230°C/350–450°F).

2. Lightly brush the spring onions with oil. Grill the red pepper planks over *direct medium heat* for 8–10 minutes, with the lid closed, until tender, turning occasionally. At the same time, grill the spring onions over *direct medium heat* for 2–3 minutes, until wilted, turning once. Cut the pepper planks into 8-mm/⅓-inch strips. Finely chop the spring onions.

3. Grill the sausage over *direct medium heat* for 12–15 minutes, with the lid closed, until fully cooked (70°C/160°F), turning occasionally. Cut the sausage into 5 mm/¼-inch slices.

4. Divide the dough into four equal pieces. Lightly brush four 23-cm/9-inch squares of baking paper on one side with oil. Roll or press each piece of dough on the oiled side of the paper into a 20-cm/8-inch circle about 8 mm/⅓ inch thick. Lightly brush the tops with oil. Allow the dough to stand at room temperature for 10 minutes.

5. Grill the dough, paper side facing up, over *direct medium heat* for 2–5 minutes, with the lid closed, until well marked and firm on the underside, rotating as needed for even cooking. Discard the baking paper. Transfer the crusts to a work surface with the grilled side facing up.

6. Top each pizza with equal amounts of the cheeses, sausage, red pepper and spring onions, leaving a 5-mm/¼-inch border. Return the pizzas to the grill and cook over *direct medium heat* for 2–5 minutes, with the lid closed, until the cheese is melted and the bottoms of the crusts are crisp, rotating the pizzas occasionally. Transfer to a chopping board. Top the pizzas with mint and basil and cut into wedges. Serve warm.

BRUNCH PIZZAS

SERVES: **4** | PREP TIME: **30 MINUTES** | GRILLING TIME: **14–20 MINUTES**

375 g/12 oz fully cooked chicken sausages
1 medium red onion, cut into 1 cm/½-inch wedges
1 large red pepper
Extra-virgin olive oil
2 teaspoons balsamic vinegar
1½ teaspoons finely chopped fresh rosemary leaves
½ teaspoon sea salt
½ teaspoon freshly ground black pepper
450 g/1 lb prepared pizza dough, at room
   temperature
300 g/10 oz Monterey Jack or Cheddar cheese,
   coarsely grated
75 g/2½ oz Parmesan cheese, freshly grated

You can use either a gas or a charcoal grill for making pizzas, but there is something really special about the way pizza dough picks up the smokiness of a charcoal grill. It is reminiscent of great thin-crusted pizzas cooked in a wood-fired oven.

1. Prepare the grill for direct cooking over medium heat (180–230°C/350–450°F).

2. Brush the sausages, onion and red pepper with oil and grill them over *direct medium heat*, with the lid closed, until grill marks appear, turning once. The sausages and pepper will take about 6 minutes and the onion will take about 10 minutes. Chop into 1-cm/½-inch pieces. Transfer to a bowl and add the vinegar, rosemary, salt and pepper.

3. To prepare the dough and grill the first side, follow steps 4 and 5 for the Merguez Sausage Pizzas (see recipe on facing page).

4. Top each pizza with equal amounts of the Monterey Jack cheese, sausage mixture and Parmesan cheese, leaving a 5-mm/¼-inch border. Return the pizzas to the grill and cook over *direct medium heat* for 2–5 minutes, with the lid closed, until the cheese is melted and the bottoms of the crusts are crisp, rotating the pizzas occasionally. Transfer to a chopping board and cut into wedges. Serve warm.

FRESH CHORIZO AND TEX-MEX POTATO SALAD

SERVES: **4–6** | PREP TIME: **15 MINUTES** | GRILLING TIME: **20–25 MINUTES** | SPECIAL EQUIPMENT: **PERFORATED GRILL PAN**

SAUSAGES

4 tablespoons finely chopped fresh coriander
2 tablespoons fresh lime juice
1 teaspoon Dijon mustard
½ teaspoon ground cumin
Sea salt
Freshly ground black pepper
Extra-virgin olive oil
½ teaspoon garlic granules
1.25 kg/2½ lb small new potatoes, 3.5–5 cm/
   1½–2 inches in diameter, each cut in half
3 fresh chorizo sausages, each about 120 g/
   4 oz, pierced several times with a fork
1 medium red pepper, cut into thin strips
1 medium red onion, cut into very thin slices

1. Prepare the grill for direct and indirect cooking over medium heat (180–230°C/350–450°F) and preheat a perforated grill pan over direct heat.

2. Whisk the coriander, lime juice, mustard, cumin, ½ teaspoon salt, ¼ teaspoon pepper and 4 tablespoons oil to make a vinaigrette.

3. In a large bowl whisk 2 tablespoons oil, ¼ teaspoon salt, ¼ teaspoon pepper and the garlic granules. Add the potatoes and turn to coat. Spread the potatoes in a single layer on the grill pan and cook over *direct medium heat* for 20–25 minutes, with the lid closed, until golden brown and tender, turning occasionally. At the same time, grill the sausages on the cooking grates over *indirect medium heat* for 20–25 minutes, until fully cooked (70°C/160°F), turning occasionally. Cut each potato half in half and cut the sausages into 5-mm/¼-inch slices.

4. Combine the potatoes, sausages, red pepper and onion. Drizzle with the vinaigrette and gently toss. Season with salt and pepper. Serve warm or at room temperature.

With your grill set up for both direct and indirect heat, you can grill the potatoes and roast the sausages at the same time.

CHICKEN SAUSAGE SKEWERS WITH NECTARINES AND HONEY-LIME GLAZE

SERVES: **4** | PREP TIME: **25 MINUTES** | GRILLING TIME: **6–8 MINUTES** | SPECIAL EQUIPMENT: **10 METAL OR BAMBOO SKEWERS**

GLAZE
1 teaspoon finely grated lime rind
4 tablespoons fresh lime juice
4 tablespoons honey
2 tablespoons finely chopped fresh coriander
1 tablespoon soy sauce
½ teaspoon sea salt

4 medium, ripe nectarines
1 tablespoon extra-virgin olive oil
10 fully cooked spicy chicken sausages,
    700 g/1½ lb, each cut into 4 pieces
Hot cooked rice (optional)

Whenever you have a sweet glaze like this one, wait until the final 3–5 minutes of grilling time to apply it or it might burn.

1. If using bamboo skewers, soak them in water for at least 30 minutes.

2. Prepare the grill for direct cooking over medium heat (180–230°C/350–450°F).

3. In a small bowl whisk the glaze ingredients.

4. Cut each nectarine into 10 chunks about the same size as the sausage pieces. In a medium bowl combine the oil with the nectarines and stir to coat. Thread the sausages and nectarines on to skewers, alternating the pieces and arranging them so they are touching but not crammed together. You can also thread them separately on their own skewers.

5. Grill the skewers over *direct medium heat* for 6–8 minutes, with the lid closed, until the sausages are heated through and the nectarines are marked in spots, turning every 2 minutes and brushing with the glaze during the last 4 minutes of grilling time. Remove from the grill and serve immediately with rice, if desired.

SAUSAGES

KIELBASA, ONION AND PEPPER SPIEDINI
WITH GRILLED GARLIC BREAD

SERVES: **4** | PREP TIME: **20 MINUTES** | GRILLING TIME: **8–10 MINUTES** | SPECIAL EQUIPMENT: **8 METAL OR BAMBOO SKEWERS**

4 teaspoons fresh lemon juice
1 tablespoon finely chopped shallots
1 teaspoon Dijon mustard
Sea salt
Freshly ground black pepper
Extra-virgin olive oil
2 large red peppers
2 medium onions
425 g/14 oz Polish kielbasa sausage,
   cut crossways into 16 pieces
4 slices artisan bread, each about 1 cm/½ inch thick
1 garlic clove, cut in half
4 large handfuls rocket leaves

1. If using bamboo skewers, soak them in water for at least 30 minutes.

2. Prepare the grill for direct cooking over medium heat (180–230°C/350–450°F).

3. Whisk the lemon juice, shallots, mustard, ½ teaspoon salt and ¼ teaspoon pepper. Slowly add 5 tablespoons oil, whisking constantly until the vinaigrette is emulsified.

4. Cut each red pepper into eight 2.5-cm/1-inch squares. Quarter each onion and separate each quarter into two segments (discard the very small pieces from the centre of the onion). Using four skewers, thread the vegetables through their centres, alternating the ingredients and arranging them so they are touching but not crammed together. Thread the kielbasa separately on to four skewers. Brush the vegetables and kielbasa with 3 tablespoons of the vinaigrette. Lightly brush the bread slices on both sides with oil.

5. Grill the skewers over *direct medium heat* for 8–10 minutes, with the lid closed, until the vegetables are lightly charred and the kielbasa is nicely browned and heated through, turning occasionally. During the last minute of grilling time, toast the bread over direct heat, turning once. Remove everything from the grill. Rub one side of each bread slice with the cut side of the garlic clove. Place a slice of bread, garlic side up, on each of four serving plates.

6. In a bowl toss the rocket with the remaining vinaigrette, and divide among the four bread slices. Set one vegetable skewer and one kielbasa skewer on top of the rocket and serve immediately.

Run the flat, cut side of a clove of garlic across a warm piece of toast for instant garlic bread. *Delizioso!*

A GUIDE TO UNDERSTANDING
SAUSAGES

For about as long as humans have been on the hunt, sausages have been on the menu.

Tasty and efficient (they were designed to use all parts of an animal, but don't dwell on that), cured and smoked meats kept our pre-fridge ancestors well fed. No doubt they would be amazed at how far sausage makers have taken this craft. We have so many types to choose from that it can be hard to know which is which. Here, then, is a little primer on four broad categories of sausages and how to cook them.

FRESH

The minced meat in these sausage casings is uncooked.

EXAMPLES (SHOWN LEFT TO RIGHT): Hot or sweet Italian sausage, fresh poultry sausage, Mexican chorizo

COOKING: Mandatory. Grill directly over low to medium heat, or roast them over indirect heat until no pink remains.

COLD SMOKED

These sausages have been smoked with some type of wood and are usually completely cooked.

EXAMPLES (SHOWN LEFT TO RIGHT): Andouille, linguica, kielbasa

COOKING: Not always necessary, but a quick grilling to warm the meat and get a good char will only make them better.

PRE-COOKED

These have been made with fresh, blended meat and were then cooked prior to packaging and distribution.

EXAMPLES (SHOWN LEFT TO RIGHT): Hot dog, pork bratwurst, veal bratwurst, mortadella

COOKING: Not required, but certainly recommended to boost flavour.

CURED

Here we have sausages that have been salted and air-dried for weeks. They enjoy long shelf lives.

EXAMPLES (SHOWN LEFT TO RIGHT): Spanish chorizo, salami, Landjäger

COOKING: Your call. They're designed to be delicious as is but can be great cooked, too.

ITALIAN SAUSAGES WITH PEPPERS, ONIONS AND PROVOLONE

SERVES: **4** | PREP TIME: **20 MINUTES** | GRILLING TIME: **8–10 MINUTES** | SPECIAL EQUIPMENT: **PERFORATED GRILL PAN**

Extra-virgin olive oil
Sea salt
Freshly ground black pepper
2 medium peppers, 1 red and 1 green,
    cut into 8-mm/⅓-inch-wide strips
1 medium onion, cut crossways
    into 8-mm/⅓-inch slices
4 fresh Italian sausages, any combination of
    sweet and hot, each about 150 g/5 oz, each cut
    lengthways in half (don't cut all the way through)
2 tablespoons red wine vinegar
1 garlic clove, crushed
1 baguette, about 225 g/8 oz and 60 cm/2 ft long,
    cut lengthways in half
4 strips provolone cheese, each about 15 g/½ oz
    and 15 cm/6 inches long
1 tablespoon roughly chopped fresh
    Italian parsley

1. Prepare the grill for direct cooking over medium heat (180–230°C/350–450°F) and preheat a perforated grill pan.

2. In a medium bowl whisk 2 tablespoons oil, ½ teaspoon salt and ¼ teaspoon pepper. Add the peppers and onion and turn to coat.

3. Lightly brush the sausages all over with oil.

4. Whisk the vinegar, garlic, 2 tablespoons oil, ¼ teaspoon salt and ¼ teaspoon pepper to make a vinaigrette. Brush the cut side of the baguette with oil.

5. Spread the peppers and onion in a single layer on the grill pan, and place the sausages on the cooking grates. Grill over *direct medium heat* for 8–10 minutes, with the lid closed, until the vegetables are tender and the sausages are browned and fully cooked (70°C/160°F), turning occasionally. During the last 30–60 seconds of grilling time, place a strip of cheese inside each sausage slit to melt, and toast the baguette, cut side down, over direct heat.

6. Transfer the vegetables to a bowl, add the parsley, and toss to combine.

7. Cut the baguette into four 15-cm/6-inch pieces. Place each sausage in a baguette piece, and top with the vegetables and a tablespoon of the vinaigrette. Serve warm.

By splitting sausages open and exposing more of the meat to the fire, you can develop more charred and smoky flavours. Just be sure to watch out for flare-ups.

SAUSAGE MIXED GRILL OVER CREAMY POLENTA

SERVES: **8** | PREP TIME: **15 MINUTES** | GRILLING TIME: **15–20 MINUTES**

SAUSAGES

DRESSING

4 tablespoons finely chopped fresh basil
2 tablespoons white balsamic vinegar
1 shallot, finely chopped

Sea salt
Freshly ground black pepper
Extra-virgin olive oil

POLENTA

1.25 litres/2 pints milk
250 ml/8 fl oz water
400 g/13 oz quick-cooking polenta
120 g/4 oz cream cheese, softened
60 g/2 oz Pecorino Romano cheese, grated

1 ring fresh sweet luganiga sausage, about
   450 g/1 lb, pierced a few times with a fork
3 fresh hot Italian sausages, about 225 g/8 oz total
425 g/14 oz Polish kielbasa sausage

1. Prepare the grill for indirect cooking over medium heat (180–230°C/350–450°F).

2. Whisk the dressing ingredients, including ½ teaspoon salt and ¼ teaspoon pepper. Slowly add 5 tablespoons oil, whisking constantly until the dressing is emulsified. Set aside.

3. In a saucepan combine the milk, water, 1½ teaspoons salt and ¼ teaspoon pepper. Bring to the boil over a medium-high heat, and then whisk in the polenta in a slow and steady stream. Reduce the heat to medium and cook for 4–5 minutes, until the polenta is thick, stirring constantly. Remove from the heat and add the cream cheese and pecorino cheese, stirring constantly until the cheeses are melted. Keep warm over low heat, stirring occasionally to prevent scorching.

4. Grill the luganiga and Italian sausages over *indirect medium heat* for 15–20 minutes, with the lid closed, until fully cooked (70°C/160°F), turning occasionally. At the same time, grill the kielbasa over *indirect medium heat* for 12–15 minutes, until nicely browned and heated through, turning occasionally. If liked, during the last 3–5 minutes of grilling time, brown the luganiga and Italian sausages over direct heat, turning once. Remove all the sausages from the grill and cut them into bite-sized pieces.

5. Spread the polenta in a thick layer on a large serving plate. Top with the sausage pieces. Whisk the dressing again and spoon it over the sausages. Serve immediately.

Luganega is a thin ring of sweet sausage that tends to be milder than traditional Italian sausage and is often flavoured with parsley and cheese. It can be found in Italian delis and some supermarkets.

LITTLE SAUSAGES WITH ONIONS, FLAT BREAD AND MUSTARD

SERVES: **6** | PREP TIME: **40 MINUTES** | GRILLING TIME: **8-10 MINUTES**

1 teaspoon finely grated lemon rind
2 tablespoons fresh lemon juice
2 teaspoons granulated sugar
Extra-virgin olive oil
Sea salt
Freshly ground black pepper
2 medium red onions, each cut in half and
 very thinly sliced

SAUSAGES

700 g/1½ lb lean pork mince
225 g/8 oz beef mince (90% lean)
5 tablespoons chopped fresh parsley leaves
6 garlic cloves, crushed
1 tablespoon smoked paprika
1½ teaspoons fennel seeds
1 teaspoon ground cumin
¾ teaspoon dried thyme
¼ teaspoon saffron threads, crushed (optional)

Flat breads
Spicy brown mustard

1. Whisk the lemon rind and juice, sugar, 1 tablespoon oil, ½ teaspoon salt and ¼ teaspoon pepper. Stir in the onions and set aside.

2. Mix the sausage ingredients, including 2 tablespoons oil, 1½ teaspoons salt and 1 teaspoon pepper, and then form into 24 sausages, each about 7 cm/3 inches long and 2.5 cm/1 inch thick, slightly compressing each sausage so they will hold together on the grill. Refrigerate the sausages until ready to grill.

3. Prepare the grill for indirect cooking over medium heat (180–230°C/350–450°F).

4. Grill the sausages over *indirect medium heat* for 8-10 minutes, with the lid closed, until cooked to medium (70°C/160°F), turning once or twice. During the last minute of grilling time, warm the flat breads over direct heat, turning once.

5. Serve the sausages warm with the onions, flat breads and mustard.

TURKEY-CORIANDER SAUSAGE TACOS

SERVES: **4** | PREP TIME: **20 MINUTES** | GRILLING TIME: **8–10 MINUTES**

SAUSAGES

SAUSAGES

1 kg/2 lb turkey mince, preferably thigh meat,
   very cold
8 tablespoons finely chopped fresh coriander
4 tablespoons finely chopped canned chipotle
   chillies in adobo sauce (include some of
   the sauce)
¾ teaspoon dried oregano
½ teaspoon freshly ground black pepper
½ teaspoon garlic powder
½ teaspoon ground cumin
½ teaspoon ground coriander
½ teaspoon sea salt

8 flour tortillas (15 cm/6 inches)
Extra-virgin olive oil
150 g/6 oz Cheddar cheese, grated
225 g/8 oz ripe cherry tomatoes, quartered
2 handfuls shredded romaine lettuce

1. Mix the sausage ingredients, and then form
16 torpedo-shaped sausages, each about 7 cm/3 inches
long, compacting the meat gently. Refrigerate the
sausages until ready to grill.

2. Prepare the grill for direct and indirect cooking
over medium heat (180–230°C/350–450°F).

3. Wrap the tortillas in an aluminium foil parcel. Brush
the sausages with oil, and then grill over *direct
medium heat* for 8–10 minutes, with the lid closed,
until fully cooked (74°C/165°F), turning once. At the
same time, warm the tortilla parcel over *indirect
medium heat*.

4. Place two sausages inside each tortilla. Divide the
cheese, tomatoes and lettuce among the tortillas and
serve immediately.

*Serving suggestion: Fresh Tomato Salsa
(for recipe, see page 236).*

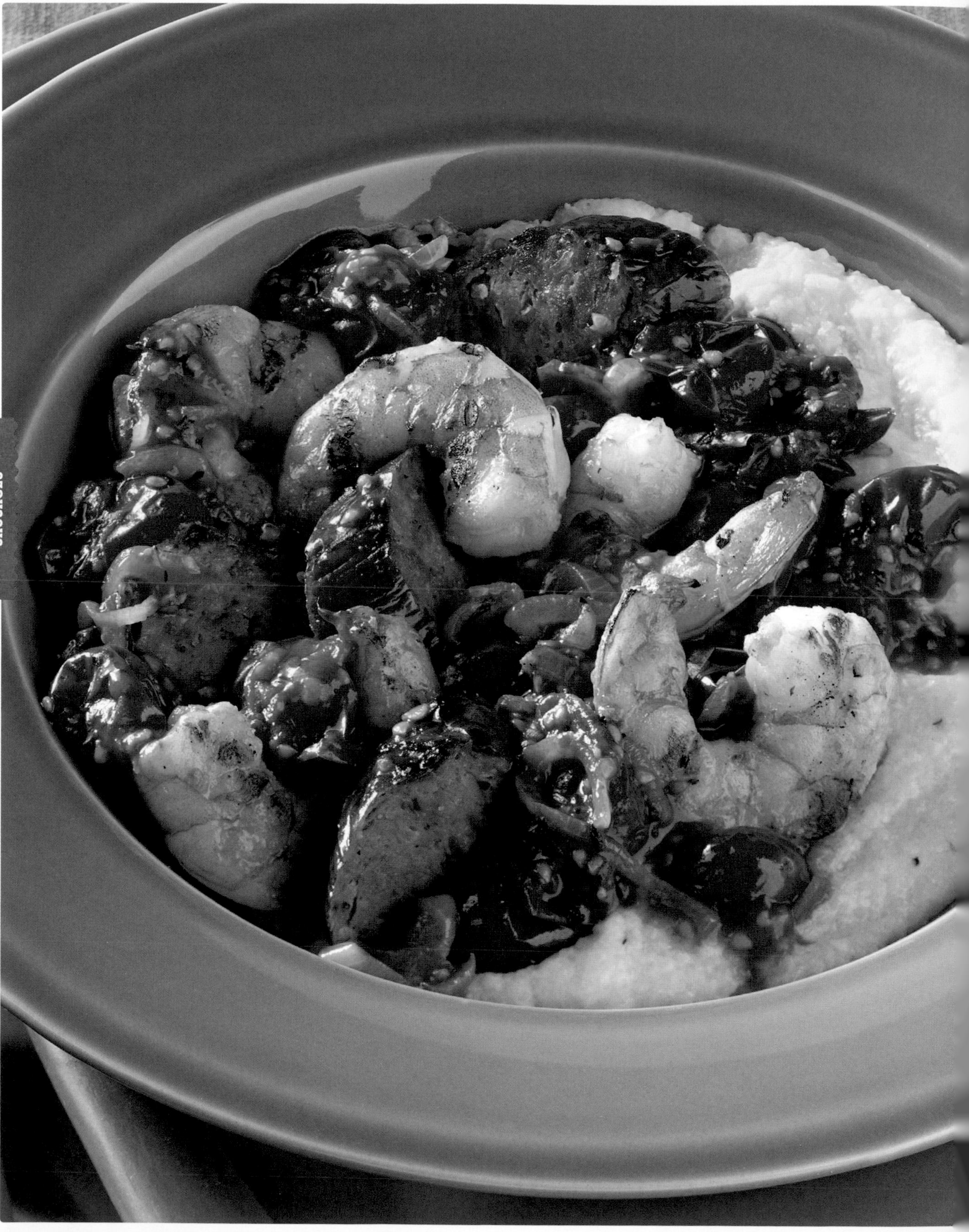

PRAWN, ANDOUILLE AND TOMATO SAUCE
OVER CHEDDAR GRITS

SERVES: **6** | PREP TIME: **30 MINUTES, PLUS ABOUT 25 MINUTES FOR THE SAUCE**
MARINATING TIME: **30 MINUTES** | GRILLING TIME: **8–10 MINUTES**

24 large prawns, peeled and deveined, tails removed
2 garlic cloves, crushed
Extra-virgin olive oil

SAUCE
1 medium onion, cut in half and
   very thinly sliced
4 garlic cloves, crushed
1 teaspoon dried basil
¼ teaspoon crushed chilli flakes
700 g/1½ lb ripe cherry tomatoes
1 tablespoon balsamic vinegar
1 teaspoon honey
½ teaspoon sea salt
¼ teaspoon freshly ground black pepper

375 g/12 oz fully cooked andouille sausage

GRITS
850 ml/1½ pints full-fat milk
40 g/1½ oz unsalted butter
¾ teaspoon sea salt
240 g/8 oz quick-cooking grits (not instant grits)
   or polenta
250 g/8 oz Cheddar cheese, grated

1. Combine the prawns, garlic and 1 tablespoon oil and toss to coat. Cover and refrigerate the prawns for 30 minutes.

2. Prepare the grill for direct cooking over medium-high heat (200–260°C/400–500°F).

3. In a large frying pan over a medium-high heat, warm 3 tablespoons oil. Add the onion, garlic, basil and chilli flakes and cook for 2–3 minutes, until the onion starts to soften, stirring occasionally. Add the tomatoes and cook for 18–20 minutes, until they burst and are very tender, stirring often. Stir in the vinegar and honey and cook for 1 minute. Remove from the heat and stir in the salt and pepper. Keep the sauce warm.

4. Grill the sausage over *direct medium-high heat* for 8–10 minutes, with the lid closed, until nicely browned and heated through, turning occasionally. During the last 2–4 minutes of grilling time, grill the prawns over *direct medium-high heat* until firm to the touch and just becoming opaque in the centre, turning once. Remove from the grill and cut the sausage on a diagonal into 1-cm/½-inch slices. Cover the sausage and prawns with foil to keep warm.

5. In a saucepan combine the milk, butter and salt. Bring to the boil over a medium-high heat, and then whisk in the grits in a slow, steady stream. Reduce the heat to medium and cook for 4–5 minutes, until the grits thicken, stirring often. Add the cheese and stir until melted.

6. Divide the Cheddar grits among bowls and top with equal amounts of tomato sauce, sausage and prawns. Serve warm.

FUN FACT

Southerners are serious about their grits. So much so that the small town of St George, South Carolina, honours the coarsely ground corn with its annual World Grits Festival – a three-day celebration with grits grinding, corn shelling and a grits-eating contest, drawing crowds that exceed 45,000.

ANDOUILLE PO'BOYS WITH CREOLE MUSTARD

SERVES: **4** | PREP TIME: **15 MINUTES** | GRILLING TIME: **4–5 MINUTES**

SLAW
5 tablespoons mayonnaise
2 tablespoons cider vinegar
½ small head green cabbage,
    coarsely shredded
1 red onion, thinly sliced
4 gherkins, drained
    and finely chopped

4 fully cooked andouille
    sausages, each about 120 g/4 oz
    and cut lengthways in half
4 submarine sandwich buns, split
4 tablespoons Creole mustard
4 tablespoons mayonnaise
24 pickled jalapeño slices
    (from a jar)

1. Prepare the grill for direct cooking over medium heat (180–230°C/350–450°F).

2. Whisk the mayonnaise and vinegar, and then add the remaining slaw ingredients. Mix well.

3. Grill the sausages over *direct medium heat* for 4–5 minutes, with the lid closed, until nicely browned and heated through, turning occasionally.

4. Spread the bottom half of each bun with 1 tablespoon mustard. Spread the top half of each bun with 1 tablespoon mayonnaise. Top each bun with a sausage, slaw and jalapeño slices. Serve immediately.

If you have trouble finding Creole mustard, substitute with Dijon mustard and add a touch of hot pepper sauce.

SAUSAGES

KIELBASA WITH PICKLED ONIONS, JALAPEÑO CHILLIES AND CHEDDAR

SERVES: **4** | PREP TIME: **15 MINUTES** | PICKLING TIME: **AT LEAST 2 HOURS** | GRILLING TIME: **9–12 MINUTES**

240 ml/8 fl oz red wine vinegar
3 tablespoons granulated sugar
1 teaspoon sea salt
⅛ teaspoon ground
   chipotle pepper
1 red onion, thinly sliced
30 g/1 oz unsalted butter,
   softened
8 slices rye bread
425 g/14 oz Polish kielbasa
   sausage
4 slices mature Cheddar cheese,
   each about 30 g/1 oz
Yellow mustard
6–8 pickled jalapeño chillies,
   each cut crossways

FUN FACT

We hope this tip cuts the mustard for you: what does that phrase mean anyway? Possibly originating in the early nineteenth century, it's a reference to the tall, fibrous, densely growing mustard plant. Cutting through the plants took skill, strength and patience – so those who couldn't hack it simply didn't cut the mustard.

1. In a saucepan combine the vinegar, sugar, salt and ground chipotle pepper. Bring to the boil over medium-high heat and then add the onions. Return to the boil over medium-high heat and cook for 1 minute. Remove from the heat and allow to stand at room temperature for at least 2 hours. Drain the onions before serving.

2. Prepare the grill for direct cooking over medium heat (180–230°C/350–450°F).

3. Butter one side of each bread slice. Cut the kielbasa crossways into two pieces, and then cut each piece lengthways in half. Grill the kielbasa over *direct medium heat* for 8–10 minutes, with the lid

closed, until nicely browned and heated through, turning once. Cut each kielbasa quarter crossways into two pieces (you should have eight pieces in total).

4. Grill the bread, unbuttered side down first, over *direct medium heat* for 30–60 seconds. Turn the bread over, top four of the slices with a slice of cheese, and grill for 30–60 seconds more.

5. Arrange the bread slices on a work surface. Spread some mustard on the four bread slices without cheese, and then top each with two pieces of kielbasa, onions, jalapeño chillies and a cheese-topped piece of bread. Serve warm.

MAPLE AND CIDER-BRAISED BRATS

WITH BACON AND FRIED SAUERKRAUT

SERVES: **6** | PREP TIME: **15 MINUTES** | GRILLING TIME: **22–23 MINUTES** | SPECIAL EQUIPMENT: **LARGE DISPOSABLE FOIL TRAY**

BRATS

6 rashers thick-cut streaky bacon
1 medium onion, cut in half and thinly sliced
3 garlic cloves, crushed
375 g/12 oz sauerkraut, drained well
500 ml/17 fl oz cider
5 tablespoons maple syrup
1 teaspoon caraway seeds
6 fresh bratwurst
6 submarine sandwich buns, split
Wholegrain mustard

1. Prepare the grill for direct cooking over high heat (230–290°C/450–550°F).

2. In a large frying pan over a medium heat, fry the bacon for 10–12 minutes, until crisp, turning occasionally. Transfer the bacon to kitchen paper to drain. Keep the bacon drippings in the pan. Return the pan to medium-high heat, add the onion and garlic, and cook for 2–3 minutes, until slightly softened, stirring often. Stir in the sauerkraut and cook for 4–5 minutes, until lightly browned. Remove from the heat.

3. In a large disposable foil tray combine the cider, syrup and caraway seeds. Add the bratwurst, place the pan over *direct high heat*, close the lid and bring the liquid to a simmer. Continue simmering for about 20 minutes, until the brats are evenly coloured and have lost their raw look, turning occasionally. Remove the brats from the pan and discard the liquid. Grill the brats over *direct high heat* for 2–3 minutes, with the lid closed, until browned and fully cooked (70°C/160°F), turning once or twice. During the last 30–60 seconds of grilling time, toast the buns, cut side down, over direct heat.

4. Spread mustard inside the buns and top each with a brat, one slice of bacon and fried sauerkraut. Serve warm.

Sauerkraut is a fantastic topping, and frying it in bacon fat takes it to a whole new level. The amount of saltiness in the sauerkraut varies by brand, so it is important to taste it before cooking to decide whether or not you should rinse it – just be sure to drain it well if you do.

HOME OF THE BRAT

A haze hovers over the small city of 51,000 that sits on Lake Michigan, just an hour north of Milwaukee, Wisconsin. Open fires blaze in backyards across the land and the local meat markets have been ransacked. Call it the bratwurst apocalypse, or simply call it summer in Sheboygan – these guys take their sausage seriously.

And for good reason. In 1860, 95 per cent of the residents in Sheboygan County's Herman Township were German immigrants. To this day, German flags still proudly fly throughout the city of Sheboygan and legendary homemade bratwurst line the butchers' shelves. Residents run the annual Brat Trot (included in your entry fee is a post-race treat: a brat-on-a-stick) and attend the Brat Days festival, featuring such delicacies as the double brat, the brat egg roll, the brat taco, brat pizza and brat jambalaya. Oh, and there was that formal legal battle with Bucyrus, Ohio, in 1970, which ultimately bestowed the coveted Bratwurst Capital of the World title upon the city of Sheboygan. The regional 'wurst pride in this Wisconsin town is real and it is relentless.

The textbook Sheboygan brat consists of coarsely minced pork that is seasoned with salt, pepper and nutmeg (and sometimes mace, garlic, sage or ginger) and stuffed into natural casings. And while pricking fresh brats with a fork and parboiling them in water, beer, or beer and onions to reduce the risk of exploding sausages) is a conventional practice across most of the United States, in Sheboygan this standard of care is considered unorthodox and borderline silly.

True Sheboyganites skip the parboiling and pricking, classically cooking their brats low and slow over a charcoal fire, which keeps the juices inside and allows the pork to absorb the fire's smoky flavour. This method (read: fat and smoke) is what makes Sheboygan sausage far more flavourful than some of our other pre-cooked, parboiled, smoked or otherwise cured brat friends. For the most authentic of Sheboygan brats, once cooked through, they must then be served in a round, split hard roll called a semmel and dressed to perfection with brown mustard, dill pickle slices and a heaped pile of grilled onions. Is your mouth watering yet?

Like Louisiana's crawfish boil, no social gathering in Sheboygan is complete without a brat fry. And by 'brat fry' we mean an outdoor get-together that involves 'frying' a massive amount of brats – without oil and without a deep fryer – but instead ... with a grill. According to the Sheboygan Convention and Visitors' Bureau, they do not grill their brats on a grill; they fry them – period. Sheboyganites unite in their brat terminology, even believing that their spelling is correct when writing: 'I fryed brats this weekend.' We'll let them have theirs, if we can keep ours. As they say, 'It's just the Sheboygan way.'

195

GRILLED BRATS WITH SPICY TOMATO-CORN CHOWCHOW

SERVES: **6** | PREP TIME: **15 MINUTES** | GRILLING TIME: **15–20 MINUTES**

CHOWCHOW

4 tablespoons cider vinegar
4 tablespoons water
3 tablespoons brown sugar
½ teaspoon crushed chilli flakes
½ teaspoon dried thyme
1 small can (198 g/7 oz)
    sweetcorn, drained
2 plum tomatoes (slightly under
    ripe), seeded and
    cut into 1-cm/½-inch dice
½ green pepper, finely chopped
¼ red onion, finely chopped
1 medium jalapeño chilli, seeded
    and finely diced

6 fresh bratwurst
6 hot dog buns, split
Spicy brown mustard

1. Prepare the grill for direct cooking over medium-low heat (150–180°C/300–350°F).

2. In a medium saucepan combine the vinegar, water, brown sugar, chilli flakes and thyme. Bring to the boil over a medium-high heat and cook for 1 minute. Add the corn, tomatoes, pepper, onion and jalapeño, and return to the boil. Reduce the heat to medium and simmer for 10 minutes, stirring occasionally. Remove from the heat and allow to cool to room temperature.

3. Grill the bratwurst over *direct medium-low heat* for 15–20 minutes, with the lid closed, until fully cooked (70°C/160°F), turning occasionally. During the last 30–60 seconds of grilling time, toast the buns, cut side down, over direct heat.

4. Place each brat in a bun and top with mustard and tomato-corn chowchow. Serve warm.

BEER BRATS WITH SAUERKRAUT, ONIONS AND JALAPEÑOS

SERVES: **6** | PREP TIME: **15 MINUTES** | GRILLING TIME: **24–26 MINUTES** | SPECIAL EQUIPMENT: **LARGE DISPOSABLE FOIL TRAY**

1 bottle (375 ml/13 fl oz) lager
Dijon or spicy brown mustard
2 tablespoons light brown sugar
½ teaspoon ground coriander
2 medium onions, each
   cut in half and thinly sliced
6 fresh bratwurst
450 g/1 lb sauerkraut, drained
2 jalapeño chillies, seeded and
   finely chopped
6 brat or torpedo rolls, split

BRATS

1. Prepare the grill for direct cooking over medium heat (180–230°C/350–450°F).

2. Whisk together the lager, 2 tablespoons mustard, brown sugar and coriander.

3. In a large disposable foil tray arrange the onions in an even layer. Add the bratwurst and pour the beer mixture over the top. Place the pan over *direct medium heat*, close the lid, and bring the mixture to a simmer. Simmer for about 20 minutes, turning the brats two or three times. Add the sauerkraut and jalapeños to the pan, and simmer for 2–3 minutes more.

4. Transfer the brats from the pan to the cooking grates and grill over *direct medium heat* for 2–3 minutes, with the lid closed, until browned and fully cooked (70°C/160°F), turning once. During the last 30–60 seconds of grilling time, toast the rolls, cut side down, over direct heat.

5. Place each brat in a roll and top with mustard and the sauerkraut mixture. Serve warm.

SIDES &
TOPPINGS

JICAMA-APPLE SLAW
WITH CREAMY YOGURT DRESSING

SERVES: **8–10** | PREP TIME: **20 MINUTES** | STANDING TIME: **20 MINUTES**

CLASSIC CREAMY SLAW

SERVES: **6–8** | PREP TIME: **20 MINUTES**
CHILLING TIME: **2 HOURS–1 DAY**

DRESSING
8 tablespoons natural yogurt
3 tablespoons extra-virgin
   olive oil
2 tablespoons cider vinegar
1 tablespoon fresh lime juice
2 teaspoons granulated sugar
1½ teaspoons sea salt
1 teaspoon ground cumin
½ teaspoon freshly ground
   black pepper

SLAW
1 small jicama, about 450 g/1 lb,
   peeled, quartered, thinly sliced
   and julienned
½ small head green cabbage,
   thinly sliced
2 large, ripe Granny Smith
   apples, quartered and thinly
   sliced
½ red onion, cut in half and
   thinly sliced
Small bunch fresh coriander,
   roughly chopped

1. In a large bowl whisk the
dressing ingredients. Add the
slaw ingredients to the bowl and
toss with the dressing.

2. Let the slaw stand at room
temperature for 20 minutes,
tossing occasionally, before
serving.

Jicama is a bulbous root
vegetable with white crunchy
flesh, popular in Mexican
cooking. White radish
(mooli) or kohlrabi could be
substituted in this recipe.

DRESSING
175 ml/6 fl oz mayonnaise
3 tablespoons white wine vinegar
2 tablespoons granulated sugar
1 teaspoon celery seeds

Sea salt
Freshly ground black pepper

SLAW
½ small head green cabbage,
   thinly sliced
3 medium carrots, coarsely
   grated
1 red pepper, finely diced
Small bunch fresh parsley leaves,
   roughly chopped

RED CABBAGE SLAW

WITH CIDER-DILL VINAIGRETTE

SERVES: **8–10** | PREP TIME: **20 MINUTES** | CHILLING TIME: **2 HOURS–1 DAY**

1. In a large bowl combine the dressing ingredients, including ¾ teaspoon salt and ½ teaspoon pepper, and whisk until the sugar and salt are dissolved. Add the slaw ingredients and mix well. Taste and add more salt and pepper, if liked. Cover and refrigerate until chilled, at least 2 hours or up to 1 day.

2. Before serving, drain the slaw in a colander and then transfer to a serving bowl.

VINAIGRETTE
5 tablespoons cider vinegar
5 tablespoons rapeseed oil
5 tablespoons granulated sugar
4 tablespoons chopped fresh dill
1 tablespoon sea salt
½ teaspoon freshly ground
   black pepper

SLAW
½ medium head red cabbage,
   thinly sliced
1 medium cucumber, thinly sliced
3 medium carrots, coarsely
   grated
6 celery sticks, thinly sliced

1. In a large bowl combine the vinaigrette ingredients and whisk until the sugar and salt are dissolved. Add the slaw ingredients and mix well. Cover and refrigerate until chilled, at least 2 hours or up to 1 day.

2. Before serving, drain the slaw in a colander and then transfer to a serving bowl.

SIDES

MODERN MACARONI SALAD

SERVES: **8** | PREP TIME: **30 MINUTES** | GRILLING TIME: **10–12 MINUTES**

DRESSING
8 tablespoons mayonnaise
1 teaspoon finely grated
  lemon rind
2 tablespoons fresh lemon juice
1 tablespoon Dijon mustard
¾ teaspoon sea salt
¾ teaspoon freshly ground
  black pepper
½ teaspoon paprika
¼ teaspoon hot pepper sauce

225 g/8 oz dried short-cut
  macaroni
1 tablespoon extra-virgin
  olive oil
2 medium red peppers
3 sticks celery, thinly sliced
3 spring onions (white and light
  green parts only), thinly sliced
60 g/2 oz kalamata olives,
  thinly sliced
Small bunch fresh parsley leaves,
  roughly chopped

1. In a non-reactive bowl whisk the dressing ingredients. Cover and refrigerate until ready to use.

2. Bring a large pan of salted water to a rolling boil. Add the macaroni and cook until al dente, 7–9 minutes. Drain and transfer to a large bowl. Toss with the oil. Cool to room temperature.

3. Prepare the grill for direct cooking over medium heat (180–230°C/350–450°F).

4. Grill the peppers over *direct medium heat* for 10–12 minutes,, with the lid closed, until blackened and blistered all over, turning occasionally. Put the peppers in a bowl and cover with clingfilm to trap the steam. Allow to stand for about 10 minutes. Carefully peel away and discard the charred skin. Remove and discard the stalk, seeds and ribs. Cut the peppers into medium dice.

5. To the bowl with the macaroni add the peppers, celery, spring onions, olives and parsley. Pour the dressing over the salad and toss to combine. Serve immediately, or cover and refrigerate until serving.

CHEF'S MACARONI SALAD

SERVES: 6 | PREP TIME: 20 MINUTES

DRESSING
8 tablespoons mayonnaise
3 tablespoons red wine vinegar
1¼ teaspoons sea salt
1 teaspoon spicy brown mustard
½ teaspoon freshly ground
  black pepper
¼ teaspoon granulated sugar

225 g/8 oz dried short-cut
  macaroni
¼ medium red onion,
  finely chopped
2 sticks celery, finely diced
Small bunch fresh parsley leaves,
  finely chopped

TOPPINGS
60 g/2 oz cooked ham, julienned
60 g/2 oz cooked turkey
  breast, julienned
1 small heart of romaine lettuce,
  julienned
1 medium, ripe beefsteak tomato,
  cored, seeded and finely diced
60 g/2 oz sharp Cheddar cheese,
  coarsely grated
2 hard-boiled eggs, finely
  chopped

1. Combine the dressing ingredients.

2. Bring a large pan of salted water to a rolling boil. Add the macaroni and cook until al dente, 7–9 minutes. Drain and transfer to a wide serving bowl. Add the onion, celery, parsley and dressing and toss to coat. Gently smooth the surface.

3. Arrange the toppings in stripes on top of the salad. Gently toss together before eating.

Whenever you are cooking pasta, add plenty of salt to the boiling water – enough that the water tastes as salty as the ocean. Why? Because this is your one and only chance to season the pasta on the inside. After it's cooked, salt will only season the outside.

ORZO SALAD WITH GRILLED FENNEL, TOMATOES AND ROCKET

SERVES: **8** | PREP TIME: **40 MINUTES** | GRILLING TIME: **ABOUT 10 MINUTES**

Large bunch fresh basil
3 tablespoons white balsamic vinegar
Sea salt
Freshly ground black pepper
Extra-virgin olive oil
1–2 fennel bulbs, about 450 g/1 lb total, trimmed, bulb(s) cut into quarters (leave core attached)
225 g/8 oz dried orzo pasta
450 g/1 lb ripe red and yellow cherry tomatoes, each cut in half
4 large handfuls rocket leaves
90 g/3 oz Parmesan cheese, coarsely grated (on the large holes of a box grater)

1. In a food processor fitted with a metal blade, combine the basil, vinegar, ½ teaspoon salt and ¼ teaspoon pepper, and pulse 10 times in 1-second bursts. With the motor running, slowly add 120 ml/4 fl oz oil through the feed tube. Continue to process until the vinaigrette is emulsified. Transfer to a very large bowl and set aside.

2. Prepare the grill for direct cooking over medium heat (180–230°C/350–450°F).

3. Brush the fennel with 1 tablespoon oil and season evenly with ¼ teaspoon salt and ⅛ teaspoon pepper.

4. Grill the fennel over *direct medium heat* for about 10 minutes, with the lid closed, until browned in spots and almost tender, turning three times. Remove from the grill and leave to rest while cooking the orzo.

5. Cook the orzo according to packet instructions. Drain and rinse briefly with cold water to cool slightly. Drain well. Transfer the orzo to the very large bowl with the vinaigrette. Toss to coat. Cut the fennel quarters crossways into 1.5-cm/¾-inch pieces (you may remove the core, if liked) and add to the bowl with the orzo. Add the tomatoes, rocket and cheese and mix gently. Season with salt and pepper. The salad can be served immediately or covered and refrigerated for up to 6 hours.

When you quarter fennel bulbs, leave some of the core attached to each piece. The core holds the leaves together on the grill.

SIDES

EASY COLD NOODLE SALAD WITH PEANUT SAUCE AND CARROT

SERVES: 4 | PREP TIME: **20 MINUTES**

225 g/8 oz dried fettuccine

1 medium carrot, peeled and thinly sliced on the diagonal

8 tablespoons smooth peanut butter

8 tablespoons unsweetened coconut milk

2 tablespoons fresh lime juice

1 tablespoon light brown sugar

2 teaspoons Asian fish sauce

2 teaspoons peeled, grated fresh ginger

1 garlic clove, crushed

¼ teaspoon crushed chilli flakes

1 cucumber, halved lengthways and thinly sliced into half-moons

3 spring onions, ends trimmed and thinly sliced

1. Cook the fettuccine until al dente, according to packet instructions. During the last minute of cooking time, add the carrot. Drain, rinse under cold water and drain again. Transfer to a large bowl.

2. In a blender combine the peanut butter, coconut milk, lime juice, brown sugar, fish sauce, ginger, garlic and chilli flakes and blend until smooth. Pour the mixture over the fettuccine, add the cucumber and spring onions, and toss well. If the sauce seems too thick, stir in warm water a tablespoon at a time until the desired thickness is reached. Serve either warm or at room temperature.

Called nam pla in Thailand and nuoc mam in Vietnam, fish sauce is an essential seasoning all over South-east Asia. You need just a little bit of it to give savoury dishes a pungent, salty accent.

DEVILLED EGGS WITH HOT SAUCE

SERVES: **6** | PREP TIME: **10 MINUTES**

6 large eggs
2 tablespoons mayonnaise
1 tablespoon finely chopped fresh dill
1 tablespoon full-fat milk
1 teaspoon Dijon mustard
Hot pepper sauce
¼ teaspoon sea salt
¼ teaspoon freshly ground black pepper
12 very small sprigs fresh dill

1. Place the eggs in a single layer in a large saucepan and add enough water to cover them by at least 2.5 cm/1 inch. Bring the water to the boil over high heat, uncovered. Then remove the saucepan from the heat, cover the saucepan, and let the eggs stand for 15 minutes. Drain the eggs and run cold water over them until cool to the touch.

2. Peel the eggs and cut each one lengthways in half. Scoop out the yolks and put them in a bowl. Add the mayonnaise, chopped dill, milk, mustard, ¼ teaspoon hot pepper sauce (or to taste), salt and pepper. Mix until well combined. Spoon the mixture into the egg whites. Garnish with dill sprigs and add another dash of hot pepper sauce, if liked.

To get the yolks to set in the middle of the egg whites, gently stir the eggs during the first couple of minutes of cooking time.

SIDES

TOMATO AND AVOCADO SALAD WITH LEMON-CAPER VINAIGRETTE

SERVES: **4-6** | PREP TIME: **15 MINUTES**

VINAIGRETTE

2 tablespoons fresh lemon juice
1 tablespoon capers,
    drained and chopped
1 tablespoon finely
    chopped shallot
1 teaspoon Dijon mustard
½ teaspoon sea salt
¼ teaspoon freshly ground
    black pepper
4 tablespoons extra-virgin
    olive oil

225 g/8 oz ripe yellow cherry
    tomatoes, each cut in half
½ red onion, thinly sliced
450 g/1 lb assorted ripe
    tomatoes, cored and each
    cut into 6–8 wedges
1–2 ripe avocados,
    cut into slices

1. Whisk all the vinaigrette ingredients except for the oil. Add the oil in a steady stream, whisking constantly until the vinaigrette is emulsified.

2. In a bowl combine the cherry tomatoes and onion with 1 tablespoon of the vinaigrette; toss well.

3. Spoon the cherry tomatoes and onion on to the centre of a large serving plate. Arrange the tomato wedges and avocado slices around the edge of the plate, and then drizzle with the remaining vinaigrette. The salad can be served immediately or covered and held at room temperature for up to 1 hour.

SIDES

CHOPPED GREEK-STYLE SALAD

SERVES: **6–8** | PREP TIME: **20 MINUTES**

DRESSING

2 tablespoons fresh lemon juice
1 tablespoon red wine vinegar
½ teaspoon sea salt
½ teaspoon freshly ground
  black pepper
1 small garlic clove, crushed
4 tablespoons extra-virgin
  olive oil

SALAD

2 hearts of romaine lettuce,
  roughly chopped
½ cucumber, cut into 1-cm/
  ½-inch dice
225 g/8 oz ripe cherry tomatoes,
  each cut in half (quartered
  if large)
1 large red pepper, cut
  into 1-cm/½-inch dice
240 g/8 oz canned chickpeas,
  rinsed and drained
120 g/4 oz feta cheese, crumbled
½ red onion, finely chopped
100 g/3½ oz kalamata olives,
  each cut into quarters
Large bunch fresh mint, roughly
  chopped
Large bunch fresh parsley leaves,
  roughly chopped

1. Whisk all the dressing ingredients except for the oil. Add the oil in a steady stream, whisking constantly until the dressing is emulsified.

2. In a serving bowl combine the salad ingredients. Add the dressing and toss well. Serve immediately.

WARM BROCCOLI SALAD

WITH CRISPY BACON, RED ONION, WALNUTS AND RAISINS

SERVES: **4** | PREP TIME: **15 MINUTES** | GRILLING TIME: **14–17 MINUTES** | SPECIAL EQUIPMENT: **CAST-IRON FRYING PAN**

DRESSING

4 tablespoons full-fat natural yogurt
4 tablespoons mayonnaise
1½ teaspoons red wine vinegar
½ teaspoon granulated sugar
½ teaspoon sea salt
¼ teaspoon freshly ground black pepper
⅛ teaspoon ground cayenne pepper

60 g/2 oz walnut pieces
6 rashers bacon
450 g/1 lb broccoli, cut into bite-sized florets
½ red onion, finely chopped
60 g/2 oz raisins

1. Whisk the dressing ingredients.

2. Prepare the grill for direct cooking over medium heat (180–230°C/350–450°F) and preheat a cast-iron frying pan.

3. Cook the walnuts in the frying pan over *direct medium heat* for 2–3 minutes, with the lid closed, until fragrant and golden, stirring frequently. Remove the walnuts from the pan.

4. Place the bacon in a single layer in the frying pan. Fry over *direct medium heat* for 10–12 minutes, with the lid closed, until the fat renders and the bacon is crisp, turning occasionally. Transfer the bacon to kitchen paper to drain. Leave the bacon fat in the pan. Add the broccoli and onion to the pan and sauté over *direct medium heat* for about 2 minutes, with the lid closed, until crisp-tender. Transfer to a large bowl.

5. Coarsely chop the bacon. Add the bacon, walnuts, raisins and the dressing to the large bowl and stir to combine. Serve warm, at room temperature, or cold.

FUN FACT

Broccoli, kale, cauliflower, kohlrabi, Brussels sprouts, cabbage: notice the similarity in taste, texture, aroma and appearance? That's not surprising – they're cousins! All are members of the genus Brassica and probably originated in a humble wild cabbage species native to southern Italy.

SIDES

SCANDINAVIAN POTATO SALAD WITH FRESH HERBS

SERVES: **8–10** | PREP TIME: **30 MINUTES** | CHILLING TIME: **1–4 HOURS**

1.5 kg/3 lb small new potatoes, 2.5–3 cm/1–1¼ inches in diameter

1 tablespoon plus 2 teaspoons sea salt

4 tablespoons extra-virgin olive oil

3 tablespoons white wine vinegar

1 garlic clove, crushed

2 teaspoons granulated sugar

2 teaspoons mustard powder

1 teaspoon freshly ground black pepper

3 spring onions (white and light green parts only), thinly sliced

4 tablespoons finely chopped fresh parsley leaves

4 tablespoons finely chopped fresh dill

4 tablespoons finely chopped fresh chives

1. Put the potatoes in a large saucepan and cover them with cold water by 5 cm/2 inches. Add 1 tablespoon of the salt. Bring to the boil. Reduce the heat to medium and boil gently for 15–18 minutes, until the potatoes are tender but not mushy. Drain and transfer to a large bowl.

2. Whisk the oil, vinegar, garlic, sugar, mustard powder, pepper and the remaining 2 teaspoons salt. Pour over the warm potatoes and then add the spring onions. Toss to combine. Cover and refrigerate for 1–4 hours, tossing occasionally. Just before serving, stir in the parsley, dill and chives.

GRILLED POTATO SALAD WITH EGGS, CELERY AND DIJON MAYO

SERVES: **6** | PREP TIME: **30 MINUTES** | GRILLING TIME: **20–25 MINUTES** | CHILLING TIME: **AT LEAST 2 HOURS**

1 kg/2 lb waxy potatoes,
   about 3.5 cm/1½ inches in
   diameter, each cut in half
1 tablespoon extra-virgin
   olive oil
2 teaspoons sea salt
2 teaspoons red wine vinegar
5 tablespoons mayonnaise
1½ tablespoons Dijon mustard
1 teaspoon freshly ground
   black pepper
2 large hard-boiled
   eggs, chopped
3 celery sticks, finely chopped
1 red onion, finely chopped
   rinsed in a fine-mesh sieve
   under cold water
Small bunch fresh parsley leaves,
   finely chopped

You can use any type of thin-skinned, low-starch (waxy) potatoes for this recipe. Just make sure to cut the potatoes into bite-sized pieces before grilling them. Avoid thick-skinned, starchy potatoes like King Edwards – those are better suited for chips or mashed potatoes.

1. Prepare the grill for direct cooking over medium heat (180–230°C/350–450°F).

2. In a large bowl combine the potatoes, oil and 1 teaspoon of the salt and turn to coat.

3. Grill the potatoes over *direct medium heat* for 20–25 minutes, with the lid closed, until golden brown and tender, turning occasionally. Return the potatoes to the large bowl. Sprinkle the vinegar over the potatoes and gently stir to combine. Cool to room temperature.

4. In a small bowl whisk the mayonnaise, mustard, pepper and the remaining 1 teaspoon salt.

5. To the bowl with the potatoes add the mayonnaise mixture, the eggs, celery, onion and parsley. Gently stir to combine. Cover and refrigerate for at least 2 hours. Serve chilled.

NEW POTATO SALAD WITH BACON AND ONIONS

SERVES: **8** | PREP TIME: **20 MINUTES** | GRILLING TIME: **30–37 MINUTES** | STANDING TIME: **1 HOUR (OPTIONAL)**

Extra-virgin olive oil

Sea salt

Freshly ground black pepper

1.2 kg/2½ lb new potatoes, about 3.5 cm/1½ inches in diameter, each cut in half

225 g/8 oz thick-cut bacon, cut into 5-mm/¼-inch dice

2 medium sweet onions, each cut crossways into 1-cm/½-inch slices

6 spring onions (white part only), thinly sliced

3 tablespoons chopped fresh parsley leaves

1 tablespoon chopped fresh thyme leaves

3 tablespoons sherry vinegar

3 tablespoons chicken stock *or* water

1. Prepare the grill for direct cooking over medium heat (180–230°C/350–450°F).

2. In a large bowl whisk 2 tablespoons oil, ½ teaspoon salt and ½ teaspoon pepper. Add the potato halves and toss to coat.

3. Grill the potatoes over *direct medium heat* for 20–25 minutes, with the lid closed, until golden brown and tender, turning occasionally. When cool enough to handle, cut each potato half into two pieces and place in a large bowl. Cover and set aside at room temperature.

4. In a frying pan over a medium heat, fry the bacon for 10–12 minutes, until crisp, turning occasionally. With a slotted spoon transfer the bacon to the bowl of potatoes; reserve the bacon fat.

5. Brush the onion slices on both sides with some of the reserved bacon fat and season with salt and pepper. Grill the onion slices over *direct medium heat* for 10–12 minutes, with the lid closed, until lightly browned and tender, turning and basting with the reserved bacon fat once. Cut each onion slice into quarters. Add to the potatoes along with the spring onions, parsley and thyme.

6. Combine the vinegar, stock, ¼ teaspoon salt and ¼ teaspoon pepper. Slowly whisk in 5 tablespoons oil. Pour the dressing over the potatoes and toss gently. Serve; or, to fully incorporate the flavours, cover and allow to stand at room temperature for about 1 hour before serving.

FUN FACT

Contrary to what you may think, new potatoes are actually the same variety as many of the full-sized red and white potatoes you see piled on your supermarket shelves. The difference is the aptly named 'new potato' is just a freshly harvested young potato with an edible paper-thin skin, a moist centre and a mildly sweet flavour.

SIDES

WATERMELON AND FETA SALAD WITH LIME AND MINT

SERVES: **6–8** | PREP TIME: **20 MINUTES**

1 small, ripe seedless
  watermelon, 2.5–3 kg/5–6 lb
5 tablespoons extra-virgin
  olive oil
½ cup fresh fennel bulb, finely
  chopped
2 tablespoons fresh lime juice
½ teaspoon freshly ground
  black pepper
¼ teaspoon sea salt
175 g/6 oz feta cheese, crumbled
Large bunch fresh mint, roughly
  chopped

1. Cut the watermelon into
2.5-cm/1-inch slices. Cut away
the rind and cut the flesh into
2.5-cm/1-inch chunks. Put the
watermelon chunks in a bowl and
refrigerate until ready to serve.

2. Whisk the oil, fennel, lime
juice, pepper and salt to make
a vinaigrette. Set aside.

3. When ready to serve, whisk the
vinaigrette again and pour over
the watermelon. Mix well. Add the
cheese and mint. Mix again and
serve immediately.

This salad is best eaten
right away. Otherwise
the watermelon juices will
break down the nice, firm
texture of the feta cheese.

SIDES

TROPICAL FRUIT SALAD WITH HONEY AND LIME

SERVES: **4–6** | PREP TIME: **30 MINUTES**

1 ripe papaya, about 600 g/1¼
   lb, peeled, seeded and cut into
   1.5-cm/¾-inch pieces
1 ripe mango, about
   450 g/1 lb, peeled and cut
   into 1.5-cm/¾-inch pieces
½ ripe, fresh pineapple, cored
   and cut into 1.5-cm/¾-inch
   pieces
3 ripe kiwifruit, peeled and
   cut into 5-mm/¼-inch-thick
   half-moons
Finely grated rind and juice
   of 1 lime
1 serrano chilli, seeded
   and finely diced
1 tablespoon white wine vinegar
1 tablespoon honey
1 tablespoon chopped fresh
   coriander or mint (optional)

1. In a large bowl combine the
ingredients. Gently toss. Serve
immediately.

The mango's flat
stone runs from top
to bottom. To cut
around it, rotate the
mango so that the
stone runs parallel
to the blade of your
knife. Cut lengthways
along each side of
the stone.

217

WHOLEGRAIN RICE SALAD

WITH HERBS, PINE NUTS AND SOUR CHERRY VINAIGRETTE

SERVES: **8–12** | PREP TIME: **40 MINUTES, PLUS ABOUT 45 MINUTES FOR THE RICE**

RICE

1.2 litres/2 pints water
2 tablespoons soy sauce
500 g/1 lb 2 oz brown rice or
 brown rice blend

200 g/7 oz dried sour cherries
200 ml/7 fl oz hot water
4 tablespoons red wine vinegar
5 tablespoons extra-virgin
 olive oil
1 large shallot, finely diced
1½ teaspoons sea salt
½ teaspoon ground black pepper
75 g/3 oz pine nuts, toasted
3 celery sticks, finely chopped
Large bunch fresh basil, coarsely
 chopped
Large bunch fresh mint,
 coarsely chopped
Large bunch fresh parsley leaves,
 coarsely chopped

1. In a large saucepan with a tight-fitting lid, bring the water and soy sauce to the boil. Add the rice, cover and simmer for about 45 minutes, until tender and most of the water has been absorbed. Meanwhile, prepare the vinaigrette.

2. Combine the sour cherries and hot water. Set aside until the cherries are plumped, about 20 minutes. Drain, reserving both the soaking liquid and cherries (you should have about 175 ml/ 6 fl oz liquid). Put the liquid in a saucepan and reduce over a high heat to 5 tablespoons, about 8 minutes (depending on the diameter of the pan). Pour the reduction into a bowl and whisk with the vinegar, oil, shallot, salt and pepper to make a vinaigrette.

3. Preheat a frying pan over a medium heat. Add the pine nuts and cook for about 3 minutes, until golden brown, shaking the pan occasionally and watching carefully to prevent burning.

4. In a serving bowl combine the rice with the vinaigrette, cherries and celery. Stir in the fresh herbs. Cool to room temperature. Serve; or cover and refrigerate for up to 2 days. Add the pine nuts just before serving.

CORN AND BLACK BEAN SALAD

SERVES: **6-8** | PREP TIME: **30 MINUTES** | GRILLING TIME: **10-15 MINUTES**

DRESSING

3 tablespoons fresh lime juice
1 teaspoon finely grated
    orange rind
2 tablespoons fresh orange juice
1¼ teaspoons sea salt
¼ teaspoon freshly ground
    black pepper

Extra-virgin olive oil

SALAD

4 corn cobs, outer leaves and silk
    removed
1 can (400 g/13 oz) black beans,
    rinsed and drained
1 red pepper, cut into
    5-mm/¼-inch dice
1 cucumber, cut into
    5-mm/¼-inch dice
½ red onion, finely chopped
Small bunch fresh basil, torn
4 spring onions (white and
    light green parts only),
    finely chopped
90 g/3 oz feta cheese, crumbled

1. Prepare the grill for direct cooking over medium heat (180–230°C/350–450°F).

2. Whisk the dressing ingredients, including 2 tablespoons oil.

3. Lightly brush the corn all over with oil, and then grill over *direct medium heat* for 10–15 minutes, with the lid closed, until browned in spots and tender, turning occasionally. Cut the kernels from the cobs over a serving bowl.

4. To the serving bowl add the remaining salad ingredients. Whisk the dressing again and pour it over the salad. Toss gently to combine. Serve immediately.

SIDES

FOOD EUPHORIA

We've all been there. The post-turkey slumber: propped up on the couch, football game on, sleepily lazy and oh-so-content after a huge holiday dinner. That sluggish, satisfied state is not just a result of stuffing yourself far beyond the socially acceptable lunch- or dinnertime dietary standards – it's a product of science. In fact, many foods create happiness, even euphoria, both physiologically (in our bodies) and psychologically (in our thoughts).

To understand the 'how' of food happiness, we must first understand that our brain is our body's control centre: it tells our hearts to beat, our eyes to blink and our mouths to chew. Our brain also regulates our moods and can tell us when we're hungry, angry ... even 'hangry' (the term used to describe a state of anger caused by lack of food – but that's another story in itself).

Happily, many foods help to produce mood-enhancing chemicals in the brain, such as serotonin and dopamine. Touted as the 'happy hormone', serotonin calms our minds and regulates our moods and sleep cycles. Foods that aid in serotonin production include turkey, spinach and bananas, among others. Turkey Burgers (page 98) or Chicken Popeye Sliders (page 109), anyone?

Dopamine, then, is serotonin's euphoric counterpart that captains our brain's reward and pleasure centres. Like what you see? *Whoosh ...* dopamine production. Neuro-imaging shows that these pleasure centres literally light up in the presence of 'naughty' foods, such as those high in fat, sugar or salt – very much like addicts' brain scans. *Zing! French fries!*

While some foods physiologically affect our moods, others make us happy simply because they are delicious and familiar. We're talking the flame-grilled cheeseburgers, the savoury casseroles, the hearty meatloaves and the ooey-gooey mac-n-cheeses of the world – yep, comfort foods.

These types of foods provide happiness on a psychological level, and studies show that perhaps the comfort foods we crave are actually artefacts from our pasts. Comfort foods trigger happy memories and provide a sense of well-being and security. Maybe it's Mum's homemade apple pie, or perhaps it's Dad's barbecued brats or Grandma's fried chicken. All of us have a certain food that 'speaks' to us, some special dish that warms our hearts on an impenetrable level ... what's *yours*?

CHILLI-SPICED FRIES

SERVES: **4–6** | PREP TIME: **25 MINUTES** | SOAKING TIME: **30 MINUTES** | COOLING TIME: **15 MINUTES**
FRYING TIME: **5–6 MINUTES PER BATCH** | SPECIAL EQUIPMENT: **DEEP-FRY THERMOMETER**

SPICES

1½ teaspoons sea salt
1 teaspoon ancho chilli powder
½ teaspoon chilli powder
¼ teaspoon ground chipotle chilli pepper
¼ teaspoon ground cumin

4 potatoes, about 1.25 kg/2½ lb total
Rapeseed or vegetable oil

1. Combine the spices.

2. Fill a large bowl with cold water. Scrub the potatoes under cold water and cut each lengthways into 5–8-mm/¼–⅓-inch slices. Then cut each slice lengthways into 5–8-mm/¼–⅓-inch strips. Transfer to the bowl of water. Leave the potatoes to soak for 30 minutes.

3. Drain the potatoes and then pat dry with a towel. Lay them out in a single layer on several layers of kitchen paper.

4. Line a large roasting tray with layers of kitchen paper. Pour enough oil into a large, deep saucepan to come 7 cm/3 inches up the side. Attach a deep-fry thermometer to the side of the pan. Heat the oil on the hob over a medium heat until the temperature registers 170°C/325°F. Working in small batches to prevent the oil temperature from dropping too much, add some of the potatoes to the pan and cook for about 4 minutes, until cooked through and beginning to brown slightly, maintaining the temperature between 150 and 170°C/300 and 325°F and moving them occasionally. Using a slotted spoon or tongs, transfer the potatoes to the prepared roasting tray. Repeat with the remaining potatoes, returning the oil temperature to 170°C/325°F between each batch. Allow all the potatoes to cool for 15 minutes before continuing.

5. Preheat the oven to 110°C/225°F.

6. Line another large roasting tray with several layers of kitchen paper. Increase the heat to medium-high and bring the oil temperature to 190°C/375°F. Divide the potatoes into three equal batches. Add one batch of potatoes to the oil and cook for 1–2 minutes, until crisp and deep golden brown. Transfer the potatoes to the prepared roasting tray to drain, then transfer to a third roasting tray and hold in the oven. Return the oil temperature to 190°C/375°F and repeat with the remaining two batches of potatoes, draining each batch on fresh kitchen paper.

7. Season the fries with the spices. Serve immediately.

Soak the cut potatoes in water for about 30 minutes to remove some starchiness, and then pat them dry with kitchen paper. The first round of frying is for cooking the fries to the centre. The second round (at a higher temperature) is for making the surfaces brown and crispy.

STEAK FRIES WITH ROSEMARY-LEMON AIOLI

SERVES: **4-6** | PREP TIME: **15 MINUTES** | GRILLING TIME: **15-17 MINUTES**

AIOLI
250 ml/8 fl oz mayonnaise
½ teaspoon finely grated lemon rind
1½ tablespoons fresh lemon juice
2 teaspoons finely chopped garlic
2 teaspoons Dijon mustard
2 teaspoons finely chopped fresh rosemary leaves

Sea salt
Freshly ground black pepper
4 potatoes, about 1.5 kg/3 lb total
2 tablespoons extra-virgin olive oil

1. Prepare the grill for direct cooking over medium heat (180–230°C/350–450°F).

2. Whisk the aioli ingredients. Season with ¼ teaspoon salt and ¼ teaspoon pepper.

3. Scrub the potatoes under cold water and dry them with kitchen paper. Cut the potatoes lengthways in half and then cut each potato half lengthways into 1-cm/½-inch-thick slices. Place in a bowl and add the oil, 2 teaspoons salt and 1 teaspoon pepper. Toss to coat.

4. Grill the potato slices over *direct medium heat* for 15–17 minutes, with the lid closed, until tender and marked by the grill, turning occasionally.

5. Serve the fries warm with the rosemary-lemon aioli.

SIDES

CURRY SWEET POTATO FRIES WITH SPICY YOGURT SAUCE

SERVES: **4** | PREP TIME: **15 MINUTES** | GRILLING TIME: **10–15 MINUTES** | SPECIAL EQUIPMENT: **PERFORATED GRILL PAN**

SAUCE

8 tablespoons natural Greek yogurt
2 teaspoons fresh lime juice
½ teaspoon red curry paste
¼ teaspoon sea salt
1 garlic clove, crushed

2 teaspoons curry powder
1 teaspoon sea salt
½ teaspoon freshly ground black pepper
2 tablespoons extra-virgin olive oil
2 sweet potatoes, about 1 kg/2 lb
   total, peeled and ends trimmed

1. Prepare the grill for direct cooking over medium heat (180–230°C/350–450°F) and preheat a perforated grill pan.

2. Whisk the sauce ingredients.

3. In a large bowl combine the curry powder, salt and pepper. Stir in the oil. Cut the potatoes into 10 by 1 by 1-cm/4 by ½ by ½-inch sticks (discard any uneven pieces, as they would burn easily). Put the potatoes in the bowl with the oil and spices and turn to coat evenly.

4. Spread the potatoes in a single layer on the grill pan and grill over *direct medium heat* for 10–15 minutes, with the lid closed, until tender, turning every few minutes to brown all sides.

5. Serve the fries warm with the spicy yogurt sauce.

FUN FACT

Curry powder is actually a blend of up to 20 different spices, which can include turmeric (which gives it the characteristic golden colour), coriander, cumin, fenugreek, paprika, pepper, cardamom, cinnamon, nutmeg, cloves, allspice and more.

SMOKY BARBECUED BAKED BEANS

SERVES: **8** | PREP TIME: **15 MINUTES** | GRILLING TIME: **1½–2 HOURS**
SPECIAL EQUIPMENT: **4 LARGE HANDFULS OAK, APPLE OR CHERRY WOOD CHIPS; 30-CM/12-INCH CAST-IRON FRYING PAN**

150 g/5 oz thick-cut bacon,
   finely chopped
1 small onion,
   finely chopped
1 medium jalapeño chilli, finely
   chopped (optional)
5 cans (each 400 g/13 oz) haricot
   beans or other small white
   beans, rinsed and drained
300 ml/½ pint barbecue sauce
240 ml/8 fl oz beef, chicken, or
   vegetable stock
5 tablespoons black treacle
2 tablespoons spicy
   brown mustard
½ teaspoon sea salt
¼ teaspoon freshly ground
   black pepper

1. Soak the wood chips in water for at least 30 minutes.

2. Prepare the grill for indirect cooking over medium-low heat (150–180°C/300–350°F).

3. In a 30-cm/12-inch cast-iron frying pan over medium-low heat, fry the bacon for about 5 minutes, until barely browned, stirring often. Add the onion and jalapeño (if using) and cook for about 3 minutes, until the onion is softened. Add the remaining ingredients and mix well.

4. Drain and add two handfuls of the wood chips to the charcoal or to the smoker box of a gas grill, following manufacturer's instructions, and close the lid. When the wood begins to smoke, cook the beans over *indirect medium-low heat* for 1½–2 hours, with the lid closed, until the sauce has thickened and the beans are fully flavoured with smoke, stirring occasionally. Drain and add the remaining wood chips after 30 minutes of cooking time.

5. Serve the beans warm.

If you're using a charcoal grill, replenish the charcoal as needed to maintain a steady temperature, adding about 8 unlit briquettes every 45 minutes–1 hour. Leave the lid off the grill for about 5 minutes to help the new briquettes light.

SIDES

SOUTHERN FRIED PICKLES WITH RÉMOULADE

SERVES: **6-8** | PREP TIME: **20 MINUTES** | FRYING TIME: **ABOUT 1 MINUTE PER BATCH**
SPECIAL EQUIPMENT: **DEEP-FRY THERMOMETER**

RÉMOULADE
240 ml/8 fl oz mayonnaise
2 tablespoons coarse-grain
  Dijon mustard
2 tablespoons tomato ketchup
1 tablespoon horseradish
2 teaspoons capers,
  drained and chopped
½ teaspoon hot pepper sauce

80 g/3 oz plain flour
1 tablespoon paprika
1 teaspoon garlic powder
½ teaspoon sea salt
½ teaspoon freshly ground
  black pepper
1 large egg, beaten
150 ml/3 oz well-shaken
  buttermilk
1 teaspoon hot pepper sauce
200 g/7 oz panko breadcrumbs
1 jar (450 g/16 oz) dill pickle
  slices, drained and patted dry
  Rapeseed or vegetable oil

1. Combine the rémoulade ingredients. Cover and refrigerate until ready to serve.

2. In a shallow bowl whisk the flour, paprika, garlic powder, salt and pepper. In a deeper bowl whisk the egg, buttermilk and hot pepper sauce. Put the panko in a third bowl. Working with a few at a time, dip the pickles into the flour mixture, turning to coat and then shake off the excess and dip them into the egg mixture. Shake off the excess egg mixture and then dredge them through the panko. Place in a single layer on a roasting tray. Repeat with the remaining pickles.

3. Preheat the oven to 110°C/225°F/ gas mark ¼. Line a roasting tray with kitchen paper and have an unlined roasting tray to hand.

4. Pour enough oil into a large, deep saucepan to come 5 cm/ 2 inches up the side. Attach a deep-fry thermometer to the side of the pan. Heat the oil on the hob over a medium-high heat until the temperature registers 180°C/350°F. Add one-quarter of the pickles and cook until golden and crisp, about 1 minute, turning once, if necessary. Place the fried pickles on the lined roasting tray to blot the excess oil and then transfer to the unlined roasting tray; keep warm in the oven. Repeat with the remaining pickles.

5. Serve the fried pickles warm with the rémoulade.

CLASSIC BUTTERMILK ONION RINGS

SERVES: **4-6** | PREP TIME: **20 MINUTES** | STANDING TIME: **15 MINUTES**
FRYING TIME: **2-4 MINUTES PER BATCH** | SPECIAL EQUIPMENT: **DEEP-FRY THERMOMETER**

500 ml/17 fl oz well-shaken buttermilk
1 tablespoon paprika
1 teaspoon ground cumin
1 teaspoon freshly ground black pepper
2 large onions
275 g/9 oz plain flour
1 tablespoon sea salt
¾ teaspoon ground cayenne pepper
Rapeseed or vegetable oil
Ranch dressing
Tomato ketchup
Barbecue sauce

1. In a large bowl whisk the buttermilk, paprika, cumin and pepper.

2. Cut the onions crossways into 1-cm/½-inch slices and separate them into rings. Add the onion rings to the buttermilk mixture and stir to coat. Allow to stand for 15 minutes, stirring occasionally.

3. Meanwhile, in a large, shallow bowl whisk the flour, salt and cayenne pepper.

4. Preheat the oven to 110°C/225°F/gas mark ¼.

5. Line a roasting tray with baking paper.

6. Pour enough oil into a large, deep saucepan to come 2.5 cm/1 inch up the side. Attach a deep-fry thermometer to the side of the pan. Heat the oil on the hob over a medium-high heat until the temperature registers 180–190°C/350–375°F.

7. Working in batches, remove some of the onion rings from the buttermilk mixture and dredge them in the flour mixture. If liked, dip the onion rings back into the buttermilk and dredge them a second time in the flour mixture. Carefully add the onion rings to the hot oil and cook for 2–4 minutes, until they are golden, turning once. Using tongs, transfer the onion rings to the prepared roasting tray and keep warm in the oven. Repeat with the remaining onion rings and flour mixture.

8. Serve the onion rings immediately with your choice of condiment.

A SALUTE TO KETCHUP

In praise of tomato ketchup ... or is it catsup? Either way, the tangy, tomato-loaded condiment seems to be the foundation upon which America has built a nation – or at least a culinary tradition.
But like many American standbys, tomato ketchup hails from far away. During their travels, eighteenth-century English explorers fell for a thin, fermented Asian fish sauce, which was brought back to Britain and adapted to eventually include tomatoes. The word 'ketchup' is derived from its original, varied pronunciations.

But things got interesting in the States when, in 1876, the H.J. Heinz Company began bottling its take on tomato ketchup, kicking off America's love affair with the condiment – which is now outsold only by mayonnaise and salsa. Beyond being tasty, tomato ketchup is full of cancer-fighting lycopenes and is shelf stable due to its high acidity. It can even be used to polish brass (seriously) – but we much prefer it on our burgers.

GRILLED AVOCADO AND JALAPEÑO GUACAMOLE

SERVES: **6–8** | PREP TIME: **15 MINUTES** | GRILLING TIME: **6–8 MINUTES** | CHILLING TIME: **30 MINUTES–1 HOUR**

3 ripe avocados, about 1 kg/2 lb
   in total, each cut in half and
   peeled
2 medium jalapeño chillies
Extra-virgin olive oil
1 white onion, finely chopped
   and rinsed in a fine-mesh sieve
   under cold water
1 ripe plum tomato, cored,
   seeded and finely chopped
Small bunch fresh coriander,
   chopped
1 teaspoon sea salt
2–3 tablespoons fresh lime juice
Tortilla chips

1. Prepare the grill for direct cooking over medium heat (180–230°C/350–450°F).

2. Lightly brush the avocados and jalapeños with oil and then grill over *direct medium heat* for 6–8 minutes, with the lid closed, until the avocados are well marked and the jalapeños are blackened and blistered, turning once.

3. Put the avocados in a bowl and coarsely mash with a fork. When the jalapeños are cool enough to handle, scrape away the blackened skin, remove the stem and seeds, and finely chop. To the bowl with the avocados, add the jalapeños, onion, tomato, coriander, salt and 2 tablespoons of the lime juice. Mix well. Add more lime juice, if liked. Place a piece of clingfilm directly on to the surface of the guacamole to prevent it from browning. Refrigerate until cold, 30 minutes–1 hour.

4. Serve the guacamole with tortilla chips.

Make sure your avocados are perfectly ripe for maximum flavour and ease of mashing. Look for skins with a dark hue that are free of indentations, which could be an indicator of bruising. The avocado should yield to slight pressure when gently squeezed in the palm of your hand – avoid using your fingers or you'll probably bruise the fruit. (For a tip on ripening, see page 157.)

SIDES

CIDER-BRAISED SAUERKRAUT

SERVES: **8** | PREP TIME: **10 MINUTES, PLUS ABOUT 30 MINUTES COOKING TIME**

30 g/1 oz unsalted butter
1 medium onion, cut in half and thinly sliced
2 garlic cloves, crushed
1 teaspoon caraway seeds
1 teaspoon fennel seeds
1 bay leaf
½ teaspoon sea salt
¼ teaspoon ground black pepper
1 kg/2 lb sauerkraut, drained and squeezed dry
500 ml/17 fl oz cider or apple juice, preferably unfiltered

1. In a heavy saucepan over a medium heat, melt the butter. Add the onion, garlic, caraway seeds, fennel seeds, bay leaf, salt and pepper and sauté until the onion is softened, about 5 minutes. Add the sauerkraut and cider and bring the mixture to the boil. Lower the heat and allow the sauerkraut to simmer for about 20 minutes, until all of the liquid has been absorbed. Remove the bay leaf.

2. Cool the sauerkraut to room temperature. Serve; or cover and refrigerate for up to 2 days. Bring to room temperature before serving.

SIDES

231

GRILLED SUMMER VEGETABLES WITH THREE DIPPING SAUCES

SERVES: **6** | PREP TIME: **45 MINUTES** | GRILLING TIME: **19–23 MINUTES (TOTAL TIME, INCLUDING SAUCES)**

6 courgettes, about 875 g/1¾ lb total, each cut
  lengthways in half (quartered if large)
1 aubergine, about 450 g/1 lb, ends trimmed,
  cut crossways into 1-cm/½-inch slices
450 g/1 lb asparagus, spears about 1 cm/½ inch
  in diameter, tough ends trimmed
Extra-virgin olive oil
1½ teaspoons sea salt
1 teaspoon freshly ground black pepper
1 baguette
2 garlic cloves, each cut in half

1. Prepare the grill for direct cooking over medium heat (180–230°C/350–450°F).

2. Brush the vegetables with oil and season evenly with the salt and pepper.

3. Cut the baguette on a deep diagonal into long 1-cm/¾-inch-thick slices. Lightly brush the baguette slices on both sides with oil.

4. Grill the vegetables over *direct medium heat*, with the lid closed, until tender and lightly charred on all sides, 6–8 minutes for the asparagus and courgettes and 8–10 minutes for the aubergine, turning occasionally. Transfer to a serving plate.

5. Toast the baguette slices over *direct medium heat*, with the lid closed, for 1 minute, turning once. Rub both sides of the baguette slices with the cut side of the garlic. Transfer to the plate with the vegetables. Serve warm with the dipping sauces.

SPICY ROASTED RED PEPPER SAUCE

MAKES: **ABOUT 300 ML/½ PINT**

2 red peppers, each 200–240 g/7–8 oz
1 large red jalapeño chilli, seeded and coarsely
    chopped (about 2 tablespoons)
2 tablespoons extra-virgin olive oil
1 teaspoon ground cumin
1 teaspoon sea salt
2 garlic cloves
½ teaspoon ground coriander
½ teaspoon freshly ground black pepper

1. Prepare the grill for direct cooking over medium heat (180–230°C/350–450°F).

2. Grill the peppers over *direct medium heat* for 10–12 minutes, with the lid closed, until blackened and blistered all over, turning occasionally. Transfer to a bowl and cover with clingfilm to trap the steam. Allow to stand for about 10 minutes. Remove the peppers from the bowl and discard the charred skin, stalks and seeds and roughly chop. Transfer to a food processor. Add the remaining ingredients. Process until smooth. Serve; or cover and refrigerate for up to 1 day. Bring to room temperature before serving.

HERBED BALSAMIC VINAIGRETTE

MAKES: **125 ML/4 FL OZ**

3 tablespoons balsamic vinegar
2 tablespoons chopped fresh basil
1 tablespoon chopped fresh parsley leaves
1 teaspoon finely chopped garlic
½ teaspoon sea salt
¼ teaspoon freshly ground black pepper
5 tablespoons extra-virgin olive oil

1. In a small bowl whisk all the ingredients except for the oil. Add the oil in a steady stream, whisking constantly to emulsify. Serve; or allow to stand at room temperature for up to 2 hours. Whisk again just before serving.

TZATZIKI SAUCE

MAKES: **ABOUT 350 ML/12 FL OZ**

½ cucumber, coarsely grated on the large holes of a
    box grater
250 ml/8 fl oz natural Greek yogurt
2 tablespoons chopped fresh mint
1 tablespoon fresh lemon juice
2 teaspoons extra-virgin olive oil
1 medium garlic clove, crushed
½ teaspoon sea salt
¼ teaspoon freshly ground black pepper

1. Place the grated cucumber in a sieve and press firmly to squeeze out the excess liquid. Discard the liquid. Transfer the cucumber to a small bowl. Add the remaining ingredients and stir to combine. Serve; or cover and refrigerate for up to 4 hours.

CUCUMBER RELISH

MAKES: **ABOUT 175 ML/6 FL OZ**
PREP TIME: **10 MINUTES**
CHILLING TIME: **1–3 HOURS**

1 cucumber, peeled, seeded and grated on the large holes of a box grater
1 teaspoon sea salt
2 spring onions (white and light green parts only), thinly sliced
2 teaspoons chopped fresh coriander
1½ teaspoons rapeseed oil
1 teaspoon rice vinegar
1 teaspoon Asian fish sauce
1 teaspoon brown sugar
½ teaspoon fresh lime juice
¼ teaspoon toasted sesame oil

1. In a colander toss the cucumber with the salt; allow to drain for 15 minutes.

2. When the cucumber has finished draining, squeeze out the excess moisture using a few sheets of kitchen paper. Whisk the remaining ingredients and fold in the cucumber. Cover and refrigerate for at least 1 hour or up to 3 hours.

SOUR CREAM RAITA

MAKES: **ABOUT 250 ML/8 FL OZ**
PREP TIME: **10 MINUTES**

½ cucumber, halved lengthways and thinly sliced
120 ml/4 fl oz sour cream
4 teaspoons fresh lemon juice
1 tablespoon extra-virgin olive oil
¼ teaspoon curry powder
¼ teaspoon sea salt
1 small garlic clove, crushed

1. In a medium bowl combine all the ingredients.

PICKLED OKRA

MAKES: **ABOUT 300 ML/½ PINT**
PREP TIME: **15 MINUTES**
BRINING TIME: **AT LEAST 1 HOUR**

225 g/8 oz fresh okra, rinsed and cut lengthways in half
5 tablespoons sea salt
350 ml/12 fl oz rice vinegar
240 ml/8 fl oz water
Small bunch fresh dill, chopped
1 teaspoon mustard seeds
1 bay leaf
½ teaspoon crushed chilli flakes
2 garlic cloves, crushed

1. In a colander toss the okra with 3 tablespoons of the salt and allow to drain for 10 minutes.

2. Meanwhile, in a saucepan combine the remaining ingredients, including the remaining 2 tablespoons salt. Bring to a simmer over a medium-high heat and cook until the salt is dissolved, stirring occasionally. Rinse the okra thoroughly under cold water to remove the salt and transfer to a non-reactive bowl or a 1-litre/2-pint glass jar. Pour the brine over the okra and cool to room temperature. Refrigerate for at least 1 hour before serving. The okra can be stored in the refrigerator in a covered container for up to 1 month.

BABA GHANOUSH

MAKES: **ABOUT 250 ML/8 FL OZ**
PREP TIME: **10 MINUTES**
GRILLING TIME: **ABOUT 20 MINUTES**

1 large aubergine
4 tablespoons tahini
3 tablespoons fresh lemon juice
1 tablespoon extra-virgin olive oil
2 large garlic cloves
½ teaspoon sea salt
¼ teaspoon ground cumin
¼ teaspoon freshly ground black pepper

1. Prepare the grill for direct cooking over high heat (230–290°C/450–550°F).

2. Grill the aubergine over *direct high heat* for about 20 minutes, with the lid closed, until the flesh is so tender that you can slide a knife all the way through it without resistance. Remove from the grill and allow to cool.

3. Cut the aubergine lengthways in half and scoop out the flesh. In a food processor fitted with a metal blade, combine the aubergine flesh with the remaining ingredients. Purée until smooth.

JALAPEÑO SPREAD

MAKES: **ABOUT 250 ML/8 FL OZ**
PREP TIME: **10 MINUTES**

1 ripe avocado, roughly chopped
1 jalapeño chilli, seeded
5 tablespoons sour cream
4 tablespoons mayonnaise
2 tablespoons fresh lime juice
½ teaspoon sea salt

1. In a blender or food processor fitted with a metal blade, combine all the ingredients and process until smooth.

SWEET AND SPICY TOMATO CHUTNEY

MAKES: **ABOUT 500 ML/17 FL OZ**
PREP TIME: **15 MINUTES, PLUS ABOUT 1 HOUR COOKING TIME**

1 tablespoon extra-virgin olive oil
2 onions, finely chopped
3 garlic cloves, crushed
2 teaspoons peeled, grated fresh ginger
¼ teaspoon crushed chilli flakes, or to taste
1 kg/2 lb ripe plum tomatoes, cored, seeded and finely chopped
1 medium green pepper, finely chopped
175 ml/6 fl oz cider vinegar
4 tablespoons honey
¾ teaspoon sea salt
¼ teaspoon freshly ground black pepper
⅛ teaspoon ground cinnamon (optional)

1. In a non-reactive saucepan over a medium heat, warm the oil. Add the onion, garlic, ginger and chilli flakes. Cook for 2–3 minutes, until the onion starts to soften, stirring occasionally. Stir in the tomatoes and green pepper, and cook for about 3 minutes, until the tomatoes start to wilt. Add the remaining ingredients. Increase the heat to high, bring to the boil and then reduce the heat to medium-low. Simmer, uncovered, for 45–55 minutes, until the mixture has thickened and reduced to about 500 ml/17 fl oz, stirring occasionally. Remove from the heat and cool completely before serving. The chutney can be stored in the refrigerator in a covered container for up to 1 week.

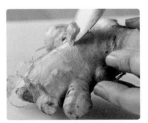

Before grating the ginger, scrape off the skin with the back of a spoon.

RED PEPPER HARISSA

MAKES: **ABOUT 175 ML/6 FL OZ**
PREP TIME: **10 MINUTES**
SPECIAL EQUIPMENT: **SPICE MILL OR PESTLE AND MORTAR**

1¾ teaspoons cumin seeds
240 g/8 oz roasted red peppers (from a jar)
1 tablespoon fresh lemon juice
1 teaspoon ground coriander
½ teaspoon smoked paprika
½ teaspoon sea salt
1 medium garlic clove
⅛ teaspoon ground cayenne pepper
⅛ teaspoon freshly ground black pepper
5 tablespoons extra-virgin olive oil

1. In a dry small frying pan over a medium heat, toast the cumin seeds for 2–3 minutes, until fragrant and slightly darker in colour, stirring often. Remove from the heat and cool slightly. Transfer to a spice mill and finely grind.

2. In a food processor fitted with a metal blade, combine the toasted cumin with all the remaining ingredients except for the oil. Purée until almost smooth. With the motor running, gradually pour the oil through the feed tube and purée until the sauce is as smooth as possible. Transfer to a bowl and set aside at room temperature until ready to serve; or cover and refrigerate for up to 1 day. Bring to room temperature before serving.

FRESH TOMATO SALSA

MAKES: **ABOUT 500 ML/17 FL OZ** | PREP TIME: **20 MINUTES**

225 g/8 oz tomatoes, roughly chopped
Large bunch fresh coriander
½ white onion, roughly chopped and rinsed in a fine-mesh sieve under cold water
1 medium jalapeño chilli, roughly chopped
1 garlic clove, roughly chopped
1 teaspoon fresh lime juice
½ teaspoon sea salt

1. In a food processor fitted with a metal blade, combine all the ingredients. Pulse until finely chopped. Refrigerate until ready to serve.

SUN-DRIED TOMATO PESTO

MAKES: **ABOUT 150 ML/¼ PINT**
PREP TIME: **10 MINUTES**

50 g/2 oz pine nuts
2 large bunches fresh basil
50 g/2 oz Parmesan cheese, freshly grated
4 tablespoons oil-packed sun-dried tomatoes
2 garlic cloves
5 tablespoons olive oil (not extra-virgin)
Sea salt

1. Preheat a frying pan over a medium heat. Add the pine nuts and cook for about 3 minutes, until golden brown, shaking the pan occasionally and watching carefully to prevent burning. Pour into a food processor fitted with a metal blade and allow to cool for a few minutes. Then add the basil, cheese, sun-dried tomatoes and garlic. Pulse until the basil leaves are finely chopped. With the motor running, gradually pour the oil through the feed tube and process until the pesto is almost smooth. Season with salt.

WEBER'S SECRET SAUCE

MAKES: **ABOUT 175 ML/6 FL OZ**
PREP TIME: **10 MINUTES**

4 tablespoons mayonnaise
5 tablespoons sour cream
1–3 teaspoons hot pepper sauce
2 teaspoons fresh lemon juice
2 teaspoons finely chopped fresh chives
½ teaspoon dried parsley
½ teaspoon onion powder
½ teaspoon paprika
½ teaspoon dried dill
½ teaspoon mustard powder
¼ teaspoon garlic granules
¼ teaspoon sea salt
¼ teaspoon freshly ground black pepper

1. In a medium bowl whisk all the ingredients.

The secret to this sauce's success is the balanced blend of herbs and spices. First try it with just a little hot pepper sauce and then add more to suit your taste. It is great on all kinds of burgers.

CHERRY COLA BARBECUE SAUCE

MAKES: **ABOUT 1 LITRE/1¾ PINTS**
PREP TIME: **10 MINUTES, PLUS ABOUT 1 HOUR COOKING TIME**

15 g/½ oz unsalted butter
2 onions, finely chopped
3 garlic cloves, crushed
750 ml/1¼ pints tomato ketchup
600 ml/1 pint cherry cola (not diet)
125 g/4 oz light brown sugar
150 g/5 oz cherry jam
4 tablespoons red wine vinegar
2 teaspoons chilli powder
¼ teaspoon ground cayenne pepper

1. In a saucepan over a medium heat, melt the butter. Add the onion and garlic and cook for 5–6 minutes, until slightly softened, stirring occasionally. Whisk in the remaining ingredients. Increase the heat to medium-high and bring to the boil, then reduce the heat to medium-low and simmer, uncovered, for 45–55 minutes, until the mixture thickens and is reduced to 1 litre/1¾ pints, stirring occasionally. Serve warm; or cool completely and transfer to a covered container. The sauce can be refrigerated for up to 1 month. Reheat before serving.

DRINKS

TROPICAL RUM PUNCH

SERVES: **8** | PREP TIME: **5 MINUTES**

300 ml/½ pint gold rum
700 ml/28 fl oz cold fresh
  pineapple juice
480 ml/16 fl oz cold mango
  nectar
235 ml/7½ fl oz cold guava nectar
60 ml/2 fl oz fresh lime juice
Ice
Ripe, fresh pineapple wedges
  (optional)
Lime wedges (optional)

1. In a large jug combine the rum, pineapple juice, mango nectar, guava nectar and lime juice; mix well.

2. Serve cold over ice. Garnish with pineapple wedges or lime wedges, if liked.

COCKTAILS THAT COMPLEMENT BURGERS AND SAUSAGES

Rather than staunchly sticking with fussy pairings, we're advocates of the 'drink what you like' style of sipping. However, we will admit: a carefully calculated food-drink match does wonders. Got robust flavours like bacon or mature cheese? Consider something with a little tartness and fizz, such as our Cape Cod Berry Spritzers (page 246). Serving up spice? Tropical Rum Punch can tame the heat with sweet. Using poultry or seafood? The Spiked Coconut Shakes (page 246) counter the leanness with some heft. And when in doubt, margaritas (page 245) are perennial winners. Bottoms (and buns) up!

VARIATION

For a non-alcoholic version, substitute 235 ml/7½ fl oz sparkling mineral or soda water for the rum, and increase the fresh lime juice to 80 ml/3 fl oz.

POMITO

SERVES: 1 | PREP TIME: **5 MINUTES**

½ lime, cut into 3 wedges
8 fresh mint leaves
1 teaspoon caster sugar
Crushed ice
1 tablespoon fresh lime juice
45 ml/1½ fl oz light rum
30 ml/1 fl oz pomegranate
   liqueur
60 ml/2 fl oz pomegranate
   juice (no sugar added)
3 tablespoons sparkling
   mineral water
1 fresh mint sprig

1. In the bottom of a collins glass, muddle two of the lime wedges with the mint leaves and sugar to extract the juice from the limes and the oils from the mint.

2. Fill the glass with crushed ice, and then add the lime juice, rum, pomegranate liqueur and pomegranate juice. Top with the sparkling mineral water and stir. Garnish with the remaining lime wedge and mint sprig.

VARIATION

For a non-alcoholic version, muddle 3 lime wedges. Replace the rum with an extra 60 ml/ 2 fl oz pomegranate juice. Replace the pomegranate liqueur with an extra 2 tablespoons of sparkling mineral water.

WATERMELON LEMONADE

SERVES: **8-10** | PREP TIME: **15 MINUTES** | STANDING TIME: **15 MINUTES** | CHILLING TIME: **1 HOUR**

SIMPLE SYRUP
475 ml/16 fl oz water
200 g/7 oz granulated sugar
Small bunch coarsely chopped
   fresh mint

1.5 kg/3 lb ripe, seedless
   watermelon cubes
350 ml/12 fl oz fresh lemon juice
Ice
Fresh mint leaves
Watermelon wedges
1 lemon, cut crossways
   into thin slices

1. In a saucepan over a medium heat, combine the water and sugar and cook for about 2 minutes, until the sugar dissolves, stirring occasionally. Remove from the heat, stir in the mint, and allow to stand for 15 minutes. Refrigerate for 1 hour. Strain and discard the mint.

2. In a blender purée the watermelon and then pour through a fine-mesh sieve set over a bowl. Gently press on the solids to extract more of the juice. Discard any remaining solids. Transfer the watermelon juice to a jug.

3. To the jug add the lemon juice and 350 ml/12 fl oz of the chilled simple syrup; mix well (add more simple syrup, if liked). Serve over ice. Garnish with fresh mint, watermelon wedges and lemon slices.

VARIATION

Substitute 1.5 kg/3 lb of honeydew melon cubes for the watermelon, decrease the lemon juice to 300 ml/½ pint, and omit the mint.

PEACH, PLUM AND BERRY ROSÉ SANGRIA

SERVES: **8** | PREP TIME: **20 MINUTES** | STANDING TIME: **15 MINUTES** | CHILLING TIME: **1 HOUR–1 DAY**

2 ripe, fresh peaches, cut
   into 1-cm/½-inch chunks
2 ripe, fresh plums, cut
   into 1-cm/½-inch chunks
125 g/4 oz ripe, fresh blackberries
125 g/4 oz ripe, fresh raspberries
125 g/4 oz ripe, fresh blueberries
3 tablespoons granulated sugar
475 ml/16 fl oz cold peach nectar
1 bottle (750 ml) chilled
   rosé wine
60 ml/2 fl oz brandy (optional)
Ice

1. Combine the fresh fruit and sugar. Allow to stand at room temperature for 15 minutes, gently folding the fruit occasionally. Transfer to a large jug.

2. To the jug add the peach nectar, wine and brandy (if using), stirring gently to mix. Chill for at least 1 hour or up to 1 day. Serve over ice.

VARIATION

For a non-alcoholic version, substitute sparkling apple juice for the wine, leave out the brandy, and add 60 ml/ 2 fl oz fresh lemon juice.

FROZEN STRAWBERRY-MANGO MARGARITAS
WITH CHILLI SALT RIMS

SERVES: **4** | PREP TIME: **20 MINUTES** | STANDING TIME: **15 MINUTES**

1 ripe mango, peeled and cut into cubes
225 g/8 oz ripe, fresh strawberries, sliced
75 g/3 oz granulated sugar
475 ml/16 fl oz ice cubes
80 ml/3 fl oz good-quality tequila
60 ml/2 fl oz triple sec
80 ml/3 fl oz fresh lime juice
2 teaspoons sea salt
½ teaspoon chilli powder
1 lime wedge
4 slices lime (optional)
4 ripe, fresh strawberries (optional)

1. Combine the mango, strawberries and sugar and allow to stand at room temperature for at least 15 minutes, stirring occasionally.

2. Transfer the strawberry-mango mixture to a blender and add the ice, tequila, triple sec and lime juice. Purée the mixture on high.

3. On a small plate mix the salt and chilli powder. Moisten the rims of four glasses with the lime wedge, and dip the rims into the salt mixture to coat. Divide the margaritas among the four glasses, and garnish with a lime slice and a strawberry, if liked.

GINGER-LIME MARGARITA

SERVES: **1** | PREP TIME: **20 MINUTES** | STEEPING TIME: **1 HOUR**

GINGER SYRUP (MAKES 500 ML/17 FL OZ)
200 g/7 oz granulated sugar
235 ml/7½ fl oz water
375 g/12 oz fresh ginger, peeled and sliced

1 tablespoon caster sugar
½ teaspoon ground ginger
2 lime wedges

MARGARITA
Crushed ice
Juice of 1 lime
45 ml/1½ fl oz good-quality tequila
3 tablespoons ginger syrup (from recipe above)

1. In a saucepan over a medium heat, combine the granulated sugar and water and cook for about 2 minutes, until the sugar dissolves, stirring occasionally. Remove from the heat, add the fresh ginger, cover and allow to steep for 1 hour. Strain, and reserve the liquid.

2. On a small plate mix the caster sugar and ground ginger. Moisten the rim of a rocks glass with one of the lime wedges, and dip the rim into the ginger sugar to coat. Fill a 350-ml/12-fl oz cocktail shaker with ice, lime juice, tequila and ginger syrup. Shake, and pour into the glass. Garnish with the other lime wedge.

VARIATION

For a non-alcoholic version, fill a 350-ml/12-fl oz cocktail shaker with ice, the juice of 1 lime and 3 tablespoons ginger syrup. Shake and pour into a rocks glass. Top with soda water and stir. Garnish with a lime slice. For a more pronounced ginger flavour, replace the soda water with ginger beer.

CAPE COD BERRY SPRITZERS

SERVES: **6** | PREP TIME: **10 MINUTES**

125 g/4 oz ripe, fresh raspberries
125 g/4 oz ripe, fresh strawberries, chopped
235 ml/7½ fl oz 100% cranberry juice
1 bottle (750 ml) sparkling apple juice
Ice
6 ripe, fresh strawberries
6 ripe, fresh raspberries

1. In a blender purée the raspberries, the strawberries and 60 ml/2 fl oz of the cranberry juice. Pour the contents into a large jug and add the remaining cranberry juice. Slowly pour the sparkling apple juice down the inside wall of the jug to prevent excessive foaming. Add ice to the jug and gently stir.

2. Fill six glasses with ice, pour an equal amount of the spritzer into each glass, and garnish with a strawberry and a raspberry.

SPIKED COCONUT SHAKES

SERVES: **2** | PREP TIME: **5 MINUTES**

475 ml/16 fl oz coconut sorbet
150 ml/¼ pint cold unsweetened coconut milk
4 ice cubes
2 tablespoons agave nectar
60 ml/2 fl oz light rum
2 teaspoons fresh lime juice
¼ teaspoon coconut extract
Toasted coconut flakes

1. In a blender combine all the ingredients, except for the toasted coconut flakes, and purée.

2. Divide the shake between two tall glasses. Garnish with the toasted coconut flakes.

VARIATION

For a non-alcoholic version, leave out the rum and increase the fresh lime juice to 1½ tablespoons.

NEW YORK-STYLE EGG CREAM

SERVES: **1** | PREP TIME: **5 MINUTES**

3 tablespoons chocolate or vanilla syrup
80 ml/3 fl oz cold full-fat milk
175 ml/6 fl oz sparkling mineral or soda water
Whipped cream (optional)
Chocolate sprinkles (optional)

1. In a tall glass combine the syrup and milk. Vigorously stir the syrup and milk while pouring in the mineral water in a steady stream. The constant stirring will help to give the egg cream its traditional creamy head of froth.

2. Garnish the egg cream with whipped cream and chocolate sprinkles, if liked.

Egg creams typically contain neither eggs nor cream. So ... why the name? One story says that this late nineteenth-century New York invention got its name from the white foam top layer, which resembles beaten egg whites.

PEACH AND STRAWBERRY SMOOTHIES

SERVES: **4–6** | PREP TIME: **5 MINUTES**

3 ripe, fresh peaches, about 450 g/1 lb total, peeled and roughly chopped
450 g/1 lb frozen whole strawberries
235 ml/7½ fl oz lemonade
125 ml/4 fl oz natural yogurt
2 tablespoons honey or agave nectar, or to taste

1. In a large blender purée the peaches, frozen strawberries, lemonade and yogurt. Add the honey. Blend once more. Divide the smoothie among four to six glasses. Serve cold.

GRILLING GUIDE

TYPE	THICKNESS/ WEIGHT	APPROXIMATE GRILLING TIME	INTERNAL TEMP
Beef, minced	1 cm/½ inch thick	**6–8 minutes** direct medium-high heat (200–260°C/400–500°F) to medium	70°C/160°F
	1.5 cm/¾ inch thick	**8–10 minutes** direct medium-high heat (200–260°C/400–500°F) to medium	70°C/160°F
	2.5 cm/1 inch thick	**9–11 minutes** direct medium-high heat (200–260°C/400–500°F) to medium	70°C/160°F
Bison, minced	1.5 cm/¾ inch thick	**7–9 minutes** direct medium heat (180–230°F/350°–450°F) to medium	70°C/160°F
	2.5 cm/1 inch thick	**8–10 minutes** direct medium heat (180–230°F/350°–450°F) to medium	70°C/160°F
Lamb, minced	1.5 cm/¾ inch thick	**8–10 minutes** direct medium-high heat (200–260°C/400–500°F) to medium	70°C/160°F
	2.5 cm/1 inch thick	**9–11 minutes** direct medium-high heat (200–260°C/400–500°F) to medium	70°C/160°F
Pork, minced	1.5 cm/¾ inch thick	**8–10 minutes** direct medium-high heat (200–260°C/400–500°F) to medium	70°C/160°F
	2.5 cm/1 inch thick	**10–12 minutes** direct medium heat (200–260°C/400–500°F) to medium	70°C/160°F
Poultry, minced	1 cm/½ inch thick	**7–9 minutes** direct medium-high heat (200–260°C/400–500°F) to medium	70°C/160°F
	1.5 cm/¾ inch thick	**8–10 minutes** direct medium-high heat (200–260°C/400–500°F) to medium	70°C/160°F
	2.5 cm/1 inch thick	**11–13 minutes** direct medium heat (180–230°F/350°–450°F) to medium	70°C/160°F
Seafood, minced	1.5 cm/¾ inch thick	**6–8 minutes** direct medium heat (180–230°F/350°–450°F)	63°C/145°F
Hot dog	75 g/3 oz link	**4–5 minutes** direct medium heat (350°–450°F)	
Sausage, raw	75 g/3 oz link	**20–25 minutes** direct medium heat (180–230°F/350°–450°F) until fully cooked	70°C/160°F
Sausage, pre-cooked	75 g/3 oz link	**8–10 minutes** direct medium heat (180–230°F/350°–450°F) until hot	

CONVERSION TABLES

CUP EQUIVALENTS FOR DIFFERENT TYPES OF INGREDIENTS

A standard cup measure of a dry or solid ingredient will vary in weight depending on the type of ingredient. A standard cup of liquid is the same volume for any type of liquid. Use the following chart when converting grams (weight) or millilitres (volume) to standard cup measures.

STANDARD CUP	FINE POWDER (E.G. FLOUR)	GRAIN (E.G. RICE)	GRANULAR (E.G. SUGAR)	LIQUID SOLIDS (E.G. BUTTER)	LIQUID (E.G. MILK)
1/8	15 g	25 g	25 g	35 g	30 ml
1/4	25 g	50 g	50 g	60 g	60 ml
1/3	40 g	75 g	75 g	80 g	80 ml
1/2	50 g	100 g	100 g	125 g	120 ml
2/3	80 g	125 g	150 g	160 g	160 ml
3/4	90 g	150 g	175 g	180 g	180 ml
1	125 g	200 g	225 g	250 g	240 ml

USEFUL EQUIVALENTS FOR LIQUID INGREDIENTS BY VOLUME

1/4 teaspoon					=	1 ml	
1/2 teaspoon					=	2 ml	
1 teaspoon					=	5 ml	
3 teaspoons	= 1 tablespoon			1/2 fl oz	=	15 ml	
	2 tablespoons	=	1/8 cup	= 1 fl oz	=	30 ml	
	4 tablespoons	=	1/4 cup	= 2 fl oz	=	60 ml	
	5 1/3 tablespoons	=	1/3 cup	= 3 fl oz	=	80 ml	
	8 tablespoons	=	1/2 cup	= 4 fl oz	=	120 ml	
	10 2/3 tablespoons	=	2/3 cup	= 5 fl oz	=	160 ml	
	12 tablespoons	=	3/4 cup	= 6 fl oz	=	180 ml	
	16 tablespoons	=	1 cup	= 8 fl oz	=	240 ml	
		2 1/2 cups	=	1 pint	=	480 ml	
		4 cups	=	1 3/4 pints	=	1 litre	
			33 fl oz	=	1000 ml	=	1 L

USEFUL EQUIVALENTS FOR DRY INGREDIENTS BY WEIGHT

To convert grams to ounces, divide the number of grams by 30.

1 oz	=	1/16 lb	=	30 g
4 oz	=	1/4 lb	=	120 g
8 oz	=	1/2 lb	=	240 g
12 oz	=	3/4 lb	=	360 g
16 oz	=	1 lb	=	480 g

USEFUL EQUIVALENTS FOR LENGTH

To convert centimetres to inches, divide the number of centimetres by 2.5.

1 in =	2.5 cm					
6 inches =	1/2 foot	=	15 cm			
12 inches =	1 foot	=	30 cm			
36 inches =	3 feet	=	1 yard	=	90 cm	
40 inches		=	100 cm	=	1 metre	

USEFUL EQUIVALENTS FOR COOKING/OVEN TEMPERATURES

	FAHRENHEIT	CELSIUS	GAS MARK
Freezing point	32°F	0°C	
Room temperature	68°F	20°C	
Boiling point	212°F	100°C	
Bake	325°F	160°C	3
	350°F	180°C	4
	375°F	190°C	5
	400°F	200°C	6
	425°F	220°C	7
	450°F	230°C	8

An Hachette UK Company
www.hachette.co.uk

First published in Great Britain in 2015 by
Hamlyn, a division of Octopus Publishing Group Ltd
Endeavour House
189 Shaftesbury Avenue
London
WC2H 8JY
www.octopusbooks.co.uk

ISBN 978-0-600-63008-1

A CIP catalogue record for this book is available from the British Library

Printed and bound in China

10 9 8 7 6 5 4 3 2 1

www.weber.com®
www.sunset.com

Author Jamie Purviance
Managing Editor (US edition) Marsha Capen
Photography Tim Turner
Photography Assistants Joe Bankmann, Christy Clow, Matt Gagné, Josh Marrah, David Raine, Meghan Ross, Donte Tatum
Food Styling Lynn Gagné
Food Styling Assistant Nina Albazi
Illustrations Linda Kelen
Contributors Lynda Balslev, Brigit Binns, Lena Birnbaum, David Bonom, Angela Brassinga, Linda Carucci, Tara Duggan, Sarah Epstein, Elizabeth Hughes, Allison Kociuruba, Alex Novielli, Rick Rodgers, Cheryl Sternman Rule, Andrew Schloss, Kerry Trotter, Abby Wilson, Terri Wuerthne

Weber-Stephens Products LLC
Chief Marketing Officer Mike Kempster
Vice President Corporate Marketing Brooke Jones
Round Mountain Media
Consulting Global Publishing Director Susan Maruyama
Oxmoor House
Publisher Jim Childs
Editorial Director Leah McLaughlin
Creative Director Felicity Keane, ,
Brand Manager Vanessa Tiongson
Project Editor Pam Hoenig,
Weber-Stephens Products (UK) Ltd
Senior Marketing Executive Helen Raison,
Director of Marketing Laura Ashall,
Director of Sales Jo McDonald,
Octopus Books
Commissioning Editor (UK edition) Eleanor Maxfield
Designer Jeremy Tilston
Editor Pauline Bache
Production Controller Sarah Kramer